THE FIGURE OF BEATRICE

A Study in Dante

by

CHARLES WILLIAMS

Copyright © 2018 Read Books Ltd.
This book is copyright and may not be
reproduced or copied in any way without
the express permission of the publisher in writing

British Library Cataloguing-in-Publication Data
A catalogue record for this book is available from
the British Library

CHARLES WILLIAMS

Charles Walter Stansby Williams was born in London in 1886. He dropped out of University College London in 1904, and was hired by Oxford University Press as a proof-reader, quickly rising to the position of editor. While there, arguably his greatest editorial achievement was the publication of the first major English-language edition of the works of the Danish philosopher Søren Kierkegaard.

Williams began writing in the twenties and went on to publish seven novels. Of these, the best-known are probably *War in Heaven* (1930), *Descent into Hell* (1937), and *All Hallows' Eve* (1945) – all fantasies set in the contemporary world. He also published a vast body of well-received scholarship, including a study of Dante entitled *The Figure of Beatrice* (1944) which remains a standard reference text for academics today, and a highly unconventional history of the church, *Descent of the Dove* (1939). Williams garnered a number of well-known admirers, including T. S. Eliot, W. H. Auden and C. S. Lewis. Towards the end of his life, he gave lectures at Oxford University on John Milton, and received an honorary MA degree. Williams died almost exactly at the close of World War II, aged 58.

For
MICHAEL
in redemption of a promise

CONTENTS

I.	INTRODUCTION	page 7
II.	BEATRICE	17
III.	THE DEATH OF BEATRICE	31
IV.	THE *CONVIVIO*	52
V.	THE NOBLE LIFE	69
VI.	THE *DE MONARCHIA* AND THE EXILE	86
VII.	THE MAKING OF THE *COMMEDIA*	100
VIII.	THE *INFERNO*	107
IX.	THE *PURGATORIO*	145
X.	THE RE-ASSERTION OF BEATRICE	175
XI.	THE *PARADISO*	190
XII.	THE RECOLLECTION OF THE WAY	224
	INDEX	233

Riguarda qual son io
    Paradiso xxiii, 46.

I

INTRODUCTION

This study of Dante is intended to pay particular attention to the figure of Beatrice and to the relation which that figure bears to all the rest. That figure is presented at the beginning of Dante's first book, for Dante is one of those poets who begin their work with what is declared to be an intense personal experience. That experience is, as such, made part of the poetry; and it is not only so, with Dante, at the beginning, but also when, in his later and greater work, the experience is recalled and confirmed.

He defined the general kind of experience to which the figure of Beatrice belongs in one of his prose books, the *Convivio* (IV, xxv). He says there that the young are subject to a 'stupor' or astonishment of the mind which falls on them at the awareness of great and wonderful things. Such a stupor produces two results—a sense of reverence and a desire to know more. A noble awe and a noble curiosity come to life. This is what had happened to him at the sight of the Florentine girl, and all his work consists, one way or another, in the increase of that worship and that knowledge.

The image of Beatrice existed in his thought; it remained there and was deliberately renewed. The word image is convenient for two reasons. First, the subjective recollection within him was of something objectively outside him; it was an image of an exterior fact and not of an interior desire. It was sight and not invention. Dante's whole assertion was that he could not have invented Beatrice. Secondly, the outer exterior shape was understood to be an image of things beyond itself. Coleridge said that a symbol must have three characteristics (i) it must exist in itself, (ii) it must derive from something greater than itself, (iii) it must represent in itself that greatness from which it derives. I have preferred the word image to the word symbol, because it seems to me doubtful if the word symbol nowadays sufficiently expresses the vivid individual existence of the lesser thing. Beatrice was, in

Introduction

her degree, an image of nobility, of virtue, of the Redeemed Life, and in some sense of Almighty God himself. But she also remained Beatrice right to the end; her derivation was not to obscure her identity any more than her identity should hide her derivation. Just as there is no point in Dante's thought at which the image of Beatrice in his mind was supposed to exclude the actual objective Beatrice, so there is no point at which the objective Beatrice is to exclude the Power which is expressed through her. But as the mental knowledge or image of her is the only way by which she herself can be known, so she herself is (for Dante) the only way by which that other Power can be known—since, in fact, it was known so. The maxim of his study, as regards the final Power, was: 'This also is Thou, neither is this Thou.'

I say 'the only way', but only to modify it. There were, in his mind, many other shapes—of people and places, of philosophies and poems. All these had their own identities and were each autonomous. But in his poetry Dante determined to relate them all to the Beatrician figure, and he brought that figure as near as he could to the final image, so far as he could express it, of Almighty God. It is, we all agree, one of the marks of his poetic genius. But it is something else also. It is the greatest expression in European literature of the way of approach of the soul to its ordained end through the affirmation of the validity of all those images, beginning with the image of a girl.

It is this particular way of approach which these pages pretend to examine. It is an accepted fact that there have, on the whole, been two chief ways of approach to God defined in Christian thought. One, which is most familiar in the records of sanctity, has been known as the Way of Rejection. It consists, generally speaking, in the renunciation of all images except the final one of God himself, and even—sometimes but not always—of the exclusion of that only Image of all human sense. The great intellectual teacher of that Way was Dionysius the Areopagite; its conclusion was summed in a paragraph:

'Once more, ascending yet higher, we maintain that It is not soul, or mind, or endowed with the faculty of imagination, conjecture, reason, or understanding; nor is It any act of reason or understanding; nor can It be described by the reason or perceived by the understanding, since It is not number, or order, or great-

Introduction

ness, or littleness, or equality, or inequality, and since it is not immovable nor in motion, or at rest, and has no power, and is not power or light, and does not live, and is not life; nor is It personal essence, or eternity, or time; nor can It be grasped by the understanding, since It is not knowledge or truth; nor is It kingship or wisdom; nor is It one, nor is It unity, nor is It Godhead or Goodness; nor is It a Spirit, as we understand the term, since It is not Sonship or Fatherhood; nor is It any other thing such as we or any other being can have knowledge of; nor does It belong to the category of non-existence or to that of existence; nor do existent beings know It as it actually is, nor does It know them as they actually are; nor can the reason attain to It to name It or to know It; nor is It darkness, nor is It light, or error, or truth; nor can any affirmation or negation apply to It; for while applying affirmations or negations to those orders of being that come next to It, we apply not unto It either affirmation or negation, inasmuch as it transcends all affirmation by being the perfect and unique Cause of all things, and transcends all negation by the pre-eminence of Its simple and absolute nature—free from every limitation and beyond them all.'

The other Way is the Way of Affirmation, the approach to God through these images. The maxim of this Way is in the creed of St. Athanasius: 'Not by conversion of the Godhead into flesh, but by taking of the Manhood into God.' That clause was primarily a definition of the Incarnation, but, being that, it necessarily involved much beside. Other epigrams of the sort are, no doubt, scattered through the history of the Church. But for any full expression of it, the Church had to wait for Dante. It may be that that Way could not be too quickly shown to the world in which the young Church lived. It was necessary first to establish the awful difference between God and the world before we could be permitted to see the awful likeness. It is, and will always remain, necessary to remember the difference in the likeness. Neither of these two Ways indeed is, or can be, exclusive. The most vigorous ascetic, being forbidden formally to hasten his death, is bound to attend to the actualities of food, drink, and sleep which are also images, however brief his attention may be. The most indulgent of Christians is yet bound to hold his most cherished images—of food, drink, sleep, or anything else—

Introduction

negligible beside the final Image of God. And both are compelled to hold their particular Images of God negligible beside the universal Image of God which belongs to the Church, and even that less than the unimaged reality.

Our sacred Lord, in his earthly existence, deigned to use both methods. The miracle of Cana and all the miracles of healing are works of the affirmation of images; the counsel to pluck out the eye is a counsel of the rejection of images. It is said that he so rejected them for himself that he had nowhere to lay his head, and that he so affirmed them by his conduct that he was called a glutton and a wine-bibber. He commanded his disciples to abandon all images but himself and promised them, in terms of the same images, a hundred times what they had abandoned. The Crucifixion and the Death are rejection and affirmation at once, for they affirm death only to reject death; the intensity of that death is the opportunity of its own dissolution; and beyond that physical rejection of earth lies the re-affirmation of earth which is called the Resurrection.

As above, so below; as in him, so in us. The tangle of affirmation and rejection which is in each of us has to be drawn into some kind of pattern, and has so been drawn by all men who have ever lived. The records of Christian sanctity have on the whole stressed the rejection. This indeed can hardly be avoided in any religion—nor perhaps outside all religion; the mere necessities of human life—change, misadventure, folly, age, and death—everywhere involve it. But even more within religion the discipline of the soul, ordinary or extraordinary, enforces it. The general praise of ascetic life and even the formal preference of one good (such as virginity) to another good (such as marriage) have themselves imaged that enforcement. On the other hand such great doctrines as the Resurrection of the Body and the Life Everlasting have continually recalled the Affirmation; with every act of charity towards others, every courtesy towards others, and even permissibly towards ourselves. The very equalling of ourselves with others and of others with ourselves is a declaration of the republic of images. No doubt these doctrines, metaphysical or moral, are to be understood after a great manner and towards God. But no doubt also every way of understanding leaves them exact in themselves. After the affirmations we may have to

Introduction

discover the rejections, but we must still believe that after the rejections the greater affirmations are to return.

In the literature of Europe the greatest record of the Way of Affirmation of Images is contained in the work of Dante Alighieri. There the facts of existence are translated into the actualities of poetry; they are all drawn, in Hippolyta's admirable definition of poetry (*Midsummer Night's Dream*, V, i) into

> something of great constancy,
> But howsoever, strange and admirable.

The 'constancy' of this work is its most remarkable characteristic—both in the sense of lastingness and in the sense of consistency. The greater, the most important, part of that work is poetry, and we must not, of course, confuse poetry with religion. We do not know if, or how far, Dante himself in his own personal life cared or was able to follow the Way he defined, nor is it our business. We do not know if he was a 'mystic', nor is it our business; and the word, having been mentioned, may now be dismissed. The present point about the work of this great poet is that it refers us not to a rare human experience but to a common; or rather it begins with one that is common and continues on a way which might be more common than it is. What we can say about Dante, and almost all that we can say about him, is that he had the genius to imagine the Way of Affirmation wholly—after a particular manner indeed, but then that is the nature of the way of the Images. If a man is called to imagine certain images, he must work in them and not in others. The record of the Dantean Way begins with three things—an experience, the environment of that experience, and the means of understanding and expressing that experience; say—a woman, a city, and intellect or poetry; say again—Beatrice, Florence, and Virgil. These images are never quite separated, even in the beginning; towards the end they mingle and become a great complex image. They end with the inGodding of man.

This, to Dante, necessary (but also voluntary) choice of images is not, of course, the only choice; it is not the only method of that Way. On the whole, the nearest thing to it which we have in English literature is in the *Prelude* of Wordsworth, and in his other lesser poems. The *Prelude* begins also with the affirmation

Introduction

of images, but this time of 'fountains, meadows, hills and groves'. Had Wordsworth been of the stature of Dante, we should have had in English an analysis and record of a Way of Affirmation comparable to the Italian. He was not; he ceased even while he spoke of those 'hiding-places of man's power' of which he desired to write. Yet the very title of the poem reminds us that he had intended no less a task; he was precisely aiming to enter into an understanding, in poetry, of 'the two great ends of liberty and power'; 'la potestate', says Virgil to Dante (*Purg.* XVIII, 70-5), . . . la nobile virtù . . . lo libero arbitrio.' 'This power . . . this noble virtue . . . (is) the liberty of the will.' Wordsworth rather reminded us of the Way than defined it for us. But he did remind us of the business of the Imagination which is the faculty by which images, actual or poetic, are understood.

> Imagination—here the power so-called
> Through sad incompetence of human speech,
> That awful Power, rose from the mind's abyss;

and again:

> This spiritual love acts not nor can exist
> Without Imagination; which, in truth,
> Is but another name for absolute power,
> And keenest insight, amplitude of mind,
> And Reason in her most exalted mood;

and again:

> Imagination having been our theme,
> So also hath this spiritual love,
> For they are each in each, and cannot stand
> Dividually. Here must thou be, O man,
> Power to thyself; no helper hast thou here;
> Here keepest thou in singleness thy state.
> No other can divide with thee this work.
> No secondary hand can intervene
> To fashion this ability; 'tis thine,
> The prime and vital principle is thine,
> In the recesses of thy nature, far
> From any reach of outward fellowship,
> Else is not thine at all. But joy to him,

Introduction

> Oh, joy to him who here hath sown, hath laid
> Here, the foundation of his future years!
> For all that friendship, all that love can do,
> All that a darling countenance can look,
> Or dear voice utter, to complete the man,
> Perfect him, made imperfect in himself,
> All shall be his; and he whose soul hath risen
> Up to the height of feeling intellect
> Shall want no humbler tenderness.

It has seemed worth while to quote at this length for two reasons: (i) because the whole passage is a description of the difficulty of the Way of the Images, (ii) because a number of the phrases are, as might have been expected, exactly applicable to that other Dantean Way. It is not to be rashly assumed that the Way of Affirmation is much easier than the Way of Rejection. To affirm the validity of an image one does not at the moment happen to like or want—such as that of one's next door neighbour—is as harsh as to reject an image—such as oneself as successful—which one does happen to like and want. 'To fashion this ability' is a personal, secret, and arduous business. It is the Purgatory of the *Divine Comedy*; just as 'the dear voice' of Beatrice assists in the *New Life*, as in the *Paradise*, in the perfecting of Dante. That Wordsworth wrote like Wordsworth and not like Dante may be a criticism of his verse but does not alter the application of the maxims.

The great resemblance between Dante and Wordsworth rather than any other of the English poets is that the work of each of these pretends to start from a definite and passionate personal experience. In that sense their work has something in common which is not, for example, in either Shakespeare or Milton, the throb in their poetry of a personal discovery. The Shakespearian world becomes gradually full of human capacities; the Miltonic is ritually aware (in the *Ode on the Nativity*) of the moment following the victory of one capacity over the others. But Dante, even in the first—call it an anecdote, is aware of three kinds of capacity all overwhelmed by a power; and Wordsworth has a similar, though less analysed, sense. The next to nearest is Patmore, but the entry of Patmore on this Way is more graceful

Introduction

and delicate; he delays, as it were, poetically, before the revelation of an 'unknown mode of being'. This 'unknown mode' which in Wordsworth is 'Nature' is in Dante Romantic Love. I keep the word Romantic for three reasons. The first is that there is no other word so convenient for describing that particular kind of sexual love. The second is that it includes other loves besides the sexual. The third is that in following the Dantean record of his love it may be possible to understand something more of Romanticism itself, and of its true and false modes of being. The word should not be too narrowly confined to a literary manner. It defines an attitude, a manner of receiving experience. I do not see any grounds on which, if we are to call the young Wordsworth a Romantic, we can deny the term to the young Dante. That there is a false Romanticism I willingly concede; that Dante denounced it I hope to suggest. But the false does not abolish the true or the value of the true, any more than the cheap use of the word Romantic spoils the intellectual honour which properly accompanies it.

Romantic Love then was the personal experience with which Dante's poetry ostensibly began; that is, the love which has been described in so many exalted terms by so many poets. Since one of the purposes of this book is to examine its nature as Dante revealed it, there is no need to delay to do so outside Dante. A question debated is whether it is, in varying degrees, a normal human experience. Those who suppose it not to be will naturally deny that an examination of the pattern of the work dealing with that abnormal state can have any general value. Those who believe that it is may agree that such an examination of a normal state may perhaps have some such value. I am not suggesting that Dante confined his attention to Beatrice alone. Beatrice, as was said above, was met in Florence; and Florence was a city; and images of cities, human and indeed divine, are part of Dante's affirmation. That affirmation was made, by him, in prose and verse; and such prose and verse was the means of his poetic images, and formed in itself an actuality of his life; that is, literature was an image, of which the greatest expression in his own work was the shape of Virgil. It is because Dante knew that there was a great deal other than Beatrice to which he must attend that his attention to Beatrice is valuable. It is that in-

Introduction

clusion which prevents his Way of Affirmation being either a mere sentimentality or a disguised egotism. He was, it must be admitted, moral, for he perceived that images existed in their own right and not merely in his.

The image of the woman was not new in him, nor even the mode in which he treated it. What was new was the intensity of his treatment and the extreme to which he carried it. In his master's great poem—in Virgil's *Aeneid*—the image of the woman and the image of the city had both existed, but opposed. Dido had been the enemy of Rome, and morality had carried the hero away from Dido to Rome. But in Dante they are reconciled; the appearance of Virgil at the opening of the *Commedia* has about it this emphasis also. Virgil could not enter the paradise of that union, for his poem had refused it. But after Virgil the intellect had had visions which it communicated to the heart, if indeed they are so far separate. Since Dante the corrupt following of his way has spoiled the repute of the vision. But the vision has remained. People still fall in love, and fall in love as Dante did. It is not unusual to find them doing it.

There are two other matters which should be touched on in relation to this particular romantic vision and marriage. The first is the error that it is, or should be, the only basis for marriage. It would be as ridiculous to assert this as it is foolish to deny that it often forms such a basis. The 'falling in love' often happens, but it is not to be either demanded or denied. There are many modulations and combinations of vision, affection, and appetite, and none of these modulations is necessarily an improper beginning for that great experiment which we call marriage.

The second, and opposite, error is that it necessarily involves marriage; it may indeed exist—as it seems to have done in Dante's own case—where, for one reason or another, marriage is not only impossible but is never even contemplated. Adoration, and it is adoration of its own proper kind which is involved, may exist between all kinds of people; that kind of secondary worship permitted, under the name of *dulia*, to saints and angels and other express vehicles of the Glory. Where this romantic adoration exists, there this proper intellectual investigation of it ought to exist. The clearest possibility of this Way, and perhaps the most difficult, may be in marriage, but the suggestion of it is

Introduction

defined wherever the suggestion of adoration is present. 'Hero-worship', and even more sentimental states, are only vaguer and less convincing images of the quality which this love is. They are often foolish, but they are apt also to have that kind of sincerity which may, one way or another, become fidelity to the image or to the principle within and beyond the image. One way or another this state is normal; what is not yet normal is the development of that state to its proper end.

It may be thought that the death of Beatrice interferes with the proposition that the way of Dante's imagination can be an image of the normal way of romantic love, whether with marriage or without. There are two answers. The first is that the death of Beatrice corresponds to a not uncommon stage in the sensible development in the Way. Something will be said about that in the third chapter. The second is that the death of Beatrice, or (let us say) the disappearance of Beatrice, does not mean the abandonment of her image; and that the *Commedia*, by its maintenance of that image, exhibits the definitions of the Way in their general application.

We have then three themes with which this book is, one way or another, intended to deal: (i) the general Way of the Affirmation of Images as a method of process towards the inGodding of man, (ii) the way of romantic love as a particular mode of the same progress, (iii) the involution of this love with other images, particularly (*a*) that of the community—that is, of the city, a devotion to which is also a way of the soul, (*b*) that of poetry and human learning. The general maxim of the whole way in Dante is *attention*; 'look', 'look well'. At the beginning he is compelled to look by the shock of the vision; later his attention is enforced by command and he obeys by choice. At the beginning, two of the three images—poetry and the city—are habitual to him though still fresh and young; they do not astonish him. But Beatrice does. *Incipit Vita Nova*. It was, with Dante as with Wordsworth,

> the bodily eye . . .
> Which spake perpetual logic to my soul,
> And by the unrelenting agency
> Did bind my feelings even as in a chain.

II

BEATRICE

The *Vita Nuova* is said to have been written when Dante was twenty-six, directly after the death of Beatrice. He is reported in maturer years to have been 'much ashamed of having made this little book'.[1] This is likely enough; Shakespeare at the time of *King Lear* probably had no great opinion of *Romeo and Juliet*. The greater the poet, the farther his later achievement from his earlier. Even in our degree, we can feel a little, from the midst of the *Paradiso*, how tender, how thrilling, but how young and small a thing it is. That does not prevent it from being much beyond our own capacities at twenty-six.

It is a conventional book; that is, it is written according to the literary habits of his time. Dante was acquainted with contemporary poets and writing more or less in their style. He himself tells us how he sent the first sonnet in it to various well-known poets, 'famosi trovati in quel tempo', and how some of them answered him, and how one answer was the beginning of a friendship between him and its writer, who became the chief of his friends. This too is natural enough; it has a kind of epistolary agreement with

> What things have we seen
> Done at the Mermaid!

or to Wordsworth reading the *Prelude* to Coleridge. But Wordsworth was then thirty-six; the *Prelude* was begun when he was thirty. The events of which he was writing had taken place some years before. It is of interest to observe that the great crisis in Wordsworth's early experience—the declaration of war by England against France; that is, against the Revolution—took place when he was twenty-three: the death of Beatrice is supposed to have taken place when Dante was twenty-four. This, at least, on the assumption that she was Beatrice Portinari. Whether she was or not, whether her actual name was Beatrice or not, is

[1] Boccaccio, *Life of Dante*.

Beatrice

another, and less important, matter. There was a girl; 'for four centuries no biographer and no commentator ... doubted the physical reality of Beatrice.'[1]

Before the experience of this great emerging Image of Beatrice is considered in detail, it is desirable to observe what Dante meant by Love. At a certain point in the *Vita Nuova*—precisely, as we shall see, after the most evangelical of all the significances in Beatrice has been defined—he breaks off his story in order to explain. He says he has been talking throughout about Love 'as if he were a thing in himself and not only an intelligent being but a corporeal being. Which thing according to truth is false, for Love does not exist in himself as a substance does but as an accident in a substance.' It is a quality; it is not, as Dante has been calling it, a living creature. 'I have spoken of Love as a man.' Dante defends this style as traditional and proper; the poets who wrote in Latin did it, therefore so may those who write in Italian. But, he adds, those who do so write must have clear reason for what they do; it is shameful for any man to write in figure and colour and not be able to strip his meaning of such decoration and say plainly what he has in mind.

Love then, however he speaks of it, is a quality—a quality of himself towards Beatrice. It is this quality, once he has become aware of it, which he is to express and analyse, by 'a passion and a miracle of words'. 'Dante', wrote Coleridge, 'does not so much elevate your thoughts as send them down deeper'; that is, make them more profound. The distinction was well made; it is not a rarefying but a deepening and enlargement of this quality and relation which is in question, until it becomes the universal relationship, in its most intense quality, of the close of the *Paradiso*.

Incipit vita nova. He was nine when he first met Beatrice and she was eight. He saw her, during the next nine years, on a number of occasions, but it was not until he was eighteen that she spoke to him. She was then walking in the street with two other ladies, rather older than she was; she had on a white dress, and as they passed him she looked at him and 'saluted' him. It was nine on a May morning of the year 1283, in a street in Florence.

[1] Scartazzini: *A Companion to Dante*; trs. by A. J. Butler. He allows one exception.

Beatrice

Those two meetings together, with all that went between, formed the 'falling in love' of Dante Alighieri, the first but obscure emergence in him of that 'quality' of love. He was full of a

> deep and undetermined sense
> Of unknown modes of being.

He was also a poet, and a particular kind of poet; what kind he describes in the *Purgatorio* (XXIV, 52–63)

> Io mi son un che, quando
> Amor mi spira, noto, ed a quel modo
> che ditta dentro, vo significando.

'I am one who, when Love breathes in me, note it, and expound it after whatever manner he dictates.' He is careful, that is, to be accurate, and he is so sure of this that he causes the redeemed soul to whom he is then talking to congratulate him on it, and to say that Dante's literary style is better than that of others only because of this. The poem of which they are both thinking is a poem which occurs later in the *Vita* and begins: 'Ladies who have intelligence in love'—'ch' avete intelletto d' amore.' It is that 'intelletto d' amore' which he now begins to expound, and which his genius supplied for the profit of later and less articulate lovers.

The appearance of Beatrice, her 'image'—'la sua immagine'—produces at their first meeting three distinguishable effects, which he attributed in the physiological and poetic habit of his day to three centres of the human body. No doubt this analysis was supplied later; we need not suppose it untrue. The 'spirit of life' which dwells in the most hidden chamber of the heart trembled and said 'Behold a god stronger than I who is come to rule over me'. The 'animal spirit' which lived in the brain where all sense-perceptions are known was amazed and said 'Now your beatitude has appeared'. The 'natural spirit' which dwelled 'where our nourishment is distributed'—that is, in the liver—begins to weep and says: 'O miserable wretch! how often now shall I be hampered!' It is something of a pity that poets in English do not any more distinguish between the heart and the liver. Aquinas called the heart 'the organ of the passions of the soul'.[1] These are the greater emotions, the nobler but also no

---
[1] *Vita Nuova*. Temple Classics.

Beatrice

doubt the worse. The liver is the seat of organic life, and in considering the whole history it would be unwise to forget that Dante allowed fully the disturbance to this third seat of his consciousness. It is not, I think, too much to say that his sex, like his intellect, was awakened. That he had, there and perhaps thereafter, no direct desire of Beatrice sexually is likely enough; first love often happens so. But that the potentiality of it was there is also likely. When, later, he says that his 'natural' spirit was 'impeded in its operations', so that he became weak and frail, and his acquaintances grew curious and even spiteful, he must mean at least that this potentiality was present. Long afterwards he was to cry out: 'The embers burn, Virgil, the embers burn', and the fire was general through him.

So much only to prevent too great an 'elevation' of Dante's thought; we are not to suppose him a mere cerebralist. When, after the second critical meeting, he dreamed of Love, and saw in a cloud of the colour of flame the figure of a lord, 'of terrible aspect to whoever should look on him', who seemed 'of such joy as to himself that it was a marvellous thing' it is his first imaginative formation of this 'quality of love'. Love speaks aloud but Dante understands little of what he says, except the words: 'I am thy lord.' This great and terrible figure, fire-shrouded, is carrying Beatrice asleep in his arm, and lightly wrapped in some crimson cloth, and in his other hand something burning, of which he cries to Dante: 'See, your heart!' Then he wakes Beatrice and causes her 'by his art' to eat, though in fear, of the burning thing; and then presently Love begins to weep, and gathers her, and still weeping ascends towards heaven.

They were, said Wordsworth, of other huge and mighty forms, 'a trouble to my dreams.' The dream is generally referred to the death of Beatrice, and so perhaps properly. But this figure is what this accident of substance, this quality of being, this new relation, is. His spiritual emotions, his intellectual perceptions, his organic sensations, all coalesce in a recognition of it and of her by whom it comes. It is no wonder he quotes Homer: 'She did not seem the daughter of a mortal man, but of God.' A kind of dreadful perfection has appeared in the streets of Florence; something like the glory of God is walking down the street towards him. It appears that this is an experience which has

Beatrice

occurred to a large number of young people besides Dante. Their elders do not encourage them to believe that the phenomenon is what it seems; the causes of their elders' hesitation are many, and some of them at any rate are exhibited in the ditches of the *Inferno* or (if they are fortunate) on the terraces of the *Purgatorio*.

This state of things is what Dante calls 'Love'. It must however be stressed that this image of Beatrice is 'of so noble a virtue' that it does not allow Love to triumph without Reason, in all things proper to Reason. This, at that moment, is not a very advanced business; indeed, an opponent might say that Reason is only there to show Dante how to carry himself towards the lady. It would be an unfair retort; at the moment certainly that is Reason's chief occupation because it is Dante's. But the part that Reason plays is the beginning of a much greater part; it is the first determination that this Love is precisely what Wordsworth said his was—

> kindred to our purer mind
> And intellectual life.

Beatrice is 'la gloriosa donna della mia mente'—the glorious lady of my mind. The development of that intellectual concern is to be shown long afterwards—in its rejection and in its affirmation. 'We are come', says Virgil to Dante at the opening of the *Inferno*, 'where I told you you should see that unhappy people who have lost the good of intellect'—'il ben dell' intelletto.' And at the close of the *Paradiso* Beatrice says to him: 'We are come to the heaven which is pure light—intellectual light full of love'—'luce intelletual piena d' amore.' In the *Vita* it is rather love (of its own proper kind) full of intellectual light. But the greatest Romantic poet, like every other true romantic, insists on the intellect at every step of the Way; of that threefold image—Beatrice, love, and intellect—no element was ever false to the others.

With the dedication of the *Vita* to Reason in mind, it is permissible to observe the kind of language that Dante uses concerning the Florentine girl. She has 'an ineffable courtesy'; she is 'la mia beatitudine'—my beatitude; she is 'the destroyer of all vices and the queen of virtue'; she is, in one remarkable poem, 'salute'—salvation. In 1576, when the *Vita* was first printed,

Beatrice

the ecclesiastical authorities revised it for the press. They removed all these semi-theological words; they substituted 'felicità' for 'beatitudine' and 'dolcezza' for 'salute', and they made other alterations. The net result was to cut out as much theology as they could. They were (it seems probable) foolish; but they were not so foolish as those other commentators who, keeping Dante's language, have assumed either (*a*) that Dante did not mean it, or (*b*) that Dante's experience was abnormal and that his language is not applicable to any other love affair. What between clerical caution and lay obtuseness, the idea that Dante's state of being is that of many others, and that the doctrine is generally applicable, and was seriously meant, has been almost lost.

But in fact Dante did mean his language. The proof of it is in the famous passage in which he describes the significance of her 'salutation'. He wished to keep his feelings about Beatrice secret —it was a convention of 'courtly love', but it is also quite a frequent human tendency, especially if combined with a tendency to talk about the beloved on every possible occasion: literary conventions (in spite of some critics) are not necessarily 'psychologically' unsound. He therefore pretended to be 'attentive' to another young woman, and (after that one left Florence) to a third. Of this third lady and Dante there was a good deal of gossip; the worst of the talk came to Beatrice's ears. She cut Dante in the street. 'She refused me her most sweet greeting in which all my blessedness lay.'

He explains what he means by blessedness, and it seems that he meant blessedness. He writes: 'Dico—I tell you when she appeared from any direction, the hope of her admirable greeting abolished in me all enmity, and I was possessed by a flame of charity which compelled me to forgive anyone who had done me an offence; and if anyone had asked me a question about anything, I should have said only *Love!* with a countenance full of humility.' The sight of Beatrice (dico—I tell you) filled him with the fire of charity and clothed him with humility; he became— and for a moment he knew it—an entire goodwill. Neither of these great virtues is gained by considering oneself; and the apparition of this glory, living and moving in Florence, precisely frees him from the consideration of himself. Love is greater than he: his soul was right when it exclaimed: 'A stronger than I

Beatrice

dominates me' and trembled, and his brain was right when it said: 'Behold your blessedness', and even his flesh when it said: 'O misery, how I shall be shaken', as in Malory 'the deadly flesh began to tremble right hard when it beheld spiritual things'. This love certainly does not exclude the physical reactions; his body, he says, was so oppressed by it, as by a surfeit of sweetness, that it felt heavy and lifeless; her greeting was too much for him; it 'passava e redundava la mia capacitade—overpassed and overflowed my capacity'. This too is not without significance when we consider the way in which, in the *Paradiso*, the body is spoken of, 'the glorious and holy flesh' (*Par.* XIV, 43); there the light, beauty, and love of the holy souls will grow greater through their bodies, and they will see more deeply into God. It is an image of this state which he already sees in Beatrice, as for a moment its actuality—humility and charity—is, so far as he can bear it, communicated to his soul.

On this particular occasion she passes and ignores him. That sudden snub, those cold averted eyes, must have struck similarly —for better or worse reasons—on numbers of young men. Dante was young; he was medieval and an Italian; he went away and cried. It did not occur to him to be ashamed of his emotions; he wept and slept—'come un pargoletto battuto lagrimando—like a beaten sobbing little child', and he had a dream of Love. The image of Love appeared to him in sleep on a number of occasions; or (perhaps more truly) he invented these dreams in order to declare something of the nature of this quality of Love. It is not possible to go over all, but this one is of importance. Love appears to him clothed in white and sitting deep in thought; presently he gazes at Dante and after a time says with a sigh: 'Son, it is time to put aside our pretences—*simulacra*', and he himself begins to weep. 'I said: "Lord of nobility, why do you weep?" He said: "Ego tamquam centrum circuli, cui simili modo se habent circumferentiae partes; tu autem non sic." Thinking over these words, it seemed to me he had spoken obscurely, and I forced myself to speak and say to him: "Lord, why do you speak to me so darkly?" And he answered me in the common tongue: "Do not ask more than is useful to you." ' After which they go on to the matter of the snub, and Love causes Dante to write a poem to put himself right with 'our Beatrice'.

Beatrice

But while Love was talking the more ceremonial Latin, what did he mean? 'I am the centre of a circle to which all parts of the circumference are in a similar relation; but you are not so.' The whole crisis is about Dante's unhappiness at Beatrice's behaviour; this saying then has some bearing on it. Dante is not like Love; he is not central to all the circumference. The earlier similitudes are to be put away; they are to speak truth, and the truth is that Dante is not Love. He moves, presumably, on the circumference; he changes and is changed with it, but Love is not. Greeting or no greeting, Love is Love.

> Love is not love
> Which alters when it alteration finds
> Or bends with the remover to remove.[1]

But Dante, for all that momentary charity and humility, is not yet in a state to recognize so much.

There was written by St. Bonaventura, about the same time, a sentence which, with a like simile, had a further aim; it was the famous 'God is a circle whose centre is everywhere and whose circumference nowhere'. The two formulae together cover almost the whole of the Way of Images—and indeed of the Way of Rejection of Images also. Dante is not in the centre; he feels great emotions varyingly; only some parts of the circumference impose goodwill. But to Love in the centre all parts are equal; it does not matter whether the lover is successful or not, happy or not. To be so—'but you are not so'—one must will charity and humility; it is not enough that they shall be communicated by joy. Beyond this again lies that further state when Love is no longer in relation to something in the soul which is not Love; charity and humility do not exist there only in relation to some other particular image; they are at all times everywhere to everyone.

---

[1] The preceding line and a half of the sonnet—
> Let me not to the marriage of true minds
> Admit impediments—

are sometimes taken to refer to two lovers. But this makes nonsense of the next lines, for then one of the 'true minds' must 'alter', or the other could not find alteration. It is rather to the union of two minds with Love that the sonnet refers, which 'bears it out even to the edge of Doom', and the meaning is not unlike Dante's dream.

Beatrice

So that, in this matter of the salutation, Dante knows the fullness of Love on occasion and by grace; but then he has to become it, without the means of that special illumination and particular initiative; and so becoming, all along the Way of the Images, he will find no separate knowledge of them, but in the end their absolute existence, as at the close of the *Paradiso*, where the Divine City exhibits them on all sides.

But at this earlier time it might almost be said that the refusal of the salutation is the second stage on the Way, and it was carried further at a certain feast. It was the wedding-feast of a friend of Beatrice, and Dante had gone there in the company of a friend of his own. He was aware (he says) of the presence of Beatrice before he saw her; his heart shook and a faintness took him. He saw her and was no longer himself, and the young women there began to smile at him and made feminine fun of him to (or with) Beatrice, but his friend seeing something was amiss drew him aside and questioned him. 'And I said: "I have set my feet in that part of life beyond which it is not possible to go with any intention of return." '

Lasciate ogni speranza, voi ch' entrate—those two states are not the same. But they have something in common, and what they have in common is finality. Nothing will ever be the same again; *he* will never be the same again—if he takes another step. There is about him an agony of choice; this now is the quality of love. He cannot bear to see her and he cannot bear not to see her; either is a little death, and all of it is one of the commonest experiences. 'I forget', he wrote in a sonnet, 'all that happens to me, when, fair Joy, I set out to see you, and when I am near you I hear Love saying: "Flee away, if you find it tiresome to perish." My face shows the colour of my heart, which faints and looks for support, and I grow drunk with a great trembling and seem to hear the very stones crying out to me: "Die, die!" ' . . . This is the present climax of self-preservation and self-loss. Love itself says 'Flee', and the stones say 'Die'. The beauty and the joy are too much for him; they are absolute over him; there is in them a high and dreadful conclusion; it is either flight or death.

But if he stays? if he dies this little death? if he, so far, understands this new centre which is Love? It is, I think, true to say that from this point the quality of Love is found illuminating in

Beatrice

a new way. We are still to suppose that Dante was right when he said that he was one who took note when Love spoke, and wrote accurately. What he writes now is the famous 'Donne, ch' avete intelletto d' amore', and it was this poem of which he was thinking in the *Purgatorio*. He remembered and ratified it there; he gave it, that is, the value of his maturity and not only of his youth, the value of his purification as well as the value of his delight. Coleridge was right; Dante does not exalt our thoughts, he makes them infinitely more profound. We ought to have taken at least this poem seriously, if we call Dante a great poet; we might have thought it was meant for all who desire to have intelligence in love, intellect in love.

Briefly, he says (addressing himself only to those ladies who have intelligence in love; it is not proper to speak to the rest), that an angel cried out in divine intellect, and said that a wonder was on earth which shone as if in heaven. Heaven itself desired her presence. But God answered that she must remain on earth a little, for one was there who expected to lose her and who should say in hell to the damned: 'I have seen the hope of the blessed—Io vidi la speranza de' beati.' She is such that whoever stays to behold her becomes a noble thing or dies; she proves her virtue, for he grows so humble that he forgets every offence; this grace God has given her, that whoever speaks with her cannot end badly. Love says of her: 'How can a mortal thing be so beautiful and so pure?' Love gazes at her (riguarda) and swears that God meant to make a new thing (cosa nuova). She has all goodness that Nature can give, and beauty proves itself by her example. This quality of Love sparkles in her eyes and touches the hearts of all who see her, and is painted in her smile which no-one can steadily look on. And Dante, speaking to his own canzone, adds that he has raised it to be a little daughter of Love, young and simple, and it is to go only among those who are courteous—'solo con donna o con uomo cortese'—and with Beatrice it shall find Love; 'recommend me to him.'

Dante wrote this when he was young; he ratified it when he was mature; he put it into the middle of the purging of the soul. He must therefore have supposed that he was talking sense, and not only sense but even holiness. Anyone who thinks him (and even anyone who calls him) a great poet will probably admit so

Beatrice

much. It may also perhaps be generally admitted that Dante did not rationally and out of love suppose Beatrice to be so much of an exception and example to all the young women of Florence as, in love but not unrationally, he imaginatively asserted that she was. The quality of love (he maintained) exhibited in her a heavenly glory. Are we to say that this was so or that it was not so? If so, was it unique, or is it general to other young lovers and other states of adoration? And if general, are we to take the glory as seriously as Dante did? and if so, why? and if not, why not?

These are the questions which, always supposing we go on calling Dante a great poet, we shall have seriously to try and answer. The answers which the present pages support are that the exhibition of glory is actual; that it is also general; that we do well to take it seriously; and for reasons these pages attempt to sustain. The immediate suggestion, put forward elsewhere, which coincides with that canzone, is that what Dante sees is the glory of Beatrice as she is 'in heaven'—that is, as God chose her, unfallen, original; or (if better) redeemed; but at least, either way, celestial. What he sees is something real. It is not 'realer' than the actual Beatrice who, no doubt, had many serious faults, but it is as real. Both Beatrices are aspects of one Beatrice. The revealed virtues are real; so is the celestial beauty. The divinely intelligent angel is quite right; the place of this heavenly creature is heaven. God, not disapproving, says that Dante will call her 'the hope of the blessed'. Beatrice then, so the quality of Love reveals, is the hope of the blessed; that is, the high and glorious Beatricean quality of Beatrice is the hope of the blessed. The phrase itself is obscure. We might allow Dante a rash, even an over-rash, phrase in his youth, but the purgatorial ratification should cause it to be considered further. It may however be left for the moment, only so that it be taken as a serious statement with all that is to follow.

Indeed there had been at least one earlier definition of the same kind. In the earlier pages of the *Vita* is a sonnet on a young lady who died. Dante had once seen her in the company of Beatrice; and (he says) 'I said something of this in the last part of the words which I composed, as clearly appears to him who understands'. The last lines are: 'I will not disclose what lady this

Beatrice

was except by her known quality. He who does not merit salvation must not hope to bear her company.'

> Chi non merta salute
> Non speri mai d' aver sua compagnia.

This, it seems, has been a difficulty to the commentators, yet, on Dante's showing, the thing is clear enough. The dead lady had been in the company of Beatrice; this, he says, is what he was alluding to. Anyone then who wished for her company must be worthy of the company of Beatrice. He who does not merit—Beatrice? say, 'salute', salvation—need not hope to find her. But this is to identify Beatrice with salvation? Yes, and this is the identity of the Image with that beyond the Image. Beatrice is the Image and the foretaste of salvation. This is not proper to say to any but those 'ch' avete intelletto d' amore.'

Of that canzone Dante wrote that he feared he had communicated its intention to too many and it would please him if any who did not understand it let it be. It seems, even in those days of love-doctrine, to have caused a certain sensation. One of his friends asked Dante to tell him then what Love was—this high accident of his substance which dared such similes and definitions, and Dante answered with the 'Love and the gentle heart are one same thing'; Love lies asleep in that heart till the beauty of a wise woman (saggia donna) causes it, by desire, to awaken, and so in a woman's heart does the worthiness of a man. But a greater sequence and one more worthy the preceding doctrine of the conclusion of the sonnet and of the whole of the canzone is in an episode that soon succeeds—the episode, as it were, of the Precedent Lady. On a particular day, Dante writes, 'I saw a gentle lady coming towards me who was well known for her beauty and was the dear lady of my chief friend. Her name was Giovanna (or Joan) but because of her beauty, as it was thought, she was often called Primavera (or Spring), and went by that name. And looking past her, I saw the admirable Beatrice coming. These ladies went by me, one after the other. Then it seemed as if Love spoke in my heart, and said: "The first is called Primavera only because of her coming to-day. For I caused the name to be given her—Primavera, or *prima verra*, 'she will come first', on the day when Beatrice shall be shown to the imagination of her

Beatrice

liege. And if you consider her first name, it is as much as to say 'she will come first', for her name Giovanna (Joan) is from that Giovanni (John) who preceded the true light, saying: 'I am the voice of one crying in the wilderness, Make straight the way of the Lord.' " And I thought Love went on to say other words, namely: "He who should consider this matter subtly would call Beatrice Love, for the likeness she has to me." '

It is at this point that Dante breaks off in order to define Love as a quality and not a thing, an accident and not a substance. He did well; the intellect had to be justified with the greatness the vision demanded. But the defined limitation of the then relation —the substance, the image, and the quality of the substance towards the image—only confirms the permissible vision. If that vision had not developed in the *Paradiso*, we should have been less certain whether we could trust it here. The sight of Joan preceding Beatrice as John preceded Christ would have been nothing but an invention, and at that perhaps a profane invention. But we know—what the young and conventionally writing Dante could not then altogether know—how he was to justify the invention, both for himself and for all future lovers of his school. Beatrice is not indeed to be, in the divine sense, Love though there is a sense in which she is the Mother of Love, the God-bearer. That quality of love which is the beginning of the New Life is to become a quality of the final Consummation. The Way to this knowledge is in the practice of charity and humility and all virtues.

The lord of terrible aspect then has so far defined himself. He is the image of a quality by which the truth of another image is seen, and that other image is a girl in Florence, as it might be in London or San Francisco, in the thirteenth century or in the twentieth. Through her there springs in Dante this new quality. But Love also defines himself as that centre of a circle, and as in some sense one with Beatrice herself. This, to make a gloss on Dante, is the point of the beginning of Romantic Theology; that is, of theology as applied to romantic experiences—as Mystical Theology is applied to mystical experiences; and Dogmatic Theology to thought about dogmas. In this interpretation Beatrice is the Mother of Love in Dante; that love has authority; it communicates and demands charity and humility; it can

Beatrice

endure without failing the application to it of such words as beatitude and salvation. In its light Beatrice is seen in something of her true celestial state; in which state she is declared by Christian doctrine to be precisely what Dante then sees her as being. She follows her precursor as the way of the Lord followed the preluding voice. The vehicle of Love moves in Florence as (after an incomparable and yet comparable manner) it moved in Nazareth. Her 'off-spring' is, beyond Dante's first meaning, indeed a lord of terrible aspect. But the first meaning is not to deny the second implication, any more than the implication of divinity is to negate the meaning of earth. 'Ego dominus tuus.'

III

THE DEATH OF BEATRICE

I. THE DEATH OF BEATRICE

There is no reason to suppose that the death of Beatrice was, in Dante's own life, anything but the death of Beatrice. The *Vita* is a work of art, written afterwards, and therefore the account of her death in it is prepared for and arranged. Hints and dreams precede it; then it follows, one might say, as the second great negative crisis of the book, the first being the refusal of the salutation. The death of her companion, the death of her father, the dream of her own death, precede it, and the significance of hers follows as she herself followed Giovanna in the street of Florence.

It was just after that death of her father that Dante had his own dream. He had been ill and was still lying weak and in pain when he suddenly thought: 'Even Beatrice will certainly die.' It came like one of Wordsworth's 'strange fits of passion', and the fit Wordsworth remembered was similar:

> 'O mercy!' to myself I cried,
> 'If Lucy should be dead!'

He, like Dante in another poem, meant this confession for 'the Lover's ear alone'; there is a confraternity of passion, and both poets belonged to it, in which such things have a simple terror. As Dante lay there, he dreamed he saw faces of women with dishevelled hair floating before him and crying: 'You too will die', and then other more horrible faces which called to him: 'You are dead'—'tu se' morto.' And in the nightmare forms of women weeping and disarrayed followed; and darkness lay on the earth, in which the burning stars seemed to be weeping, like the lord of terrible aspect in the first dream, and there seemed to be earthquakes, in the midst of which a friend of his came up to him and said: 'What! don't you know? your wonderful lady has gone from this world.' He remained staring up to heaven, and all his images of her so combined that he saw a little cloud of great whiteness,

The Death of Beatrice

and flying after it a mass of angels; they were singing gloriously 'Hosanna in the highest!' His doctrine was strong in him; there was more to the dream, for he seemed to see her dead body, her face having an appearance of such humility (tanto aspetto d' umiltade) that she seemed to be saying: 'I am come to see the beginning of peace'—but then he was wakened by those who were watching him just as he cried out: 'O Beatrice, blessed are you!' It was, in the *Vita*, directly after this that the day came on which Beatrice should be 'shown' to her liegeman—almost as if he had not seen her before—following Joan, as the True Light followed John, and was told that if he considered subtly, he would do well to call Beatrice Love. It may be added that, in the ecclesiastical revision of the *Vita*, the censors cut out the Hosanna of the angels, and also the whole passage of Joan, John, and the True Light. It was the less excusable because they had then the *Commedia* also at hand, if they chose, and could have seen that all this was something quite other than a blasphemous amorousness. One must not deny that possibility; it was a danger; it could, with another mind, have been—but with Dante it was not. In an anxiety to control the flesh they did away with everything except the flesh. Something of that habit still lasts among our instructors.

Such was the dream. Now it happened. The news came to him when he was in the middle of a poem. The actual poem is significant. He was writing at this point in the *Vita* of her reputation among other people in Florence, and finding a 'mirabile letizia', 'a wonderful gladness' in the pleasure others took in her. In the first vision of Love, the terrible lord had had 'such joy in himself that it was marvellous', and here it is renewed—the joy with which the adorer hears the adored praised by others. The gay and handsome gentleness, the modesty and full goodness, of the Florentine girl roused a general liking and pleasure in all who knew her. She herself went on, 'coronata e vestita d' umiltà', crowned and clothed with humility. Because of her, other ladies were praised and honoured more; indeed, Dante goes so far as to say in one poem that these other ladies felt no envy, but went along with her in nobility, in love, and in faith. It seems almost as if a Saturnian age of love lived in Florence, where a glory lay on the city because of the princely young miracle that walked in it.

The Death of Beatrice

All this is natural and beautiful. The sweetness—dolcezza—of love trembles and sighs everywhere, but in the full sunlight, not in any wistful shadows. It is sweet and generous and noble, full of humility, honour, and courtesy. They are no dilettantes who so move and sigh and study, but wise women and men of worth; such as, if they had not been so wise and so worthy, would have made the harsh and bloody Florence of history. Here Dante is not talking about the Florence of history; he is, for a moment, seeing in a certain image of youth and love, the Florentine type of the divine City.

Every young lover in Florence perhaps felt the same about his lady; most young poets wrote as if they did. It was a convention of verse, a convention both shaped by and shaping natural truth hitherto unshaped. The golden haze of virtue that hangs over Florence is not in itself untrue; all that matters is whether a true Romanticism examines it or a pseudo-Romanticism is blinded by it. 'Look; attend.' The poems at this point—exaggerate? no; but they stress a single perception, the perception of the young and vivid City lit by the young and vivid Beatrice. Dante's was perhaps in at least a poetic danger of universalizing her influence overmuch, true though he was to human sensibility; he returned from it in a charming phrase to his own immediate state. 'It seemed to me that I had not described how at this time she affected me, and as I could not say this in the shortness of a sonnet I began a canzone.' He wrote the first stanza, which still returned to the same subject—humility. Umil, umile, umiltà—the words throng through prose and verse, so much that we might easily believe that Dante was so conscious of it because he found it of all things the most difficult. Yeats has said that Dante, being a daimonic man, desired his antithesis.

> He set his chisel to the hardest stone.
> Being mocked by Guido for his lecherous life,
> Derided and deriding, driven out
> To climb that stair, and eat that bitter bread,
> He found the unpersuadable justice, he found
> The most exalted lady loved by a man.

It is true that he accused himself of pride. It is our surest evidence; certain stories we have of him suggest the same thing,

The Death of Beatrice

though they would hardly, of themselves, prove it. Yet Milton talked of chastity; we are not therefore to suppose him lecherous. There is no rule; look and pass.

He wrote the first stanza, and then the news came. It was the evening of the eighth of June, 1290. A blank breaks the canzone, and then he turns again to the great Latin, to a sentence from Jeremiah: 'Quomodo sedet sola civitas . . .' 'How doth the city sit solitary, that was full of people! how is she become as a widow, that was great among the nations!' 'The Lord of Justice called this most gentle lady to be glorious under the ensign of that queen, the blessed (benedetta) Mary, whose name had the greatest reverence in the words of this blessed (beata) Beatrice.' It was more proper than perhaps she knew; not than he. At the end of the *Paradiso* the only eyes to which the eyes of Beatrice give place are the eyes of Mary. He was 'abbandonata dalla sua salute'—abandoned by her—whatever exact meaning we give to 'salute', for the light of her humility—'luce della sua umilitate'—had struck through the heavens (a new and substituted canzone sang) so strongly that the eternal Father himself had wondered and had called to himself so great a 'salute'—'tanto salute'. The word recurs as the word 'humility' recurs; it is another quality of Beatrice—salutation in courtesy, salvation in blessedness. It is no wonder the censors cut it out, thinking it too full of meaning; we, leaving it in, make it meaningless. Yet it is the crux of the whole matter.

It had been particularly her quality towards Dante, the quality of her image—la sua immagine—which his own quality of love had revealed to him. His love had somehow seen his most courteous salvation, make what we will of the words. It was gone now, with the actual death of an actual woman, the actual disappearance of an actual joy. The Lord of Justice had called its visibility to himself. Beatrice is dead. Let us forget for a moment that this is Dante and recapitulate as if it were any young man. He has met a young woman; he is attracted to her; his emotions are moved, his sensitiveness increased, his intellect excited, and that dim state of being which we call his soul purged and cleared. He is 'in love'. He is concerned (perhaps) to ask questions about this new quality of life. It seems to him to have a terrible power, grand but (in a sense) ominous, related to every recognizable

The Death of Beatrice

element in him. The girl seems to him something like perfection —though, of course, he knows quite well that she is not, and may even (if he is on more intimate terms with her than ever Dante was with Beatrice) experience quite sharply that she is not. The vision of perfection does not at all exclude the sight of imperfection; the two can exist together; they can even, in a sense, co-inhere. To suppose anything else would be a false romanticism of the worst kind. Proper Romanticism neither denies nor conceals; neither fears nor flies. It desires only accuracy; 'look, look; attend.'

She dies. Innumerable young lovers have mourned such a death. Innumerably more have regretted the disappearance if not of Beatrice yet of that quality in Beatrice, the particular glorious Beatrician quality. Innumerably more again have not regretted it, have almost not noticed it, or have noticed it and easily reconciled themselves to it. It is from that too-easy reconciliation that all aged imbecilities arise, and even the not so aged. 'Young love', 'calf-love', 'it won't last', 'you mustn't expect', 'a quiet affection', and all the rest of the silly phrases—silly not in themselves but in their sound, borrowing silliness from the voices that sound them.

'It won't last.' Or, at least, it does not. An opaqueness, even if a beautiful and dear opaqueness, takes the place of that translucency. The sensitive awareness of perfection disappears, and the spring joy of Beatrice and Love arriving at once. Why then? There are, no doubt, many reasons. Time seems to change it, and custom—'heavy as frost and deep almost as life.' One grows (despite oneself) tired of beholding beauty; the mere monotony of the revelation wearies, and beauty ceases, in one's own sight, to be beauty, and the revelation to be revelation. It may be added, for fairness, that Beatrice—in a closer and more prolonged life than Dante was permitted—is not always celestial. Sin on both sides—original or actual—is a fact; we are too quickly 'disobedient to the heavenly vision'.

Wordsworth said the same thing, in the special terms of his own romantic exploration—

> There hath passed away a glory from the Earth . . .
> At length the Youth beholds it die away
> And fade into the light of common day.

The Death of Beatrice

Say 'the woman' or 'the man' instead of 'the Earth' and the principle is still the same. What then? Nothing; a particular phenomenon has disappeared. It is for us to decide whether its disappearance makes nonsense of its first appearance. If we choose to think so, then for us, no doubt, it will be so. If we choose not to think so, then for us, no doubt, it will not be so. But in itself it is so or not, and whether it is in fact so or not does not at all depend upon our thinking. In this, as in so much, we have on inadequate evidence to make up our minds on the principles of things; it is the old gamble. 'Then the wise course is not to gamble.' 'Yes, but you must; you are not free to choose.' The agnostic, the anti-romantic, gambles as much as the believer and the romantic—nor is he any more certain of the great classic end. He is indeed less certain, for he has ceased to explore the distances; he has given up measuring the times; he has, that is to say, abandoned proportion. But on proportion the classic whole depends. That whole has a place for the romantic beginning; it puts the romantic into its place certainly, and firmly keeps it there. But the anti-classic has no place for any image at all—either of the beginning or of the end, only for a makeshift.

The Beatrician quality has disappeared. But the things that have been said and done in the light of that quality remain; vows, if they have been serious vows, remain. If under the influence of the centre where Love is, we have wished to be at the centre with Love, then we have to get to the centre. It was not by accident that Dante was so intensely aware of humility. Humility has to do with things as well as persons.

There may, in the light of that humility, be something else at work. The fault, wherever it is, if there is a fault, is indefectibly linked to purposes of redemption. The clouding of the translucency may be at the will of the translucency, and the withdrawal of the glory at the will of the glory. Here too, if we may continue the similitude of the young Beatrice with the True Light, it is perhaps the glory which says: 'If I go not away, the Comforter will not come unto you, but if I depart, I will send him unto you.' Similitude? yet the image of the True Light comes in the *Vita* after Love has warned Dante that it is time to put away similitudes and speak plainly. The young lament the vision; the old warn the young—sometimes with tenderness, sometimes

The Death of Beatrice

with abominable gusto—that the vision will go. Few remit to the vision itself the control of its own manifestation.

The purpose of the withdrawal, by whatever power, is evident. There was, in the early days, communicated not only a vision but a conversion. The quality of love which springs from Beatrice and beholds Beatrice seems to 'drive far off each thing of sin and guilt'. It communicates to the worshipper and lover either repentance or virtue or perhaps both. Dante himself, at the girl's greeting, becomes love. That moment may last for the flash of her smile or for an evening or for six months. But it desires more than such a miracle; it desires the total and voluntary conversion of the lover. Dante has to become the thing he has seen in Beatrice, and has, for that moment, been in himself. The maxim: 'This also is Thou, neither is this Thou' applies here. Love is at the centre of the circle, and Dante has to get there; this is the significance of the romantic distances. The sensitive knowledge is withdrawn. There is perhaps another contributory reason—the difficulty of co-ordinating the physical and mental satisfactions. Saint Thomas Aquinas long ago stated that physical intercourse caused a submergence of the rational faculty, which was an evil though no sin. The two climaxes of power seem to be a little opposed. The clear serenity of the intellectual adoration, which is an element in it however intense it may grow, is hidden and pent by the night of desire. The night of desire is thinned and (in a sense) impoverished by the intellectual lucidity. Our virtues are not at ease together. The habit—selfish or generous or both— of physical intercourse, once established, is apt permanently to cloud the intellectual and to make the memory of it weaker. I am far from saying that the eventual good it brings is not necessary and greater than that it seems temporarily to remove. If we take into account children and the co-inherence of married bodies (if fortunate), there is no doubt that it is necessary, and only perhaps in very few cases could the intellectual remain effective in its own scale without that friendship of the body. All that I say is that the lack of immediate co-ordination, natural to us now, is apparently part of the general clouding of the vision. The maintenance of a mutual memory of that intellectual glory might be one of the methods, in due time, of a re-quickening of the vision.

For there remains always the certain knowledge of what has

The Death of Beatrice

been and there remains the free will. In one of the poems of the *Vita* Dante calls Beatrice 'nobile intelletto'. It may be seen presently how this aspect of their relation runs through all; it is sufficient here to feel that the quality of Beatrice is not only a sensitive but an intellectual thing. The recollection of her moves the rational part, even if she no more affects the sensitive, and this rational part can, to a certain extent, still loose her image on the sensitive. It is by that recollection that the lover is helped towards becoming 'a flame of charity', 'a vesture of humility'. He must, without a miracle, become the perfection he has seen.

This removal of the image does not set up a contradictory image; that comes later. The real and extreme contradiction of Beatrice in Dante's work does not lie in her death but in his later civic frustration and banishment from his city. To speak again in the terms of Romantic Theology, this disappearance of the Beatrician quality is not in correspondence with the death of our Lord, but rather with the beginning of his ministry. The wonders of the birth and the hiddenness of the childhood are done. Love must, in every sense, be about his Father's business. The real work of conversion is about to begin. It is one of the duties of marriage—one of those quiet and long duties which make marriage the great business it is—or of whatever state of vigilance corresponds to marriage. It might almost be said that the formal rite of marriage corresponds to the public baptism of our Lord.

> Public profession, vows, the ring, we twain
> A single household; so, he lives again
> His first presenting, and his Temple stay,
> The three years following his baptismal day.

The ceremony is not, in the strictest sense, necessary any more than that Baptism;[1] in both, Love submits to a Rite—'thus it becometh us to fulfil all righteousness.' It does; that is why it seems to withdraw; that is why its power remains.

---

[1] That is, 'the ministrants of the sacrament are the contracting parties themselves.' (*The Church and Marriage*, S.P.C.K., 1935, App. I. *Short Notes by a Roman Theologian*.) But the Roman Church decrees that the contract must be made before a priest 'under penalty of non-validity for lack of form'. I quote this that no-one may accuse me of wishing to make Dante an Anglican.

The Death of Beatrice

II. AFTER THE DEATH OF BEATRICE

The image of the City of Florence had existed all this time in the background of Beatrice and as a background to Beatrice. There were a great many other young women, of whom the young Dante obviously had a very clear awareness. So much has been tiresomely said about Dante's 'spiritual and ideal' love that we are apt to overlook this human and normal quality in him. It would not be altogether surprising to find that Beatrice had more reason for her snub than is usually supposed; she may even have known her Dante better than we do; or she may have been misinformed on the particular facts of that episode and yet have been intelligent in her general understanding of the situation. Or she may have been simply and heartily, and as innocently as possible, jealous. At any rate, of the young women of Florence Dante was very precisely aware—as nobly as you like, but still aware. They are part of the massed background; part, that is, of the general and still undefined mass which is, presently, to be analysed and defined into the City—first the Italian, then the mythical, then the divine. And then there are the other poets his friends, and Beatrice's father, and the 'people of importance' who came when he was drawing an angel. (But Browning was inaccurate in his gibe; he supposed them *not* to be of importance, but what Dante says is 'I saw men to whom it was proper to do honour'—'uomini a' quali si convenia di fare onore.' They were gentlemen of standing in the City.)

The death of Beatrice removes, for readers of Dante, the single image which stands between them and the image of Florence; we have to make what we can of the hints scattered through Dante's work before we can decide what then happened. Florence consisted of men and women; we are more or less clear on what happened between Dante and the men, but not at all so clear on what happened between him and the women. It will perhaps be convenient briefly to sum up the first before saying anything on the great disputes which continue regarding the second.

There is no need to plunge into Italian politics. In 1289, during the Beatrician period, he had taken part in a military campaign, and fought in a battle—mounted and in the front line. He saw a fortress surrender, and watched and took part in all the move-

The Death of Beatrice

ments of the Florentine forces. In 1295 he took up politics seriously, joining the popular as against the aristocratic party. 'Popular' however in a limited sense; there was nothing of the demagogue in him, and very little of democracy in our common sense of the word. He says in the *De Monarchia*: 'It is only when a monarch is reigning that the human race exists for its own sake, and not for the sake of something else. For it is only then that perverted forms of government are made straight, to wit, democracies, oligarchies, and tyrannies, which force the human race into slavery.' Like Shakespeare and Milton Dante firmly believed in degree, though he also passionately believed in the individual. And there may be quoted here that great sentence which is a governing clause in all his thought: 'Unde est, quod non operatio propria propter essentiam, sed haec propter illam habet ut sit.' 'The proper operation (working or function) is not in existence for the sake of the being, but the being for the sake of the operation' (*De Monarchia*, I, iii). This is true of Beatrice and Virgil and the Blessed Virgin and all his friends and enemies and himself also. Dante was created in order to do his business, to fulfil his function. Almighty God did not first create Dante and then find something for him to do. This is the primal law of all the images, of whatever kind; they were created for their working and in order to work. Hell is the cessation of work and the leaving of the images to be, without any function, merely themselves.

It was the function of Dante, or so he thought, to be political. We know that from 1295 to 1296 he played a part in the various Councils which helped to govern the city; he re-appears in 1300 when he was sent on a mission, and in the same year he became one of the 'priors'. These priors were six in number; they held office for two months. So that the number of priors and past-priors in Florence was high. He held office from 15 June to 14 August 1300—the year in which the vision of the *Commedia* is set. The whole city was then in tumult and civil struggle. The two factions —the Whites and the Blacks—were at grips, with the Pope (Boniface VIII) supporting the Blacks. In the year 1301 the crisis developed; in June Dante in council opposed the requests of the Pope; on 28 September in the same year he spoke there for the last recorded time. On 1 November Charles of Valois, summoned by the Pope, entered Florence in support of the

The Death of Beatrice

Blacks. The Whites were driven out, and on 27 January 1302 sentence was passed against Dante. He was accused of corruption and fraud, of having disturbed the peace, and of other high misdemeanours. He was sentenced to a fine of five thousand florins, two years' exile, and perpetual exclusion from any office in Florence. On 10 March it was further decreed that he and fourteen others should be burned alive if they should at any time be captured by Florence. On 19 May 1315 the exiles, however, at another crisis, were offered a recall on payment of a small fine, a formal imprisonment, and a ceremony of submission; Dante refused the conditions. But the sentence seems to have been reduced to detention in an appointed place; for further contumacy however he was further condemned, with his two sons, to decapitation.

For nineteen years he lived in exile, passing from town to town for a longer or shorter time. In 1321, on the night of 13 September, he died at Ravenna. He was then fifty-six years old.

This is the history of Dante in relation to the men of the actual city. It is not very much, yet the other stories are mostly disputed and uncertain. Of his history in relation to the images of women in the city we know even less. Outside his own work we know only that he married Gemma di Manetto Donati. He is thought to have been betrothed to her as early as 1277 when he was twelve; the marriage itself was before 1297. During the exile she seems to have remained in Florence. They had three children—two sons, Jacopo and Pietro, who afterwards joined him at Ravenna, and a daughter, Antonia, who, it is thought, entered religion at Ravenna and took the name of Beatrice—'Suora Beatrice', a Dominican nun.

So much for the—it would unfortunately be rash to call them facts, but reports as near facts as can be managed. It is possible now to return to Dante's own work with the original question—What happened after the death of Beatrice? When that image was withdrawn, did others appear? and if so, how?

What then it seems happened was something like this. A little while after the death of Beatrice Dante saw at a window the face of a young woman who was looking at him with great pity and compassion. ('Pietade' is his word; that word which covers so much, due and not due, propriety and generosity.) He found

The Death of Beatrice

himself, in his state of desolation, much moved by that silent gaze, and as he went on he said to himself: 'Surely most noble Love must dwell with so compassionate a Lady.' His thought thus directed to her, he observed, whenever he met her, that her pity seemed to grow. She was of a paleness which seemed 'color d' Amore', 'the colour of Love', and he remarked it the more because Beatrice had been of a like pallor. If 'a sorrow's crown of sorrow is remembering happier things', this visible recollection of Beatrice at once accentuated and eased the pain. It enabled and soothed his grief. Others besides Dante have discovered this, and the delicate self-deceit (could one say so!) which it holds. Dante himself, like those others, discovered that he was in fact finding not merely ease of grief but a good deal of delight in seeing the lady. This discovery of his dishonesty shocked and angered him; he turned against himself, 'Vanità', vanity! he wrote; but now that the delight was discovered, it still recurred, and he even thought that this was 'per voluntà d' Amore', 'by the will of Love', in order that his life might reach repose.

It is, in view of the *Convivio*, important to remark that he thus raised the reference of the Lady of the Window to Love. Love must (I suppose) at this point in the *Vita* be still that kind of quality which it has been defined as being. It is not for us to diminish the augustitude which the lord of terrible aspect has taken on. Dante's difficulty is that he suspects himself to be tempting himself with a kind of false pretence, an encouragement of a pseudo-identity of Love. This encouragement seemed to him for a little 'a gentle thought'; he composed a sonnet on it; 'it', he imagined himself saying to the Lady of the Window, 'speaks of you . . . it reasons so dulcetly of love that it causes the heart[1] to consent. . . .' Then the heart says to the reason: 'O pensive Reason, this is a new breathing of Love . . . his life and all his worth spring from the eyes of that compassionate one who was so disturbed at our torment.'

'A vile sonnet' he called it—*vilissimo*. It can only have been so vile because he was trying to persuade himself of the identity of a Love which was not in fact there; that love, that high vision, was still with Beatrice. 'Against this enemy of Reason'—the words are to be noted; it is intellect and knowledge which are

[1] Here, he says, 'heart' means appetite.

The Death of Beatrice

offended—there came to him one morning about nine o'clock an intense visual recollection of his first meeting with Beatrice; from that he thought again of all the order of those times that were now over, and set his heart and mind again on her. The end of the *Vita* holds, not merely that resolution, but the result of that resolution. The last sonnet is very remarkable. It was written for two ladies who wished to have some verse of his; and his respect for them was such that he determined to write them a new poem. This was the poem:

'Beyond the farthest sphere, the Primum Mobile itself, the sigh passes which issues from my heart; it has a new intelligence which Love in tears has given it, and this draws it upward. When it has come where it desires to be, it sees a lady so honoured and so shining that this pilgrim spirit wonders at her splendour. It sees her such that, when it tells its knowledge again to me, I cannot understand it, so subtly does it speak to the sorrowing heart which causes it to speak. I know that it speaks of that noble lady for it often recalls Beatrice—so that then I understand well, dear ladies mine.' 'My thought', he added as a comment, 'rises to her quality in such degree that my intellect cannot comprehend it, for our intellect is to those blessed souls as our weak eyes are to the sun—and this Aristotle says in the second book of his Metaphysics.'

It was directly after this that there was given to him 'a very wonderful vision'—and he determined to write no more of her till he could write worthily, and then 'such things as have never yet been written of any woman'. The sonnet, with its Aristotelian reference, is hardly to be separated from the vision. He had, in some way poets may understand and the rest of us believe, gripped the principle of the *Commedia*; it was to be *this* and nothing else, dim as the method, uncertain as the details, might be. He had refused the false persuasion, the too-easy inclination, the pseudo-image; he was given the true result of the true image.

If everything had stopped there, it would have been much, but both he and we were given more. He finished the *Vita* on that high note. Years afterwards he sat down to the *Convivio* and there, serious and unashamed, told us the rest. This book was to be an arrangement, with long prose commentary, of fourteen canzoni; but only the introduction and the treatises, or chapters, on the first three poems were finished. It seems likely that Dante

The Death of Beatrice

abandoned it in favour of the *Commedia*. Its date is supposed to be during the early years of the exile, though some of the poems were written earlier. 'It is', says Dr. Gardner, 'the first important work on philosophy written in Italian—an innovation which Dante thinks necessary to defend in the chapters of the introductory treatise, where he explains his reasons for commenting upon these canzoni in the vernacular instead of Latin, and incidentally utters an impassioned defence of his mother-tongue.' He says of it indeed, in a sentence which relates the image of speech to the image of Beatrice: 'This my native speech drew me into the path of knowledge which is our particular perfection, for by her aid I began Latin, and by her aid learned it—that Latin by which I was able to go farther, so that all can see, and I myself acknowledge, that she has been my benefactor in the greatest degree.'

It was, however high the phrases, the common thing from which Dante always started, as it was certainly the greatest and most common to which he came. His images were the natural inevitable images—a girl in the street, the people he knew, the language he learned as a child. In them the great diagrams are perceived; from them the great myths open; by them he understands the final end. The *Convivio* was meant to be for the common folk (not necessarily the poorest). Dante wrote of it that it should be the barley bread through which thousands should be filled, and baskets of it remain over for him. It should be 'a new light and a new sun, to shine when the old sun should set, and to give light to those who were in darkness because that old sun did not shine for them'. Italian instead of Latin? no doubt. Explication of the principles of existence? philosophy? no doubt. But perhaps also some intuition, some seizure by the Imagination, of the union of all those Images, without loss of any, in the in-Godding, and the relevance between them on the Way.

The new book was to deal with the same subject as the old—that is, love and virtue. The fourteen odes had been admired by many, but rather for their beauty than their goodness—say, their doctrine. Now their meaning is to be explained. 'And if in the present book the theme is treated more virilely than in the *Vita*, I do not intend that as any derogation from that earlier book, but rather that that should be helped by this.' It is reasonable that

The Death of Beatrice

the *Vita* should be fervid and passionate, and that the *Convivio* should be temperate and masculine. Style of speech and action changes as one's age changes; 'in the former work I spoke when I was entering on my youth, now in the latter when it has gone by.' The canzoni, he adds, have a different intention from their apparent meaning; he will discuss both—the allegorical and the literal. He has been reproached for having yielded to such a passion as the canzoni suggest; he will show now that it was not passion but virtue which moved him—'la movente cagione.' The noun is worth remembering for the *Commedia*.

The *Vita* and the *Convivio* then are on the same subject; they treat 'di amore, come di virtù'. The *Vita* had been (say) feminine and passionate; the *Convivio* is to be masculine and intellectual. The poems (in both? certainly in both) have two meanings—literal and 'allegorical'; he will deal with both. It is perhaps worth while pointing out that when a poem is said to have two meanings, both are included in the poem; we have only one set of words. The meanings, that is, are united; and the poem is their union. The poem is an image with many relevancies, and not only so, but it is itself the expressions of the relevancy of its own images each to other. The poem, not the literal or allegorical meanings, is the existing thing, the image we have to deal with; the meanings assist and enrich the line; they do not replace it (which is the danger of all—even necessary, even Dante's—criticism and comment). One goes outside the poem, in following the meanings, but only to return; only to centre again what, for a good purpose, has been de-centred. Poetry also, as Virgil might have said, 'is at the centre of a circle to which all parts of the circumference are equal, but with criticism it is not so.'

This then is the kind of work the *Convivio* is to be; the definition is laid down and the introductory treatise ends. We come to the first canzone and the Second Treatise, and again to the Lady of the Window. She is introduced as ceremoniously and astronomically as Beatrice had been. 'The star of Venus had twice revolved ... since the passing of that blessed Beatrice who lives in heaven with the angels and on earth with my soul, when that gentle Lady of whom I spoke at the end of the *Vita* first appeared to my eyes accompanied by Love, and took some place in my mind.' This means three years after the death of Beatrice—a

The Death of Beatrice

considerable time after the apparent close of the *Vita*. He says here, as he said there, that her tenderness greatly moved him; he rested in her compassion, her 'suffering with' him; and from that he came to take pleasure in being 'a disposari a quella immagine', at the disposal of that image. There was a long struggle, which the canzone describes. But (as he frankly says) the image of her was strengthened day by day, whereas even his memory could not so strengthen the image of Beatrice. So that, at last, 'with a kind of cry, to excuse myself for what seemed to me a weakness, I turned my voice to the quarter from which proceeded the triumph of the new thought, which was greatly victorious, being a heavenly virtue.'

The new thought—'nuovo pensiero'—is virtuous; the new love —'nuovo amore'—is perfected—'fosse perfetto'. All this is summed up in the phrase which he would not certainly use in the *Vita*, and the equivalent of which he will use here: 'most noble Love was with her.' It is not surprising that a young man, after the death of his girl, should fall in love with another girl; it has been known to happen even before the death of the first. The fact that Dante took three years over it is a considerable tribute to his firmness; it is also a tribute to his determination to mean by Amor here what he had meant by Amor before. 'Repetition', wrote Kierkegaard in his *Journals*, 'is a religious category,' but it was distinguished from mere change. It is the renewed investigation of that Amor to which Dante turns.

It will be convenient to postpone any remarks on that investigation for a brief discussion of what we may call the general principle of the Second Image, since that, whatever Dante may be, seems as much a contemporaneous problem now as at any time. We are hampered in discussing Dante's biography (and most fortunately) by three things. (i) We do not know what eventually happened to him and the Lady of the Window. The *Convivio* was never finished, where we might have had some information, and after the *Convivio* she is not named. (ii) We do not know what part Gemma Donati, whom he married before 1297, played in his imagination. It has been suggested that she and the Lady of the Window were the same; nothing could be more pleasantly attractive, but there is nothing to show it, and the balance of critical opinion is against it. There is no need at all to assume an unhappy marriage;

The Death of Beatrice

we are gradually coming to believe—especially since Sir Edmund Chambers rehabilitated 'the second best bed'—that Shakespeare's may not have been, and we might leave ourselves an equal freedom with Dante. That Gemma remained in Florence while he was in exile tells us nothing certain either way. (iii) When, abandoning the *Convivio*, he devoted the energy of his genius to the *Commedia*, he returned to the earlier Beatrician image. From all that he says it seems as if that particular passion, sometimes obscured, sometimes outshone, burned to the end: 'conosco i segni dell' antica fiamma'—'I know the signs of that ancient flame,' he cried out in the *Purgatorio* (XXX, 48). And at that, for the moment, it must be left.

Beatrice is dead; the Lady of the Window appears; Dante, at first maintaining a fidelity, at last finds that the same noble Love that he had known dwells with her also. This is simple enough. But suppose Beatrice is not dead? Or rather, supposing she is dead only in the sense suggested earlier—that the Beatrician quality has been withdrawn? that Amor, the god, has clouded himself from operative physical sight? what then?

The original Beatrician experience—the knowledge of the quality of love off-springing from the quality of Beatrice, and the quality of Beatrice off-springing from the quality of love ('figlia del tuo figlio')—was felt at first to be a unique thing. Certainly that first communication of charity and humility, that first sensible coming of the Holy Ghost, is, in terms of time, unique. But terms of time are not the only measurement; and even in terms of time the principle of that first exposition reaches everywhere. It may be well enough for those who do not believe in the objective reality of the glory to be content with their chance sensations, to be pseudo-romantically discriminatory towards one or pseudo-romantically indiscriminatory towards all. The first is ideal sentimentalism; the second is ideal promiscuity. But the doctrines of Romantic Theology will have no such easy satisfaction. Maintaining that the beloved is there seen in her proper and heavenly perfection, they maintain also that such a perfection is implicit in every human being, and (had we eyes to see) would be explicit there. The Christian religion declares as much. It is certain that many lovers have seen many ladies as Dante saw Beatrice. Dante's great gift to us was not the vision but the

The Death of Beatrice

ratification, by his style, of the validity of the vision. Where we ignorantly worship, there he defined. But, on that Christian showing to which he was committed, his style and those other lovers' insight are themselves only valid because that perfection is the arch-natural state of human beings as such, seen after that arch-natural manner. It is everyone's or it is no-one's; on that there can be no compromise.

But then why do we not see it always, everywhere, and in all? Because the Divine Mercy intervenes. Mercy? Mercy assuredly. 'We cannot', wrote Dante in the third Tractate of the *Convivio*, 'look fixedly upon her aspect because the soul is so intoxicated by it that after gazing it at once goes astray in all its operations.' The first manner in which it goes astray is in a tendency always to extort from the glory its own satisfaction with the glory. The alternative to being with Love at the centre of the circle is to disorder the circumference for our own purposes. This—the perversion of the image—is in fact the sole subject of the *Inferno*, although Beatrice herself is hardly mentioned there. If such a perversion follows so easily on a single seeing, would it be less likely to follow on a multitudinous? If the gazing fixedly on one divine aspect is apt to intoxicate the soul and send it reelingly astray, what chaos would follow if all men and women were so beheld, what sin, what despair! Dante himself had seen the danger in the *Vita*; the *Donne, ch' avete intelletto d' amore* is to go only to those who are courteous; to the rest it was not proper to speak. While we are what we are, the Divine Mercy clouds its creation. In the old myth, the Adam, once they had insisted on seeing good as evil, were mercifully ejected from Paradise; how could they have borne with sanity that place of restrained good, all of which could be known as unrestrained evil? So we, being also with the Adam in the Fall. In the *Commedia*, it is only at the end of the Way of Affirmation, and of its rejections, purgations, and indoctrinations, that the light of all the saints is seen united with that of Beatrice, and the humility and charity of all the City burns sensitively on human eyes.

This universalism, by the Mercy, does not endanger us; it is a truth clear to our intellects, obscure to our flesh. It serves however to direct attention to the problem, after the Beatrician revelation and the Beatrician withdrawal, after vows taken to Beatrice, of

The Death of Beatrice

the appearance of the second image of the Beatrician kind. If, as has been suggested, this quality of love lies at the root of many marriages, then the problem is contemporary enough and urgent enough—and perhaps in other fidelities of the soul, but let us say marriage and mean (as far as may be) all. The Christian Church has insisted that certain conditions are necessary for the carrying out of that great experiment of marriage: free choice, intention of fidelity, physical capacity. The physical union which is permitted, encouraged, and indeed made part of the full 'salute' of that first experience is to be forbidden to any other. Why, if the vision is credible and identical? if (in terms of Dante) 'most noble Love' indeed abides with the Lady of the Window?

The aim of the Romantic Way is 'the two great ends of liberty and power'—'la podestate', 'la nobile virtù', 'lo libero arbitrio.' To be free one must have power to accept or reject. Having thriven in one manner, we are offered the opportunity of thriving in another; we are offered the opportunity of being free in the glory. The second image is not to be denied; we are not to pretend it is not there, or indeed to diminish its worth; we are only asked to free ourselves from concupiscence in regard to it.

> The rash oath of virginity
> Which is first love's first cry

must have a lofty education—more perhaps than it or we wished. That first oath had in it no Gnostic denial of earth, nor must its later ratification have; we are not, in the words of an ancient canon, 'blasphemously to inveigh against the creation.' The first image was towards physical union; the second towards its separation. It repeats the first, in an opposite direction. But both movements are alike intense towards most noble Love: that is, towards the work of the primal Love in the creation.

Natural jealousy and supernatural zeal—the zeal of the officers of the supernatural rather—have brought us to regard that great opportunity of the second image rather as a sin than as a goodness. Of the two jealousy is the more potent. It is a form of envy, and in the *Commedia* it is properly exhibited by the livid colour of the stone on that terrace in Purgatory where it is lived through, by the haircloth and the eyes sewn up with wire: 'luce del ciel di sè largir non vole' (*Purg.* XIII, 69), 'the light of heaven does not will to give largely of itself.' The doctrine of largesse is here objectively contradicted as it was subjectively in the sin; but a voice cries out: 'they have no wine', recalling the largesse of our courteous Lord. Jealousy is the old man on the new way, who does not know courtesy even there, the courtesy which Virgil shows and Beatrice and all the blessed. Not to be jealous, it is often supposed, condones the sin, if sin there be. That anyhow is false; to be jealous only increases the first sin of infidelity to the Image by developing elsewhere another, that of infidelity to most noble Love. But there need not be sin; to observe and adore the glory is not sin, nor to receive the humility and charity shed from the glory, of the second image, or indeed any number—say, up to that seventy times seven in a day which our Lord chose as the only limit of the exercise of love. It has often been the habit of lovers, in the first rush of love, to cry out that they will not be rancorous, even if their lovers find another image. That they are not usually able to manage it is no spoiling of that first goodwill; a later impulse does not destroy the validity of the original impulse. He who hates the manifestation of the kingdom hates the kingdom; he is an apostate to the kingdom.

Saint Augustine is reported to have said that he often could not make adulterers understand that they were doing wrong. There was perhaps more excuse for them than the great doctor altogether guessed, especially if among the cares of the Church (and there was every excuse for him) he had forgotten his African love, or had perhaps loved her without the quality of the new life. However much excuse, they were still wrong. But perhaps denunciation is not the best way of correcting the error; or perhaps the error cannot be properly corrected until jealousy is denounced as strongly as adultery (whether with or without divorce). An awful truth lurks behind the comic figure of the complacent husband or wife; they are indecent, but the true decency is on the farther side. If it were possible to create in marriage a mutual adoration towards the second image, whenever and however it came, and also a mutual limitation of the method of it, I do not know what new liberties and powers might not be achieved. Meanwhile, so limiting the method, we must wholly practise passion without concupiscence wherever the principle of all the images appears.

The Death of Beatrice

Marriage is the great example, in this sense, of the Way of Affirmation. The intention of fidelity is the safeguard of romanticism; the turning of something like the vision of an eternal state into an experiment towards that state. Once that experiment has been formally begun, it cannot be safely abandoned, or so the Christian Church maintains. No other experiment of the same complete kind can be begun in the Omnipotence, once the Omnipotence has conjoined itself with the lovers' assent to the first.[1]

The appearance of a second image however is not in itself a beginning of a second experiment; it might be a desirable prolongation and enlargement of the first. The Way of Affirmation is, in this small detail, enlarged to include the Rejection; and how? by a preference of the principle of satisfaction to satisfaction itself. So to unite all, so to press towards what (in the doctrine) is the truth of the whole City, is to take a step towards unity. Fidelities are of many kinds; much more than marriage is sealed in them. Our functions are not in existence for the sake even of our immortal beings, but our immortal beings for the sake of our functions. To love is to love and serve the function for which the loved being was created, whatever that may mean or involve; this is the definition of the Way, the end of which is in that point from which heaven and all nature hangs: 'depende il cielo e tutta la natura.'

[1] It is true that the Church, in spite of the Montanists, has not disapproved of second marriages. But in those cases it is held that the first experiment has been concluded by death, which is the intervention of Almighty God, though by that outrage which he himself endured; and that the very conditions of the great experiment are therefore removed. Marriage is, partly at least, a recovery of matter; where there is no matter there is no marriage.

IV

THE *CONVIVIO*

The Lady of the Window then has been accepted as a vehicle of most noble Love. That is simple and credible. What had burst on Dante with a profound shock in the person of Beatrice had in this other appearance been a matter of slow growth. His reluctance had taken three years to recognize the identity. It is perhaps a hint that, at certain times, we too may have to exercise patience and goodwill, and another hint that, given goodwill, the nature of Love is always discoverable. I should not find it impossible, though I concede that it is the opposite of Dante's problem, to draw a further lesson and apply it to Beatrice herself. When she is 'dead', when her quality has been withdrawn, then comes the time to assert that humility and charity. Charity, in this sense, begins at home. The second image, so, would be more like a second coming of Love, more like the Parousia itself. Even that perhaps is more at our disposal than we know, and may deign to depend, at least in part, on the liberty and power of the faithful. Where Love has once been, it does not—except in hell—refuse to return.

But other things had been happening during those three years. Dante, recording them, proceeded to involve generations of commentators in a difficulty. He says (II, xiii) that after the death of Beatrice he turned for consolation to various books; notably Boethius' *Consolation of Philosophy*. Boethius was a Roman who had written this book while in prison and under sentence of death; it was an effort, and a very noble effort, to actualize to himself the principles in which he had supposed he believed. The great attempt profoundly affected Dante also. Love-in-grief, as he had said in the *Vita*, gave him a new insight; his desolation opened out into comfort and more than comfort—power. 'I found', he says, 'the vocabulary of authors, of sciences, of books.' More than ever before, he discovered and understood words. 'Visionary power,' wrote Wordsworth,

> Attends the motions of the viewless winds,
> Embodied in the mystery of words:

The Convivio

> There, darkness makes abode, and all the host
> Of shadowy things work endless changes—there,
> As in a mansion like their proper home,
> Even forms and substances are circumfused
> By that transparent veil with light divine,
> And, through the turnings intricate of verse,
> Present themselves as objects recognized
> In flashes, and with glory not their own.

Something of this sort happened to Dante; but where Wordsworth was talking chiefly of great poets, Dante was talking chiefly of great philosophers. Both of them, however, received an *'increase of enduring joy'*. 'Light divine' is peculiarly appropriate to Dante, for to him it was not only a divine light; it was also in particular the light of divinity; that is, of the study of divinity. His new and enlarged imagination of philosophy drove him to go 'where she is truly revealed—to the schools of the Orders of religion and the disputes of the philosophers'. He spent in all this study some thirty months, by the end of which time he was wholly devoted to it. He thought of it 'as a gentle and compassionate lady'; 'love of her drove out and abolished every other thought'; 'I felt myself raised from the thought of my first love to the power of this.' Three years and thirty months are as near the same as makes no matter. It was after three years from the death of Beatrice that he had celebrated in a canzone the victory of the 'new thought' of the Lady of the Window; it was after thirty months from the same time that he celebrated—in the same canzone—the triumph of the lady Philosophy. Are they then the same? Apparently. 'I declare and affirm that the lady of whom I was enamoured after my first love was the most fair and noble daughter of the Emperor of the Universe, to whom Pythagoras gave the name of Philosophy.' 'Dico e affermo che la Donna, di cui io innamorai appresso lo primo amore, fu la bellissima e onestissima figlia dello Imperadore dell' universo, alla quale Pittagora pose nome *Filosofia*.'

It could not be more definitely put. When great poets make such clear statements, we should in general simply believe them. Yet a certain school of critics has consistently refused to believe that the Lady of the Window was nothing but Philosophy. They

The Convivio

think she was, in fact, what Dante originally said she was—a lady of Florence who looked at him compassionately from a window. She may—or rather the image of her in Dante's mind may, they admit, have been in some sense Philosophy also. But they suggest that Dante, in the reasons he gave for explaining the canzoni wholly in this philosophical sense, 'gave himself away.' What he says is that he was afraid people would misread the canzoni, and would suppose that he was entirely dominated by 'passion', and not by virtue (I, ii); that in fact his readers have so misunderstood the poems (II, xiii); but that now he will explain, beside the literal meaning, the allegorical, and then everyone will know what he is truly writing about. Love of a mortal woman? No; how could they think so? It is true that, as the editor of the Temple *Convivio* says, 'he had never till now made the experiment of telling them anything else,' so that his readers' error was not altogether surprising. But now he will be clear; it is this compassionate lady Philosophy whom alone he loves.

It would have been easier to believe, whole-heartedly, if Dante had left the particular Lady of the Window out of the *Convivio* altogether, if he had not made an effort to include in this new explanation the episode at the end of the *Vita*. We should then have been quite willing to believe that after the death of Beatrice and the rejection of the other Lady, he had turned wholly to Philosophy. But he will not make it easy for us in that manner. He will have it that the other Lady was Philosophy throughout; that is the only reason apparently that the Lady of the *Vita* is brought into the *Convivio* at all. But it is almost impossible, whatever Dante says, to believe that she was only Philosophy in the *Vita* (where no suggestion of the kind is made) and therefore it is difficult to believe that she is nothing but Philosophy in the *Convivio*. Is there any reconciliation?

Let us ask first what difference it makes. We are not here concerned with Dante's biography as such; only with it (in what he says of it) in relation to his work. The pattern of that work is more credible—it has less violence imposed upon it—if we allow that the second Lady was a real woman in the *Vita* and therefore in the *Convivio*; that he was still pursuing, though after another manner, the great study he had begun in the *Vita*; but that he was pursuing it after a different manner, merely because he was

The Convivio

himself older and himself more philosophical. The difference that it makes is simply that in the one case he is attending only to Philosophy; in the second case, he was attending to a woman and to Philosophy at the same time. The difference is very small, and yet perhaps to us important. Dante imagining Philosophy as a woman is doing what great poets do, and conveying to us by a poetic image the sensibilities of his intellectual concern. Dante discovering a woman to be Philosophy is doing the same thing, no doubt, but he is also setting us an example, if we are of the kind that wishes for such an example. The one is a great invention; the other is a knot of union. Of the first we say: 'How beautiful!'; of the second: 'How true!' It is therefore this second possibility which carries the greater intensity. It is this also which fits better (before and after) with the image of Beatrice in the *Vita* and the image of Beatrice in the *Commedia*. Sooner or later, denying the actuality of the Lady of the Window, we are driven very near to denying also the actuality of Beatrice; for the *Convivio* is a discourse on that development of the soul into Perfection which it was Dante's task to describe (and to be), the plan of the way to the centre. As for reconciliation, it is not unlikely, even if we take that point of view, that Dante was annoyed with the interpretations put upon the canzoni. If you are seriously engaged on the attempt to analyse a real woman as philosophy and philosophy as a real woman—it is disconcerting to have it generally supposed that you are completely taken up by a carnal passion for her. The Lady of the Window—unknown even beyond Beatrice, young, compassionate, noble, and the subject of so high an experiment—gleams for a moment and disappears. Perhaps she too was disappointed; perhaps this intense intellectual passion was not at all that for which she had looked. Or perhaps she was not; perhaps it was more than all. There is an Ode, a canzone—the sixth of those which were to be commented on in the *Convivio*—in which Dante complains of her cruelty, and sighs for revenge. It does not read as if he were then brooding on the difficulties of study, on the remoteness of philosophy, or the unfriendliness of Saint Thomas Aquinas. On the other hand, in the fourteenth canzone of the same series, written for those who are 'enamoured', 'in love', he says that to men virtue was given, and to women beauty, and to Love power to make the two one. The

The Convivio

Convivio may be read as an effort, at least intellectually, to express that union of the two. It was abandoned, perhaps because it was already failing, perhaps because the difficulties of explaining some poems were too great, perhaps because a greater method was taking its place. We do not know what happened to the Lady of the Window. She had had at that moment a great vocation; she was then at the beginning of a movement in the mind of man, of which we do not yet know the end; happy those who have a part in it. Wish her well, and pass.

Let us say then that this was the effort—the union of virtue and beauty. It is, I think, true that virtue eventually runs away with the book; in that sense Dante was quite right. Philosophy—lady or no lady—is the vaster subject matter. But his descriptions and explanations of philosophy are often put in terms applicable to the woman, and sometimes astonishingly so. The Lady—Beatrice or she of the Window; say, the woman—is defined, or her function (for which she was created, and not her function for her) is defined, and even more exactly than in the *Vita*. That was a vision; this is much more like a diagram. But it is a living diagram; it still eats and speaks and moves in Florence. Or so (for the purpose of this chapter) we have decided to believe.

At the beginning of the second treatise, just before he takes up the theme of the Lady of the Window, Dante explained the four senses in which books may be understood. They are the literal, the allegorical, the moral, and the anagogical. The first 'goes no farther than the letter as it stands'. The second is the literal sense translated into and applied to things of the intellectual and, as it were, abstract life; the third is the literal sense applied to moral life; the fourth, the literal sense applied to—what we may call the spiritual life. Dante gives an example of each of the last three, and unfortunately a different example; it would have been more convenient here if he had shown us the different meanings of the same phrase. He did it later, in the letter to Can Grande della Scala, which dedicated the *Paradiso* to him. There he takes the sentence: 'When Israel went out of Egypt, the house of Jacob from a strange people; Judah was his sanctuary, and Israel his dominion.' He says of this: 'If we consider the literal sense alone, the thing signified is the going out of the children of Israel from Egypt in the time of Moses; if the

The Convivio

allegorical, our redemption through Christ; if the moral, the conversion of the soul from the grief and misery of sin to a state of grace; if the anagogical, the passage of the sanctified soul from the bondage of the corruption of this world to the liberty of everlasting glory.'

These four meanings—of which one only is literal, and all the others are in a sense 'allegorical'—rule the interpretation of the canzoni as of the *Commedia*. But we may go a little further. 'It is clear that the subject,' says Dante in the *Letter*, 'in relation to which these alternate meanings have their movement, must be double (*duplex*).' The feminine form about which the *Convivio* is discoursing must be duplex. The great difference between the two schools of thought on Dante may be summed up by asking: is the actual form of a woman in this sense duplex? or is it not?

The last sonnet of the *Vita* had spoken of a perception which had been led by Love-in-grief up to heaven and had there seen Beatrice in glory, with splendours about her. It had been overwhelmed by her light; afterwards in the *Commedia* Dante was to speak of the 'luce intellectual plena d' amore' which Beatrice shows him in heaven; it was at that moment that he at last, and for the first time, abandoned the effort even to hint at her face and her smile. The intellectual light full of love is also the love of the good full of ecstasy. In the sonnet all this is undefined; we are told only that when this perception, or thought, speaks of that feminine form, so seen, it speaks of things Dante cannot follow. As with the terrible figure of Love when it first appears in a dream, there is heard a throng of words of which only a few could be understood—the presaging '*Ego dominus tuus*', so in the sonnet all he can catch is the reverberation of the name of Beatrice it brings to mind. It is speaking of the secret of that high state, of Beatrice in heaven. The first canzone of the *Convivio* takes up the same theme. It is addressed to those Intelligences who move the third heaven, and it speaks of a thought which often took its way to God, where it saw 'mia Donna gloriar', and so speaks of her that Dante desires to be there. But now comes another spirit, who lords it over Dante so greatly that he trembles; and this spirit says: 'He who would see salvation (la salute), let him look on the eyes of this lady, if he is not afraid of agony of sighs'; and then the poem goes on to say how wise and

The Convivio

courteous this lady is, and how, if Dante does not deceive himself, he shall see an adornment of high miracles, and say: 'Love, true lord, behold thy handmaid; do what thou wilt.' The saying is again a variation on the great phrase of 'her, the sister'd yet the sole'—'behold the handmaid of the Lord; be it unto me according to thy word.' We must suppose, as before, that Dante knew very well what he was doing when he used the phrase, and that he did it deliberately. But here it is he who is to say it; his own soul is to be the feminine, the God-bearer, the mother of Love. In this sense there is already proposed that mortal maternity of God which is fully exposed in the conclusion of the *Paradiso*.

This lady also then is to reveal to him an adornment of high miracles. The perception which Love-in-grief had launched, which sees Beatrice in glory, is counter-acted by this other spirit, who brings him to Philosophy, included in which is the philosophy of this matter also; and in speaking of this lady who is visible and yet philosophical he, and we, are to trace the path to thse miracles. The Intelligences of the third heaven have been invoked; 'ye who by thought move the third heaven'; it is they who have brought Dante into this experience. They are the angels proper to this heaven.

The third heaven has its own particular attributions. It is, to begin with, the heaven of Venus, and (as we find in the later *Commedia*) it is that heaven where the shadow of earth, reaching like a cone into the deep skies, finally ends. Earth itself is not, of course, done with there; but, in spatial terms only, it is left behind. The woman whom Dante is studying expresses this borderland between heaven and earth. But also there are the great sciences of learning which correspond, by their nature, to the opening intellectual powers, and in this hierarchy the third heaven corresponds to rhetoric, for Venus is 'more pleasant to behold than any other star' and Rhetoric is 'the most pleasant of all the Sciences, for its chief aim is to please'. And then, besides these meanings, is one in which the divine subjects of contemplation fit for this heaven are named; for of the nine heavens, the highest three contemplate the supreme power of the Father, and the second three the wisdom of the Son, and the third three 'la somma e ferventissima Carità dello Spirito Santo'—and these last three are nearest to us and give to us of what they receive. These

The Convivio

last three contemplate the Spirit in three different modes—as he is in himself, and as he is in his union with and distinction from the Father, and as he is in his union with and distinction from the Son. But whether the third heaven contemplates the Spirit in himself or in his relation to the Father, I do not see that Dante makes clear.

These then are the four meanings—the lady herself, philosophy itself, rhetoric, the contemplation of the high fervent love of the Spirit, and all these are inter-related, but especially they are all contained in the literal; that is, both in the literal sense of the verse, which is what Dante says, and in the visible appearance of the lady, which he does not say, but it is, I think, an inevitable result of the affirmation of that physical image and of what he does say. He does continually refer to its greatness of communication; thus, when he speaks of courtesy, (and it is inevitable that we should remember 'la sua ineffabile cortesia' of the first greeting in the street between the two young creatures of eighteen), he says: 'There is nothing better in a woman than courtesy. And let not wretched ordinary folk deceive themselves with this word, and think that courtesy only means largesse, for largesse is one special kind of courtesy, and not courtesy in general. Courtesy and propriety (onestade, decency, honour, *pietas*)—it is all one; and since in courts of old virtue and fine customs were in use (as now the contrary), so this word was taken from courts, and was as much as to say courtesy, the use of courts. But if the word were taken from the courts of to-day, especially in Italy, it would mean nothing but shamefulness.' And he goes on, thinking thus both of courtesy in a woman and the most courteous doctrines of philosophy, to denounce those high-seated wretches who, 'mad, foolish, and vicious,' expose their evils by their temporal grandeur, quoting the bitter sentence of Ecclesiastes: 'There is a sore evil which I have seen beneath the sun, namely, riches kept for the owners therefore to their hurt.'

This courtesy is a kind of heavenly largesse of behaviour, not only the largesse of money. It was what Beatrice had when she greeted him, and the other lady when she showed her compassion, and (afterwards) Beatrice again when she moved so quickly to Virgil in the *Commedia*, and Virgil himself when he went to meet Dante. 'Love', wrote Tyndale, translating Saint Paul,

The Convivio

'suffereth long and is courteous'; it has this largesse of the spirit, and where that largesse of the spirit is, there is love. The girls express this and philosophy teaches this, and rhetoric must have it also in order to please, and certainly (in so far as may be) the contemplation of the Divine Spirit's fervent love is a contemplation, and even an exchange, of courtesy.

It would take a volume much longer than the *Convivio* to work through all these identities of virtue in their separate categories; and when it was all done, there would be nothing comparable to the *Convivio*. There is no point in vulgarly re-writing Dante; that, to him and to the reader, would be quite the opposite of.'la sua ineffabile cortesia'. A few separate points may be noted before we come to the conclusion of the treatises we have; always remembering that Dante himself was aware that he was trying to do more than he could. He says in the beginning of the second canzone: 'Love that with desire discourses to me in my mind of my lady often there moves such things concerning her that my intellect goes astray; . . . if I wish to treat of what I hear of her, I must first dismiss all that my intellect cannot take in, and much even of what it can, for I should not know how to say it.' The terrible lord who spoke so much that Dante could not catch, the percipient thought whose messages were too subtle to be caught, are here confirmed. 'I say all this truly', he wrote in the commentary, 'because my thoughts, in reasoning about her, often wished to come to conclusions about her which I could not understand———.' The difficulties of the *Summa*, considered as a compassionate lady? yes, no doubt, but also the mysteries of a compassionate lady seen as another kind of *Summa*. Of those two powers, contrasting and complementary, it may be said, in phrases which Dante does not here quote: 'The heavens declare the glory of God, and the firmament sheweth his handiwork. One day telleth another, and one night certifieth another. There is neither speech nor language, but their voices are heard among them.' Certainly it is not surprising if, labouring towards conclusions which his intellect did not yet understand, Dante was annoyed to find all his phrases of exploration treated as testimonies to a sexual passion limited to carnality. He protested; he protested extremely, and with the result that ever since his protest many of his critics, even of those who accept the actuality of

The Convivio

the ladies, have forgotten it with their admission and confined their own comments to Boethius, Aristotle, and Saint Thomas.

It is a largesse of spirit—courtesy, generosity, humility, charity—which is seen in the corporal vehicles—say, the carnal vehicles, of the women. They define the doctrine in their gestures; the mind apprehends it. It is the same doctrine which is defined intellectually, and so again apprehended, by the philosophers, especially by the Christian philosophers. What is Christianity but a doctrine of largesse? The doctrine of the Trinity is a doctrine of largesse; the doctrine of the Incarnation and the creation is a doctrine of largesse; the doctrine of the Redemption is a doctrine of largesse; the doctrine of heaven is every way a doctrine of largesse. Add that the doctrine of all true adoration—single or mutual—is a doctrine of largesse. This great doctrine is expounded by the science of theology, which lies around and beyond all other sciences as the empyrean about all other heavens; as the second treatise says: 'The empyrean heaven in virtue of its peace is like the divine science, which is full of all peace . . . because of the most excellent certainty of its subject-matter which is God. And he himself said of it to his disciples: "My peace I give unto you, my peace I leave with you", giving and leaving them his teaching, which is the science whereof I speak... this makes us see the truth perfectly, wherein our soul is quieted.'

It has seemed to modern commentators fanciful to work out the relation of the nine heavens to the nine great sciences, as Dante does; it has seemed to them far too fanciful to see them all expressed, one opening from beyond another, in the woman's form; and it need not be attempted here. It is sufficient that she is, in her first motions of love, correspondent to rhetoric; say, to the rhetoric of love; which indeed her body is, lucid, adorned, persuasive, noble; and in her final great state, to theology, which indeed we know from the fact of Saint Mary. And because all humans are, in that sense, feminine to God, therefore Dante can properly use the phrases of Saint Mary of himself. But a woman, Beatrice or she of the Window or any other, is more easily contemplated so, because she wholly expresses the prime feminine idea, and especially in that physical image by which it becomes visible. She is 'the demonstration to the eyes,' 'which is the immediate cause of this enamourment.'

The Convivio

The process of indoctrination with this largesse of spirit continues through the third and fourth treatises of the *Convivio*. The third, on the whole, continues to be an analysis of the duplex feminine image. The fourth is an analysis of virtue in man, which Dante here calls nobility. He had, in the *Vita*, in the sonnet 'Amore e cor gentil', *Love and the gentle heart*, spoken of the beauty of a 'wise woman, saggia donna', awakening love in a man, and so in a woman the worthiness of a man; and it would not be improper to see these treatises as separately continuing that idea. By so doing, they do another thing also, for they bring the reader near and nearer to that other image of the City which is the necessary complement and balance to the image of the woman, or (making such modifications as are proper) of the man.

The second canzone, and the third commentary, begin with this sense of the intellect labouring under something too great for it. It is perhaps almost the beginning of what Wordsworth called 'the feeling intellect'; there is a sensation of significance, and some, but not sufficient, understanding. After this Dante comes to a discussion of Love, which is here both a quality and an act conditioned by that quality: 'Love is nothing else than the spiritual union of the soul with the object loved.' 'And since the constitution of the divine nature is shown in the excellences of nature, therefore the human soul unites herself spiritually with them the quicker and the closer as they themselves appear more perfect' (III, ii). And 'this lady' exhibits the pattern of man's essence as it exists in the divine mind (III, vi). This is to repeat formally what has been asserted often enough in the *Vita* to be seen in Beatrice. She is the heavenly norm; she is what everyone ought to be; 'she is as completely perfect as the essence of man can possibly be.' There is nothing new or uncommon about this experience; it is in a great many novels and films and plays and songs; our modern songs hold it as much as the lyrics of the metaphysicals. All that is new is the seriousness with which Dante treats it and the style in which he expresses it. The lady creates in her lover the sensation of supreme content. It does not last. Why not? Dante, at least, had a perfectly definite answer (III, vi). Everything desires its own perfection: 'in this all desires are appeased and for the sake of this all is desired.' This desire causes every delight to lack something, 'for there is in this

The Convivio

life no delight so great as to assuage our souls' thirst, so that this longing for our own perfection is not always in one thought.' Our desires are everlasting, and to see an image of perfection is not the same thing as to be perfect ourselves, which until we all are, possession, even the possession of Beatrice, must lack perfection. This is what all the talk of 'the ideal' comes to; the ideal can never satisfy us until we are ideal. He who pursues any hope of satisfaction without his own conditioning perfection is bound, sooner or later, straight for the *Inferno*.

Yet certainly this outer perfection (III, vii) calls us to that; 'her aspect aids our faith.' Philosophy does it by reason, and she does it through vision. She is, as it were, the substance of spirit and the visibility of spirit; in that respect she is an arch-natural thing. The divine light 'radiates into her—I mean, in her speech and in those acts which we call her bearing and her behaviour'. It has been held by some that something like light shines from the beloved, and that her physical vehicle is lucent with it. A thousand songs repeat it; it is taken as light talk, but it may be the lightness of grave truth. Her speech, 'per l' altezza e per la dolcezza sua,' 'by her loftiness and sweetness, nourishes a thought of love in the mind of the listener'; her acts, 'per la loro suavita a per la loro misura,' by their suavity—smoothness—and by their measure—propriety—waken love and bring it to awareness wherever in a good nature its possibility has been already sown. This appearance of a harmony of sensitive good arouses in us the faculty by which we escape from eternal death and reach eternal life—'per la quale campiamo da eternal morte e acquistiamo eternal vita.' Nothing less than this is the claim; it was made in the *Vita* and it is now repeated. A noble propriety of good becomes visible. Her modesty is made magnificent by God; her God-given magnificence becomes modesty in herself; the great laws of exchange begin. All this—to say it once more—may happen anywhere at any time between any persons. Romantic love between the sexes is but one kind of romantic love, which is but a particular habit of Romanticism as a whole, which is itself but a particular method of the Affirmation of Images. And—to say this also once more—all this involves no folly of denial of the girl's faults or sins. The vision of the perfection arises independently of the imperfection; it shines through her body whatever she makes of her body. Thus chastity is exhibited in the lecherous, and industry in the lazy, and humility in the proud, and truth in the false. Duplex in this also, the single image moves. The task of Beatrice or her of the Window was, in actual life, the same as the task of Dante. Her lover's testimony told her what, in fact, the image of her was; it was for her too to make haste to become it—perhaps when in some sullenness of his own, or because of some other function of his own, or through some rejection of hers, the testimonies had temporarily ceased.

The divine beauty of this most gracious being appeared in her speech and her acts. But also it appeared in the different members of her body. The body 'has organs for almost all the powers' of man; and these organs were, for Dante, of a nature as everlasting as his desire for God; they were indeed part of his desire for God: 'the organs of the body', says the *Paradiso*, 'shall be strong for all that means delight.' Dante himself did not go far in the analysis of the human body itself; much there remains to be done.

Wordsworth, in a profound phrase (*Prelude*, VIII, 279–81), said:

> The human form
> To me became an index of delight,
> Of grace and honour, power and worthiness.

The operative word is *index*; an index refers us to the text for full treatment of its items, but the names of the items, verbally treated in the text, are verbally repeated in the index. The subjects exist in the index in the manner that they do in the text—briefly, it is true, though a good index will generally indicate the development of the subjects on any particular page, and the good student will be always attentive to the index. It is very much in this sense that the human body contains and indicates the virtues. Dante confines himself to two of those entries in the index; they contain each a joy, which points to fuller joy; things appear there 'which reveal some of the joys of Paradise'. But we must go to the text of philosophy to understand the subjects actually present in the index of the body, the body in itself being part of the philosophical volume. His stress on the whole philosophical volume was very necessary. The great doctrine lies between the spiritualizers and the carnalizers—the idealists and the sensualists; it is explained away by both, yet for ever 'it

The Convivio

trembles yet it does not pass away'. Nor, speaking generally, does it fare much better when it is called sacramental. Technically, the word might serve, but in popular use it dichotomizes too much; it divides, while professing to unite; and, in popular use, it throws over the light of the serious object a false light of semi-religious portentousness. It overwhelms the gay and lordly body with its own significance; no doubt, as Dante says, the everlasting contentment which that foreshadows cannot fall to anyone here, but we do less than proper honour to our present delight if we are everlastingly reminding ourselves of its limitation. We are bound to be—except in the laughter of the lady—self-conscious, but we should carry it as lightly as possible. To be mocked by her in love is a divine experience; perhaps that was why the deepening smile of Beatrice is one of the loveliest properties of heaven.

The two points to which Dante chooses to direct attention are the eyes and the mouth. These the soul mostly adorns; there she bestows most of her subtlety; there she shows herself 'as on a balcony'—'per bella similitudine', adds Dante rather pleasantly, 'to use a beautiful simile.' From the first balcony, that of the eyes, her passions show—goodwill, jealousy, compassion, envy, love, and shame. She can, it is true, keep them from showing, but only by the exertion of great power. We may conclude that some part of that becoming other which is a duty for Dante and for all is precisely the exercise of that power when it is desirable; and this adds another relevance to the sewing-up of the eyes of the envious spirits in the *Purgatorio*; until they can control the appearances in those balconies, the balconies themselves are not to be opened.

On the mouth Dante himself had better be quoted. 'The soul demonstrates herself in the mouth, as colour does under glass. And what is laughter but a coruscation of that delight of the soul, as a light appearing without according as it exists within? And therefore it is becoming to a man to let his soul show in a tempered joy, laughing in moderation, and with frank restraint, and only with slight movement of the face; so that the lady (the soul) who there shows herself should seem modest and not uncontrolled . . . O marvellous smile of my lady, of whom I speak, which is only communicated through the eyes!'[1] (III, viii).

---

[1] 'che mai non si sentia se non dell' occhio'—which means, I am told, 'is not felt itself if it were not through the eye.' This might mean

The Convivio

This paragraph, short as it is, is one of those that knots all. Its four meanings are bound up with it here before they are carried on into the *Paradiso*. First, it is a description of the gay and glorious young creature laughing in Florence, the mirth of whose delight scintillated in her mouth and eyes; we may allow ourselves the belief that the young Beatrice smiles so much in heaven partly at least because she had smiled so much on earth. Into this single sweet and silent laughter the joyous happiness of all lovers seems to move, and all that has been said about it in high verse; so that the earth is full of it. Secondly, it is a description of that kind of joy which accompanies the intellectual formulation of philosophy: 'dimostrare'—almost 'demonstrates herself' in figures of geometry. This demonstration is the half-concealed smile of the divine science, theology, which like the empyrean holds all peace of knowledge, and only shows herself to us in such satisfying scintillations of mouth and eyes as gleam in the syllogisms of the great Scholastics, or what other method other philosophers use. Thirdly, there is the moral meaning, which is here that of a courtly reticence of largesse. Laugh with a charming dissemblance of laughter; give all, but give princelily; and let the great laws of control exhibit themselves immingled with what they control. Fourthly, it is the soul taking a joy in her being, and rendered in her own modesty into the magnificence of the Creator, scintillating courtesy back to our most courteous Lord, so that laughter is a proper off-springing from a largesse of spirit. These are the meanings, but they are all included in each, for there is only one paragraph, and in whichever direction that paragraph is turned the three other implications lie within it. This unity of (here) quadruplicity gives to the experience of the thought a particular quality; it arouses a sensation much like the sensation of some poetry, especially of Dante's poetry. For when we talk of Dante setting the experience of beatitude in intellectual knowledge, we have to remember that it was the intellect of poetry; that is, that it had a much greater emotional sensitiveness about it than thought for us usually has. In the fourth treatise Dante spoke of philosophy becoming 'enamoured of

the lady's eyes or the lover's eyes, and does probably mean both. It either way expresses the extreme joy which dances in eyes and mouth, too full and rich for sound.

The Convivio

herself'. A girl takes more pleasure in her beauty when her lover admires it; and great philosophical poetry may, in some sense, be imagined as the admiration which the lady Philosophy has for herself. There, at least, we can feel both the act of knowing and the thing known with our bodily capacities.

Could it be so held and applied, there is no doubt that this early wisdom would do what Dante says the appearance of the girl can do—'her beauty has power to renovate nature in those who behold her, which is a marvellous thing. . . . She was created not only to make a good thing better, but to turn a bad thing into a good.' 'La sua bellezza ha podestà in rinnovare natura . . . fare della mala cosa buona cosa.' The lady cannot do it without philosophy; the literal without the allegorical. On the other hand philosophy is seen to start in the lady, and the perfection of its end is seen in the lady. It is love and wisdom which are described in the end of the third treatise. 'Philosophy has wisdom for her subject matter and for her form love, and for the composition of the one with the other the practice of speculation' (III, xiv); it would not perhaps be too bold to call this imagination—the faculty which deals with images and their relation. Faith indeed is much the same capacity whenever it is recognized as having authoritative control over our actual lives; but of authority something must be said in the next chapters. Here Dante defines, in a sentence or two, the whole high process (III, xiv). He has reverted again to the thought that 'her aspect'—let us leave it at that word 'her' with its four relevancies—'her aspect helps our faith'; and he goes on to say: 'As by her much is perceived in reason and sequence which without her would seem miraculous, so through her we may believe that every miracle may be rational for a loftier understanding and in consequence may exist. Whence our excellent faith has its origin, from which again comes the hope that desires things foreseen, and from hope is born the operation of charity. By which three virtues we rise to be philosophers in that celestial Athens where Stoics and Peripatetics and Epicureans, by the art of eternal truth, concordantly unite in one will.' Christ was afterwards to be called the chief Roman in the heavenly Rome; here he is the chief Athenian of the celestial Athens. It is a noble passage; and the nobler for its universality. The Florentine—the London, the San Franciscan—girl seems a

The Convivio

miracle, but she is accounted for in a more lofty understanding and may therefore so indeed exist; hence arises our duplex faith—in what she seemed, therefore in the doctrine of what she seemed; and from that our hope in the coming of the things foreseen in her; and from that the operation of universalizing love. This is the affirmation of all images, in the way of the soul to the city of all true lovers of the way.

There wisdom is perfectly seen which is here only desired. Her eyes are her demonstration, her smiles her persuasions. The last chapter (xv) of this treatise is to be studied in all its meanings. The beauty of wisdom is in morality; the moral virtues give pleasure which is sensibly perceived—'piacere sensibilmente': what else had the girl precisely done? Every soul must gaze on this example—Beatrice? philosophy? morality? wisdom? all in one, one in all. The beauty of the soul consists in its manners; to improve our manners we must study wisdom in its aspect of humility—that is, of morality—profound similitude! we must be modest to events. Umil, umile, umiltà—the words throng still; so only is the magnificence of the God-bearer revealed. Wisdom is the mother of all principles, all origins—'di tutto qualunque principio.' 'She was in the divine thought, which is Intellect itself, when he made the world. Whence it follows that she made it—onde seguita che ella lo facesse.' The Florentine, or what other of her kind? philosophy? morality? wisdom? all in each, each in all. We have seen them like this, in any room or street, at any meeting; our minds, like the divine poet's, laboured with thoughts we could not understand. The image of an awful Origin came down the road; it seemed to hint at a saying of that True Light of which it was a—similitude? Love would not let Dante say so: 'he who would consider subtly would call Beatrice Love for the likeness she has to me.' The saying? 'Before Abraham was, I am.' Humility is the only true opportunity of largesse; she sprinkled courtesies in that quality of love; the quality of eternity was in a communication of love; how to be everlastingly communicated but by a death and a life? But still how? it was time again to define. Dante wrote: 'It is time, in order to proceed farther yet, to bring this treatise to a close.' He opened the fourth with a different canzone.

V

THE NOBLE LIFE

With the fourth treatise of the *Convivio* there enters into the work of Dante a new element—the element of the mass. This, as was said before, already exists in allusion—the other girls, the other poets, the gentlemen of standing, the philosophers, Beatrice's father, Dante's best friend, and other even more casual groups, pilgrims and rich men. They have been a background to the protagonists. There has been also a suggestion of the intellectual mass, the weight of past thought; indeed, one description of the *Vita* and the *Convivio* might be precisely the bringing into relation of the single girl and the communion of intelligences, pre-Christian and Christian, who formed for Dante an orthodoxy of the brain. She had been the occasion by which Dante had discovered this orthodoxy; the spirit who at the beginning of the *Vita* had cried out 'Now your beatitude has appeared!' meant it of his own intellectual concern as well as of Dante's whole being, of that part as of the whole. But this new mass is something different.

The appearance of this mass is in most of the great poets, though it is managed differently. In Shakespeare it is there from the beginning; it might indeed be argued that it is the only thing that is there from the beginning, and that the individuals are gradually evoked from it. In Wordsworth it is also there throughout—the mass of mankind against the mass of nature, and Wordsworth their junction. In Patmore it appears equally with the individual, lightly in the *Angel* and the *Victories*, weightily in the *Odes*. In Keats it is hardly there at all. In Virgil it is always already a city; the alteration from one form of it to another, from Troy to Rome, is his subject. Shakespeare and Wordsworth manage their synthesis of its existence by the introduction of a kind of natural *pietas*, against which Othello, Lear, and Macbeth rebel, and which the French Revolution attempts and fails to establish. In Dante the poetic effort is more philosophical, though both natural *pietas* and a revolution (at least, a desired revolu-

The Noble Life

tion) come in; he moves from the intellectual mass to the actual mass.

Wordsworth wrote

> My soul diffused herself in wide embrace
> Of institutions and the forms of things;

the second line is noble, but perhaps the word 'diffused' unduly weakens the first. Dante's method was the opposite of diffusion; he so concentrated the idea that he personified it, and that not only by an abstract name, however effective. The personification comes later, at the beginning of the *Commedia*; there, between the disappearance of Beatrice and the re-appearance of Beatrice, the City appears in the form of a man. It lives as a man; it lives as Virgil. Virgil, like all the rest, has at least four significances; he is Virgil, and poetry, and philosophy, and the Institution or the City. 'Tu se' lo mio maestro e il mio autore' (*Inf.* I, 85); this is true in all the meanings. An Institution is the nurse of souls. It would have been every way impossible for Virgil to enter the *Paradiso*; he and the other, the redeemed, City must have collided poetically.

We have heard a great deal of courtesy—'la sua ineffabile cortesia'—and are to hear more. At the beginning of the *Vita* it is this quality which Dante marks in Beatrice, and at the beginning of the *Commedia* it is the same quality which Beatrice is caused to remark in Virgil, at the moment when she herself is on a most courteous errand, the salvation of her lover. She salutes him with the same adjective, adding—perhaps by an undeliberate collocation—the name of a city: 'O anima cortese Mantovana' (*Inf.* II, 58), 'O courteous Mantuan soul.' The juxtaposition serves as a reminder that courtesy is one of the chief virtues of the City. Beatrice and the other Lady—but from now on we may say Beatrice alone, since Dante chose it so, and since it is a principle of the whole Way of Affirmation—are always full of courtesy, and it was once communicated to Dante by a miracle. Virgil is courteous, and so is our Lord. This doctrine of largesse ranges from the girl's body to the mystery of the Trinity. But how, having for a moment known it, ourselves to continue courteous? how to bring all men to courtesy? This is the problem of the making of the City.

The Noble Life

The third canzone opens with a new note. Something disdainful and fierce has appeared in the lady, and has put a stop, as such moments will, to his accustomed habit of speech. He must give up his 'dulcet rhymes of love' and 'lo mio suave stile', his persuasive style. Instead of this, he will use a different sound, harsh and subtle, 'aspra a sottile', to tell of the 'valore' by which men are truly 'gentle'. This will refute the false and vile judgement which supposes that 'gentilezza' is based on the principle of 'ricchezza', that high spirit depends on wealth—wealth meaning, no doubt, chiefly money, but having a side fling at every kind of false possession, even of mental qualities. He invokes that Lord who so dwells in the eyes of the lady that she is enamoured of herself—'s' innamora'.

This is all, no doubt, chiefly philosophical, but a good deal of Beatrice has got in. The undeserved snub, the remote gaze, even the inimical chatter at the party, still—we must not say rankled, but they still exhibited another aspect of Beatrice. She was more like Imogen than Ophelia; she was 'a fair warrior', and less submissive than Desdemona, whom Othello rather flattered by calling her so. The lady whom Dante admired was a lady worthy of Dante in her highness as well as her softness. When, in the second canzone, he had said that her beauty 'rained down little flames of fire', he was speaking of her character and behaviour as well as of her appearance. When she returns in the judgement of the *Purgatorio* she is not different; the young girl in Florence had not then caught the later grand style, but the *principium* had been there. Her silence, in that moment of the snub, said the same thing—'Yes, look: this is I; I am Beatrice.' It is a reminder of, and a summons to, an almost irrational fidelity, a fidelity only recorded in 'a loftier understanding', for they were bound by no vows and held by no institution. Yet her demand was to be justified—by the spectacle at the opening of the *Commedia* when, in the moment of his need, she immediately precipitated herself to his help. 'No-one', she says, 'for any gain or any escape ever moved so quickly' (*Inf*. II, 109–10) as she to be of use to 'l' amico mio', to my friend. It is this great fidelity of Beatrice, it is because even in universal heaven she can still say 'my friend', which justifies through the whole work her unstressed acceptance of the whole adoration. We need not think

The Noble Life

that she had no duty; Dante imagined that she kept and fulfilled her duty, and it is at her passionate summons that Virgil, that the poetry and prophecy of Virgil, deign to move and speak. Virgil brings Dante to her, but she has deliberately as well as undeliberately sent Virgil to Dante.

It is in answer to this disdain that Dante's masculinity is heightened; the thing that moves in his mind is 'valore'—worth, value, valour. Her beauty springs fierce before him and he answers by declaring the particular virtue of a man. In the allegorical sense, something similar happens. Philosophy is not expressing itself in such attractive and dulcet demonstrations, but is now, as it were, imperious and almost arrogant. His reason is committed to a state which is in truth 'onesto' (IV, ix)— say, noble, but it appears to him disdainful and fierce. There are indeed moments in studying, say, the *Summa* when, if we could attribute feminine characteristics to that admirable work (it is not our habit? no, but it was Dante's), we should certainly describe it as disdainful and fierce; it is very high-sprung and awful, and to get on with it we must summon up all our intellectual 'valore'. And so with the other allegorical meanings. It is in this moment of pause that we can recognize what 'valore' is; another word for it, and the one he now uses is *nobility*, and nobility is later defined as 'perfezione di propria natura in ciascuna cosa', 'the perfection in each thing of its proper nature' (IV, xvi). 'A man speaks of a noble stone, a noble plant, a noble horse, a noble falcon, whenever it appears perfect after its own nature.' This certainly is Philosophy loving herself, when her high threats produce a philosophical demonstration of the nobility of man's nature; it has sometimes been held that, in a different kind, the disdain of a woman is not always displeased to provoke a serious augustitude—the perfection of his nature—in her lover.

Before however he enters on that discussion, Dante is deflected by having made an allusion in the canzone to the Emperor Rudolph of Suabia. The Emperor, when asked to define nobility, had said that it lay in 'ancient wealth and gracious manners', and some of his courtiers had gone further by omitting the second clause. Dante is thus led into a discussion of the imperial authority, and so of authority as a whole. He defines it as 'that act to which

The Noble Life

faith and obedience are due'—'atto degna di fede e d' obbedienza' (IV, ix). 'It is clear that Aristotle is the most worthy of faith and obedience; his words are the supreme and highest authority.' This is the philosophical sphere which must govern all others, and is not opposed to the imperial authority; they are indeed necessary to each other, for the imperial without the philosophical is in a state of some peril, and the philosophical without the imperial is weak; but when both are conjoined, they are in full vigour. The fourth treatise goes on to deal with the kind of life which philosophy indicates to be wholesome; the *De Monarchia* to express the external means by which that life may be mediated to the world.

The 'worth' then by which man is 'truly gentle' is nobility, and nobility is perfection of nature. This opinion is not always, or even often held; many men (even including the Emperor Rudolph before-mentioned) think it consists in lineage or riches. But as far as lineage is concerned, we see that descendants of great men are often base in spirit; and because they have such examples, the basest of all; so that they may rightly be called 'dead' even while still alive. 'Life in man is the exercise of the reason; if his life is his being, then to renounce the exercise of reason is to renounce existence, and this is death' (IV, vii). This is clear especially in the man who with the footprints of an example before him, does not follow them: 'the man is dead but the beast survives.' There are two relevancies here to Dante's other work. The first is in the image of the dead man living; afterwards, at the bottom of the *Inferno*, Dante accentuated it. There are seen certain souls whose bodies still walk the earth above, but devils inhabit those bodies, and they are no longer men but diabolic organisms (*Inf.* XXXIII, 122–150); it is one of the few instances of terrible exchange in hell. The second is the matter of the example. Dante is here talking of fathers and ancestors; natural duty as well as supernatural virtue is in question. But it can hardly be forgotten that the great example in much that has gone before has been the phenomenon of virtue in the image of the woman. Reason, as Dante said at the beginning of that Way, went with Love in all things in which Reason could be helpful; the renunciation of the exercise of Reason is that which makes a man a beast; therefore the renunciation of

The Noble Life

the exercise of that particular Reason is that which helps to make a man a beast. Reason-in-Love is only a part of universal reason, just as Beatrice is only one image of true philosophy. Still, that she was; the sighs in the *Vita* (XXXV) which most lamented her death were those which called her 'nobile intelletto', noble intellect. Indeed, this early experience goes still deeper, for the first knowledge of that something other to which faith and obedience are due had been, if not through Beatrice, at least through the light in Beatrice. The *Vita* lies pulsatingly below all this discussion of philosophical and imperial authority; in the girl authority had first appeared. So that here too, as experience, we have the four shapes of authority; the literal being Beatrice, the allegorical philosophy, the moral the Emperor and the anagogical, God. The omission there of the Pope is for two reasons: first, Dante has not yet come to discuss Papal authority; second, the serious problem of the time was whether that authority could most properly be considered as belonging to the third or fourth divisions. This was the real division between the Guelfs and Ghibellines, and therefore that which most affected Dante. For if the Papal authority was (in this vocabulary) 'moral', it was on a level with the Emperor; if 'anagogical' it was superior. One could argue about this, but Beatrice was, at bottom, unarguable.

The influence of that vision appears again when Dante proceeds to quote Saint Thomas—that 'to know the relation of one thing to another is the proper act of reason'; this, he adds, is discrimination—'e quest' e discrezione'; discrimination is the fairest branch of reason; and the fairest fruit of discrimination is reverence. This might, could Dante have then thought of it, have been put as a preface to the *Vita*, though it may be the philosophical discovery was not made till after the *Vita* was written, and the Second Lady was more closely understood in intellectual terms. The two terms now used are 'discrezione' and 'reverenza'. He uses both in demurring to the saying of Rudolph of Suabia, and if it seems strange that he should take so much trouble to refute a mere opinion of the Emperor's, we have to remember that, since Dante took authority seriously, it was important to him to know where that authority appeared. The phenomenon of Beatrice had made authority visible, and had at the same time encouraged discrimination within authority. It was not a conflict

The Noble Life

between authorities of which he wished to be aware, but one authority ('to which trust and obedience are due') operating in different manners. Our habit is to think of 'authorities' and always regard them as potentially in conflict, but with Dante it was not so. The unity of a poem which directed itself into various meanings, the unity of the humility of Beatrice which had many courtesies, the unity of the doctrine of largesse which is in many operations, are all similar to the unity of authority.

It is not to the point to follow Dante through the long discussion by which he proves that neither riches nor high descent are the cause of true nobility; we must take it up again when he returns to his affirmations. In the 16th chapter of the treatise he says we must think of nobility as 'the perfection of man's nature', and defines this by its fruits. What then are those fruits? They are, according to Aristotle, eleven; they are:

(1) Courage—which controls rashness and timidity.
(2) Temperance—which controls indulgence and abstinence.
(3) Liberality—which controls giving and receiving.
(4) Magnificence—which incurs and limits great expense.
(5) Magnanimity—which moderates and acquires honour and reputation.
(6) Love of honour—which moderates and orders us as regards this world's honours.
(7) Mansuetude—which moderates our anger and our overmuch patience with external evils.
(8) Affability—which makes us 'con-vivial' or companionable with others.
(9) Truthfulness—which prevents us in our talk from pretending to be more or less than we are.
(10) Pleasantness (eutrapelia)—which sets us free to make a proper and easy use of amusement ('sollazia'—solace).
(11) Justice—which constrains us to love and practise directness in all things.

These are the eleven virtues of largesse; these are the powers which are provoked into action by the girl's challenge, because they are the 'valore' of a man. It is indeed these which Beatrice, consciously or unconsciously, encourages, and in which she takes delight. They have a particular beauty when considered precisely

The Noble Life

as a definition of behaviour towards her, though there they have just so much intimate and exquisite colour of a particular kind as is in the 'l' amico mio' of Beatrice when she precipitates herself from heaven. The Italian language has, in those phrases, an advantage over the English, for Beatrice, speaking Italian, must say 'the lover of mine', thus making 'of mine' or 'my' a mere definitive adjective rather than the possessive pronoun of English. So far—to the extent of that special description—their special relationship is, even in heaven, justified. The largesse between them demands a special kind of courage, of liberality (as well in taking as in giving; a man is not to be selfishly generous), of magnificence (which properly incurs great expense), of mansuetude and affability and pleasantness (a man is not to be a boor or a fool—and we must, in all the Beatrician relationship, give and take a proper solace: it is one of the great maxims of sex as of sanctity upon this Way). This list indeed might be called a lover's handbook. Dante calls them the moral virtues of the active life and so they are, but two lovers are in an active life towards each other, and their reciprocal duty is to see that their powers of magnificenza and of the sollazia are adequate.

But of course the great catalogue is not meant only for Beatrice. It is dictated by Love ('I am one who when Love breathes in me take note and write as he dictates'), but also by Aristotle. It has its four relevancies; it is to be read as Beatrician, Aristotelian, imperial, and holy. These virtues are the rule of man as a rational being, but also as a civic being and a spiritual being. The eleven notes are in Virgil as well as in the lady; they are, after a lofty manner, in Saint Mary as well as in Virgil; they are even, all ways, in Christ, our most courteous Lord. They are therefore relevant to the City, human as well as divine. The effect of Beatrice on Dante is to arouse his 'valore' or nobility; these are the virtues of nobility, and these virtues are the method of interchange with other men to shape the City. The City then will be noble; it will have the perfection of its nature, and that nature is incidentally described in a paragraph which had better be quoted, both for its relevance here, and because it holds a poetic image which afterwards became one of the most famous in Dante. He has been saying that nobility has a larger scope and is more fundamental than the particular

The Noble Life

virtues, for it comprehends them all. He goes on: 'Certainly it is a heaven in which many different stars shine; in it shine the intellectual and moral virtues; in it shine all good dispositions instilled by nature—as piety and religion, and also those emotions mostly of praise—as shame and compassion and many others; in it shine the bodily excellencies—as beauty, strength, and (as far as may be) continuous health. The stars that are spread in this heaven are so many that it is no wonder if many different fruits thrive upon human nobility, so many are their natures and influences, gathered and unified in one simple substance.' These are the stars which shine afterwards in the *Commedia*—the hints and gleams of perfection, showing in separate virtue from the deep nobility of creation. But here on earth this nobility is not imparted to every man and woman, for some (by defects of nature or the time) are not so disposed that its light can shine in them directly, though it may do so indirectly and by reflection. So that, from all these considerations, we come to a second definition of Nobility (IV, xx), which is 'lo seme di felicità messo da Dio nell' anima ben posta', which is what the canzone had sung on which all this is a commentary—'the seed of felicity sent by God into a well-disposed soul.' This seed springs in the light of Beatrice and is nourished by philosophy; the imperial power protects its growth, and its final fruition is in God.

This nobility, this seed of blessedness, is communicated to a man or woman at the time of his generation. It is therefore in a particular sense related to Beatrice. She who had been the image of Love to Dante and the mother of Love in his soul is (do things so determine) to be the mother of children to whom, by her husband, the seed of felicity is communicated. This high occasion may be the opportunity for very much: 'there are some', says Dante, 'who think that if all the aforesaid powers (animal, intellectual and divine) should agree together to produce a soul when they were best fitted for the task, so much of the Deity would descend into the soul that it would almost be another God incarnate' (IV, xxi)—'un altro Iddio incarnato.' This sentence again is a union of the vision of Beatrice-in-perfection and of the knowledge of philosophy-in-perfection. The actual Incarnation itself shows for a moment, arch-natural and not alien from our commonalty, a thing (as it were) all but seen happening, a marvel

The Noble Life

of the flesh as the flesh truly is, a credible and shy simplicity, its own modesty magnificent, its own magnificence modest. 'Behold,' said our courteous Lord, looking round on the world, 'behold my mother and my brethren.' It is at the moment of Beatrice that he may say the same thing to anyone and be infinitely believed.

The remaining seven chapters of the *Convivio* are taken up by two things (i) a discussion of the two modes of life called the Active and the Contemplative, (ii) a survey of the noble life in its four chief stages. The first distinction is ancient, but it is in general perhaps over-simplified. The broad opposition of manner between the Contemplative Orders and, say, married people and politicians is not to hide the fact that each vocation must, to an extent, include the other. As is said about the Sacred Eucharist itself, 'he is received perfect and entire under each species.' The Contemplatives themselves must work exteriorly; the Actives must study interiorly. The image of Beatrice does two things. First, it raises the art of meditation which, it is generally agreed, the Actives should practise into something more like that other, more intense, state. The intensity of the vision demands the greater act. 'Look, look well, we are, we are indeed Beatrice,' is a command as continual as the power that answers to it. Second, it almost always involves an active *amicitia*, duties if not always of marriage yet always of this world's kind. It is an activity in matter; without matter there is no marriage, and the duties of marriage and all such states of *amicitia* involve matter. This is generally accepted; the state and duty of the contemplation of Beatrice-in-glory and of glory-in-Beatrice is not so generally accepted. It is regarded usually as dream or reverie, as indulgence; so it may sometimes be, but its reality is not so. Activity and Contemplation are each part of the work, but then everything is, or may be, part of the work, even the recurrent proper forgetfulness of the work; which is why Dante set Pleasantness among the stars in the heaven of our perfected nature; and Love-in-Pleasantness is one of the subjects of Contemplation. It has subjects enough; nothing of the Active life is alien from it. It and the Active life continually exchange powers. 'These two operations', wrote Dante, 'are the quickest and most direct paths to bring us to the supreme Beatitude which we cannot possess here.'

The Noble Life

We come after this to the spectacle of the whole of life seen in the depth of nobility. Dante's own work had begun with a use, among other important words, of that one, and it was to use it again in the yet unimagined maturity of its close. The small Beatrice had come before him 'vestita d'un nobilissimo colore umile ed onesto sanguigno', clothed in a most noble colour, a subdued and clear crimson. She could hardly have done better; every word is rich with significance. Those who deny her actuality will say that so much significance helps to disprove her, or perhaps that Dante, more than nine years afterwards, dressed her as his imagination chose. But, there being no other evidence, we may as well believe what we have. A colour of nobility, of the frank and modest blood, was what her mother that day chose for her to be mortally immortal in; she changed it for pure white later, as if earthly nobility became a spiritual translucency. It is all we know of her Florentine wardrobe. But at the opening of the last canto of the *Paradiso* the word, given such energy in the *Convivio*, returns. Speaking to the single perfected God-bearer, and invoking her with that phrase which defines also Beatrice and all saints—'daughter of thy son', 'figlia del tuo figlio'—Saint Bernard says:

> 'Tu sei colei, che l' umana natura
> nobilitasti sì, che il suo Fattore
> non disdegnò di farsi sua fattora.

You are she who has so ennobled human nature that its Worker did not disdain to become its work.' It is the infinite depth of this nobility which has made the infinite Incarnation possible. In the *Vita* is the symbolical and becoming vesture; in the *Convivio* is, as it were, the Rite of the mysterious deepening; in the *Paradiso* the consummate outspringing from within the noble and crimson depth.

The four periods of the noble life are Adolescence, or Increase, which lasts till the age of twenty-five; Youth, which lasts till forty-five; Age, which lasts till seventy; and then (corresponding there to the nine months of our in-wombing) ten years, more or less, of decrepitude. Plato, who 'is to be regarded as of a most excellent nature', lived to be eighty-one, and Dante adds his own belief that 'if Christ had not been crucified, but had lived for

The Noble Life

the full time possible to his nature, he would at the same age have transmuted his mortal body to an eternal'. Not choosing to do this, he seems to have left us, as it were, ourselves to redeem Age and Decrepitude, in which the apocryphal stories suggest that his mother was the first worker.

There remains to pass under view the several virtues naturally predominant at the different stages of this noble life. In the first, which is Adolescence, there are obedience, suavity (or, let us say, a sweet courtesy), shamefastness, and 'adornezza corporale', physical beauty. This life, at its opening, must be obedient to its father and teachers; it must speak and act sweetly and courteously, 'dolce e cortesemente' (IV, xxv). This is the perfection of the small Beatrice, together with the kind of modesty proper to that age; that is, a capacity for admiration—'stupor'—before all great and wonderful things. This kind of awe, this proper romanticism, is a part of nature's contribution to a noble life; we ought then to be capable of practising wonder and reverence, and to push those virtues further—to desire to be wise in them; so that such stupor is the proper beginning of wisdom. I do not know that Wordsworth put it differently when he wrote:

> Fair seedtime had my soul, and I grew up
> Nurtured alike by beauty and by fear.

This particular shy adoration is accompanied by that other modesty which is 'a shrinking of the mind from foul things, and by that shame which arouses penitence for faults committed'. This excellency of spirit is accompanied by an excellency of body; the noble life is physical in its beauties—health, alertness, comeliness. This Aristotle declared and this Beatrice was; the 'stupor' she caused was the beginning of wisdom.

But neither the noble life nor romanticism can stop with adolescence. The Way of Affirmation, in all its opening aspects, possesses the qualities defined in that earliest stage. It has them even in its literary sense; it is obedient to all proper high tradition, but not to any false images of it—that is why it is so often in apparent revolt; it must have a 'stupor' before greatness and a repugnance to foulness—but it is a spiritual foulness which it mostly hates; it has all proper adornment and alertness of its vehicle. It is not always those who have trodden one Way of

The Noble Life

Affirmation who are best at judging another and a newer, but the success of any romanticism will depend upon its having these qualities after its own manner, and on its proceeding to develop others. So we come, in the period of Youth, to those others—temperance, courage, love, courtesy, loyalty. Loyalty here means 'to follow and put in action what the laws bid', and this is particularly fitting to youth, for Adolescence ought to be easily pardoned, and the man of age (or, say, maturity) should have so trained his mind that it and just laws are one, so that 'as if without any law he should follow his own just mind'. This is the hint of the crowning and mitring at the end of the *Purgatorio*. But then this man, in whom the nobility of nature later reaches the time of Age, is (IV, xxvii) marked by other virtues—especially by prudence, justice, largesse, and that joy in hearing and telling the good of others which is called Affability. He should be, by now, adult in love. Romanticism has explored its distance and doctrines; the affirmations have kept faith. Thus a man's own proper perfection has been, as it were, acquired in Youth; now he is concerned with a wider, and therefore a greater, perfection. 'Man', Dante quotes here from Aristotle, 'is a civic animal,' but Aristotle's phrase is quickened and illuminated by Dante's. The man of nobility now is 'like a rose opening'. He is to—what? do good? yes, but as no more conscious of it than a rose, which is casually there for anyone who goes by. We are not to sell our wisdom 'a figliuoli di Colui che te l' ha dato', to the children of that One—that is, God—who gave it us. Or, we might add, in a more earthly sense, to the children of those men who gave it us, and what men did not? from whom, even our enemies, are we so divided that we have not been indebted to them for ourselves also? Was Beatrice miserly? is Aristotle enclosed? Some specialized learning, relating to our own callings, we may indeed sell, but then only so that we give freely of it also to the poor. This unnoticed enlargement of the mind is the working within us of the primal moment of courtesy and goodwill; then, when he was asked a question, Dante could only answer 'Love'. The phrase may—it would have been a pity, but it may—have then sounded a little comic. It does not so sound in the light of this larger state; for the noble answer now to all questions is only a kind of unnoticed effluence of love. Having this largesse of love, the soul

The Noble Life

has the justice and the authority of this way of love. It delights to hear and speak good. Therefore, Dante says in a phrase too august for most men to bear—'E più belle e buone novelle pare dovere sapere per la lunga esperienza della vita.' 'It ought to have fair and noble things to tell because of a long experience of life.' Its authority is the other side of its early obedience; authority cannot be perfected in act until some obedience answers to it. An act to which faith and obedience are due is not fully an act until they are paid. Faith cannot, though Obedience may, be enforced. Thus, in the noble life, generally considered, authority is always a mutual act; we ought not to think of it one-sidedly. Like pardon, it is a welding of wills, and an exchange of largesse. He or she who obeys is a servant of largesse as much as he or she who rules. It is this that Dante felt in his obedience to the glory-of-Beatrice: all the virtues interchange. These things are like the stars we heard of earlier in the heaven of nobility, but now we are in that heaven itself, we are indeed the heaven, and the hints of perfection shine out from us on to the world.

All through this chapter Dante denounces his own City of Florence. It was the Florentine girl who first exposed to him the possibility of so much greatness; it is the apostate City which perverts and rejects it. We shall see in the next chapter the intense relation of the two. Here it is enough to remark that at the height of the philosophical vision, he saw the actuality betraying itself on earth. 'O you, ill-starred and ill-born, who snatch and disinherit, who rob and seize'; they do all sorts of things which they call 'generous'. They think themselves following the doctrine of largesse. 'O misera, misera, patria mia!' Even in Dante there are few more piercing cries. But after Age it is not primarily a time to name virtues. The heaven of nobility itself seems to be moving inwards; all the circumference on which, long since, in his love's adolescent days, the lover moved, is now in like relation to the centre, and drawing inwards towards the centre. It goes softly, like a vessel entering port, when the shipman has let down the sail, gently, and with a slight headway —'soavemente con debile conducimento' (IV, xxviii). This movement towards God is not praised for any qualities except the peace which is bestowed on it and is yet its duty. Within this last experience the other citizens of nobility move to meet it—

The Noble Life

'cittadini della eterna vita, the townsmen of eternal life.' He names two who moved in this quietude, one from myth and one actual. 'Certainly the lord Lancelot would not enter with a high sail, nor our most noble Latin, Guido of Montefeltro.' Both these gave themselves to an Order of Religion. 'Sir Lancelot', says Malory, 'took the habit of priesthood of the Bishop, and a twelve-month he sang mass.' There follows a great maxim of the Way of Affirmation: 'ma eziandio a buona e vera religione si può tornare in matrimonio stando, chè Iddio non vuole religioso di noi se non il cuore,' 'but they who are married may also be professed of a good and true Order, for God wills nothing but that we should be professed in heart.' It is this heart-profession to which the long novitiate—in chamber and city—has led. The first call to that vocation is far away; it would have been more than sixty years, had Dante lived, since he had first seen the Revelation hued in a noble blood-colour till the opening of these final vows. It was compressed in him; the imagination of poetry—'so called Through sad incompetence of human speech'—involving its own prayer and fasting was allowed perhaps to take its place. Dante would hardly have thought so; he never confused poetry and religion; it is why one might think the dispensation allowed him. Like all other of these images it will not come if it is demanded. There are always two ways only by which the revelation may come; one is by free gift, the other by fidelity and attention and love. There is now no question to which 'love' is not the answer, but the word must be adult. The life of this Religious Order is in marriage, but Lancelot was not married; it is not only in marriage, for it has a wider and (one could almost say) even stricter morality. Something of it was in that other great Romantic, Wordsworth, when he renewed his vows:

> And O ye Fountains, Meadows, Hills, and Groves,
> Forbode not any severing of our loves . . .
> Thoughts that do often lie too deep for tears.

The thought that had sprung from Love-in-grief had pierced far, but the thoughts of this age spring from the centre itself. The very word Romantic is left behind; such things belong to the past and the Way. So the noble soul in this last period blesses the

The Noble Life

bygone times—'and well she may—e bene li puo benedire.' She revolves them in her memory and she recalls her truth—her 'dirette operazione', her direct work. So that she blesses the whole Way; one might say almost that the only sounds heard in that great peace are her own voice blessing, and the greetings of those other souls who softly and interiorly greet it in what is already the eternal City, as the white-clad girl had first opened her lips to her lover some fifty years before. The sentence in which the *Vita* described it is so full of hints of this fulfilment that it may be quoted again: 'e per la sua ineffabile cortesia, la quale è oggi meritata nel grande secolo, mi saluto virtuosamente tanto, che mi parve allora vedere tutti i termini della beatitudine.' The words themselves are sufficient witness of the intimate relation of the two periods—'her ineffable courtesy, which is rewarded in the great cycle, saluted me so that I thought I saw the very limit of blessedness.' Blessing back in all, the soul so first blessed moves on. It is sometime said that the old 'live in the past'. The saying may have a deeper meaning than we usually give it. The recollection, even (in some sense) the repetition, of the past, may then be for the noble soul the means by which it draws near to that gathering-up of the whole mortal life which is at once justice and mercy. It could not bear so much but for Redemption. It approaches a kind of image of eternity, in the living classic whole, proportioned and complete. It was meant to live more intensely so; happy if it can.

There is but the end of the canzone left for comment, the last six lines which made the *tornata* or formal conclusion of its hundred and forty-six. 'Song, go forth against the erring ones; and when you are come to the region where our Lady is, do not keep your business secret from her. You may say to her surely: "*I go speaking of your friend.*"' The phrase 'against those who err', Dante says, 'is the title of the whole poem', chosen deliberately as a parallel to Saint Thomas Aquinas's *Against the Gentiles*; this poem too is to confute all those who wander from the Faith. The Faith, here? 'I command the poem to show its business where this Lady, that is, Philosophy, can be found; and this most noble lady will be found where her chamber is; that is, the soul in which she lodges. And this philosophy lodges not only in sages, but also, as was proved earlier in another treatise,

The Noble Life

wherever the love of her lodges. And to them my song is to show its errand, for these will profit by its message and these will gather it in. And it is to say "I go speaking of your friend", for nobility is a friend, since nobility always demands her, and philosophy shows her sweet gaze nowhere else. How great an adornment is given her—to call her the friend of her whose true house is in the most secret place of the divine mind—è nel secrettissimo della divina Mente.'

It was what he had always done, whichever her of all the three he at any moment meant.

VI

THE *DE MONARCHIA* AND THE EXILE

On 8 June 1290 Beatrice died. Dante, it will be remembered, had in the *Vita* quoted Jeremiah: 'Quomodo sedet sola civitas . . .', 'How doth the city sit solitary, that was full of people! how is she become as a widow that was great among the nations!' He says there that he wrote a letter to the principal men in Florence, speaking of its condition. It can hardly be supposed that this letter to the priors or the chief lords dilated on the loss Florence had sustained by the death of the actual Beatrice, and we must take it that it already seemed to him that Florence without Beatrice was a type of Florence without justice or peace. His own personal light had vanished, and so had the more general light of civic virtue. This is confirmed by a letter which he wrote twenty-four years later. It was 1314; he was in exile, and had been for twelve years. The Pope Clement V, who had made his residence at Avignon, had just died; the Cardinals met near Avignon for the Conclave. Dante addressed an Epistle to them: 'Cardinalibus Italicis Dantes Alighierus de Florentia'— 'Dante Alighieri, a Florentine, to the Cardinals of Italy.' It began: 'Quomodo sedet sola civitas . . .', 'How doth the city sit solitary, that was full of people! how is she become as a widow that was great among the nations!'

The City then in question was Rome. She had been left 'widowed and deserted'—'viduam et desertam'—by the removal of the Apostolic See to Avignon. There may have been two women, there were certainly two cities, who meant a very great deal to Dante's heart and mind; one was Rome and one was Florence. Their images equalled Beatrice and her of the window. The double use of the sentences from Jeremiah exhibit to us Dante's double distress. But the desolation of Florence in the death of Beatrice was not so intense to him as the desolation of Rome in the departure of the Pope. There were three reasons

The De Monarchia *and the Exile*

for this. The first was that Dante never felt his own personal affairs to be as important as the affairs of Christendom. The second was that Beatrice had departed by the Will of God; but the Pope and the Cardinals had left Rome (as he says in this letter) because they had disobeyed the Will of God—'quod, male usi libertate arbitrii, eligire maluistis,' 'you have preferred to choose this, making evil use of the freedom of your wills.' The third was that Dante was a maturer man, and his distress was greater.

The disobedience, however, lay not merely in the removal from Rome; it was in the cause of that removal. At Avignon the Apostolic See lay under the close influence of the French Court. It was against all Dante's principles that that See should be subject to any throne but that of the Emperor himself—and it was not subject even to that for it was equal in authority and superior in honour. For the Apostolic See to place itself under a throne which was, in Dante's view, vassal to the Emperor, was apostasy. The Pope had abandoned his function; he was behaving as if his function had been created for him, and not he for his function; and now that the Pope was dead, the apostate Cardinals were persevering in the sin. It has been asked whether the use by Dante at this crisis of the sentences he had used for the death of Beatrice would not have seemed to him a kind of profanation, and the question has been used as an argument against the authenticity of the letter. The letter may be unauthentic, but such an argument will not prove it so. It is precisely, only even more intensely, applicable. The distress of a young man, even of a young poet, even of Dante, at the death of his love is not comparable with his pain at the treachery of his love; still less with the pain of a mature poet at such a treachery; and again, still less with the pain of a mature political poet at the treachery of his City—meaning a town or a Church; much less if that political treachery is, in the greatest sense, *urbi orbique*, to the City and the World. We may judge this if we imagine the sin of a man who, in order to gain possession of his love, should betray his country to its enemy; it is generally recognized not only as treachery, but as treachery of a peculiarly horrible kind. It may be a temptation; anything at any moment may be a temptation; it is therefore comprehensible, and in a sense even

The De Monarchia *and the Exile*

natural. Such things undoubtedly are natural. But we shall only feel the final depth of the *Inferno* if we understand that to Dante's mind the earthly city—Florence, let alone Rome—was as much greater than the earthly Beatrice as the Divine City was greater than the divine Beatrice. Beatrice had been the illuminated union of earth and heaven to his own eyes, but the Pope and the Emperor were the declared and decreed union of earth and heaven to all mankind.

This balance and contrast of the girl with the city is important to the whole of Dante's work, and that for a proper literary reason. There is in Dante as there is in some other poets the expression of a great contradiction.[1] One series of experiences is followed by another, and quite different, series of experiences. The first is sensitively good; the second sensitively evil. The two remain in intense conflict. This is sometimes called 'disillusion', but the term is nonsense; what happens is either worse or better than that. 'Disillusion' would mean that the first series of experiences had become invalid, but this is not so at all. They remain entirely valid, only their entire opposite has suddenly also become entirely valid. This state has been put to us most clearly in two places in English verse; the first is in Shakespeare's *Troilus and Cressida*; the second in Wordsworth's *Prelude*. In *Troilus* it is defined in relation to Cressida herself. When Troilus sees her yielding to Diomed's love-making, he says:

> This she? no; this is Diomed's Cressida.
> If beauty have a soul, this is not she.
> If souls guide vows, if vows be sanctimony,
> If sanctimony be the gods' delight,
> If there be rule in unity itself,
> This is not she. O madness of discourse
> That cause sets up with and against itself:
> Bifold authority! where reason can revolt
> Without perdition, and loss assume all reason
> Without revolt: this is, and is not, Cressid.
> Within my soul there doth conduce a fight
> Of this strange nature, that a thing inseparate

[1] I have discussed this, as far as English poetry is concerned, in *The English Poetic Mind* and in *Reason and Beauty in the Poetic Mind*. I touch on it here only so far as is needful to show it in Dante.

The De Monarchia *and the Exile*

> Divides more wider than the sky and earth;
> And yet the spacious breadth of this division
> Admits no orifice for a point as subtle
> As Ariachne's broken woof to enter.

Cressid at once is and is not; that is, Troilus's awareness of her fidelity and of her infidelity exist at once. She is 'inseparate', like Beatrice, but that indivisibility is at the same time divided. Troilus is not less conscious of either because of the other. Since there is 'rule in unity itself', this cannot be Cressid; but this is certainly Cressid, therefore there is no rule in unity itself. 'Bifold authority!'

A similar crisis is in the *Prelude*, discovered when Wordsworth heard that the English Government had declared war on the French Revolution:

> What then were my emotions when, in arms,
> Britain put forth her free-born strength in league—
> O pity and shame!—with those confederate Powers.
> Not in my single self alone I felt
> But in the minds of all ingenuous youth
> Change and subversion from that hour. No shock
> Given to my moral nature had I known
> Down to that very moment . . .

and he concentrates the moment on his hope for the defeat of the English—

>   It was a grief—
> Grief call it not! 'twas anything but that—
> A conflict of sensations without name,
> Of which *he* only who may love the sight
> Of a village steeple, as I do, can judge
> When in the congregation bending all
> To their great Father, prayers were offered up,
> And praises for their country's victories,
> I only, like an uninvited guest
> Whom no-one owned, sate silent—shall I add,
> Fed on the day of vengeance yet to come?

This moment, in its place, is not unlike the moment when Dante invoked the Emperor Henry VII to move against Italy and

The De Monarchia *and the Exile*

Florence. 'O misera, misera, patria mia!' It is still more like the preceding moment when he had found himself banished from Florence, by the evil in Florence. He was worse than 'an uninvited guest'; he was an exiled son. In a phrase used by Patmore in one of those political odes which break in on the Beatrician love-development of the *Unknown Eros*, Dante saw himself one of the few

> outlaw'd Best, who yet are bright
> With the sunken light,
> Whose common style
> Is Virtue at her gracious ease.

The *Vita* had contemplated no less, in Beatrice and (less defined) in Florence, than the 'common style' of Virtue at ease; he had felt it in himself as her smile saluted him. In proportion as his philosophical study confirmed and developed his sensitive knowledge of this pattern of Virtue, he expected it in Florence, and believed in it in Florence. The contrary image, the image of the apostasy, did not appear to him in Beatrice, nor (it seems from his work) in any woman. The opposing image was the image of the apostate city—the image which hovers within *Lear*, *Macbeth*, and *Coriolanus*, but the shock of which impinging on the single sufferer is better defined in the two quotations above. *Troilus* gives us the more metaphysical, the *Prelude* the more humanhearted, definition. The image of the apostasy is the image of the state when there is unimaginably felt to be no 'rule in unity itself'.

The phrase is exactly applicable to Dante in two senses: (i) the unity of Beatrice and Florence, (ii) the unity of the Pope and the Emperor. The first has been indicated in the *Convivio*; the second was defined in the *De Monarchia*, which is supposed to have been written during the exile, and perhaps at a time when the Emperor was already projecting his expedition to Italy, an expedition from which Dante hoped much, but which in fact failed to justify his hopes.

The *De Monarchia*, like the *Convivio*, is unfinished. We have three books of it. Its concern is to discuss the single authority as mediated through the Institution—or Institutions, the State and the Church. They are, but here in a noble and holy sense, in-

The De Monarchia *and the Exile*

separate and yet separated; just as Beatrice and the City are; and just as our duties towards Beatrice and the City are. The final unity of these apparent divisibles—final not in the sense of conclusion but in the sense of perfection and perpetuity—is hardly apprehensible in this life; it is an element of the blessedness which is eternal. The nearest we can get to it is a philosophical apprehension, when it is for a moment seized by 'the feeling intellect'. To know it properly would demand the fullness of 'the unitive life', another kind of life than that we habitually endure (which the Lady Julian of Norwich called 'our penance'). Until this unitive life is achieved the unity of which it is at once a part and an apprehension cannot be known.

Some such statement as this is continued in the opening of the *De Monarchia*. It is in the third chapter of the first book that the great sentence concerning function occurs, and this leads to the question: what is the function proper to humanity as a whole—'propria operatio humanae universitatis'? It is 'esse apprehensivum per intellectum possibilem', to be apprehensive by the possible, or potential, intellect. The chief business of man is at any moment to be realizing his powers of intellectual apprehension—to understand, to the utmost of his capacity, things as they are. For this two things are necessary, peace and direction. It is along these lines that Dante proceeds to develop, by more or less credible arguments, his view of the office of temporal monarchy; that is, as controlling all other temporal monarchs, of the Emperor. We are not here concerned to discuss those arguments in detail. Many of them are based on hypotheses which we should not admit and on a history which we should deny. They are related to the *Vita* and the *Convivio* chiefly by the image of authority which was, in the *Vita*, conveyed through Beatrice, and in the *Convivio* through the duplex Beatrician and philosophical unity, and here becomes the Imperial power—'to which trust and obedience are due.'

This authority exists in order that every man may reach his own 'liberty and power'. It is, where and as necessary, to control the three classes of men. Those three classes, as we saw in the *Convivio* (Dante does not define them here), are (i) those who have nobility in themselves, (ii) those who have a reflected nobility, learned indirectly by the observation of others, (iii) those who reject nobility and prefer greed. The first two classes are to be encouraged and directed; they are to be given opportunity. The third is to be controlled and compelled. Concord may thus be established (I, xv) everywhere: what is concord? 'Omnis concordia dependet ab unitate quae est in voluntatibus'—'all concord depends on that unity which is in wills.' Concord indeed is the expression of that unity, and the unity of man (so expressed in concord) is the reflection of the unity of God. 'Sed genus humanum maxime Deo adsimilatur quando maxime est unum; vera enim ratio unius in solo illo est.' 'But human kind is most like God when it is most one; for the true principle of unity is in him alone' (I, viii). Dante deduces from this that the human race is nearest unity where it is all subject to one prince. But there is another possibility of likeness to the divine unity (not formally mentioned by Dante) which consists in a likeness to the manner by which it exists. That manner is said to be by the 'co-inherence' of the Divine Persons in each other,[1] and it has been held that the unity of mankind consists in an analogical co-inherence of men with each other; so that the great sentence which Dante here quotes: 'Faciamus hominem ad imaginem et similitudinem nostram,' has this peculiar significance. He adds that we must not say 'ad imaginem' of anything lower than man, but we may say 'ad similitudinem' of anything, since the whole universe is 'vestigium quoddam', a certain footprint of the divine goodness. But we are not concerned with such similitudes; as Love said, 'it is time to put them aside,' and it is with the image of the co-inherent Godhead which is in mankind that we have to deal. The chief reason for mentioning that co-inherence here is that it is an idea similar to that carried by the Beatrician and Marian title: 'figlia del tuo figlio.' Being theirs, it is also all mankind's; it is the intended principle of our being; it is the function for which we were created, and not it for us. The Incarnation, or rather the motherhood of the Incarnation, is the function for which we were created, and not it for us—or say, not primarily

[1] See *God in Patristic Theology*: G. L. Prestige. Heinemann, 1936: chap. XIV, Co-inherence. This is the clearest exposition I know of the theological definition of the Divine Life in this sense. Humanly, the word stands for the idea of the 'in-othering' and 'in-Godding' of men which appears in Dante. See especially chap. XI *infra*.

The De Monarchia *and the Exile*

for us, but primarily that the Divine Being might itself fulfil those functions it had (as one might say) decreed itself to fulfil.

After he has proved the necessity of the Emperor, Dante proceeds in the second book to prove that this Empire and Emperor belong by right to the Roman people. He shows this by arguing from their inherent nobility, of which he gives examples; from miracles which accompanied their history; from their public spirit; from the principle that whoever contemplates a rightful end—and this the Romans did—must needs contemplate it rightly; from the success of the Roman people in many wars; and from the submission of our Lord, both in his birth (under the laws of the census) and in his death (under the sentence of Pilate) to the Roman sovereignty. Of these arguments, few to-day will sound even plausible without a complete revolution in our manner of thinking, which this is not the place to institute. What is important is the emergence of the image of the imperial dignity—say, simply, of the Emperor; and as the *Vita* and the *Convivio* are necessary to the *Commedia* if we are to understand there the image of Beatrice, so the *De Monarchia* is necessary if we are to receive the full impress of the image of the Emperor. The image of the Pope is equally important, but it is much more easily obtained. Many of Dante's readers, even of those who are not Roman Catholics, and even of those who are not Christians, have a sufficiently powerful imaginative grasp of the Papal image (even if they mistake in detail) to feel the poetry concerned with it. But, on the whole, we accept the doom of Brutus and Cassius at the end of the *Inferno* with an only half-willing 'suspension of unbelief'. This is, no doubt, partly Shakespeare's fault—because of *Julius Caesar*; Dante could not have reckoned on Shakespeare, and Shakespeare (for all we can see) never knew that he had to reckon with Dante. So that we have to do all the reckoning for both of them. We need not, however, make Shakespeare responsible for our own incompetence, and it is our incompetence which weakens for us that image of 'the Roman prince', of Caesar.

The image of that prince then is, for Dante, no modern image, deriving only from the five-centuries-old Charlemagne. It comes from Charlemagne certainly, but (eight hundred years before Charlemagne) from Julius Caesar himself; and even before

The De Monarchia *and the Exile*

Julius, though there is no Emperor, yet there is the nobility of the Roman people, and right back at their beginnings is Aeneas, and beyond Aeneas is Troy. The image of the Emperor derives through such progenitors. An appearance of infinite time, of infinite jurisdiction, stretches backward; a key to the *Commedia* is in the *De Monarchia*, but the key to the *De Monarchia* is in the *Aeneid*. The appearance of Octavius at the battle of Actium, in that august poem, is near to the expression of the same image. There the young Caesar, the successor of Aeneas, with the star of Julius shining in the heavens above him, leads the decent gods and households of a noble and domestic people into battle against monstrosities and furies; what Virgil and Dante meant by that warring shape Shakespeare, in another play than *Julius Caesar*, put into a line and a half:

> Prove this a prosperous day, the three-nook'd world
> Shall bear the olive freely.

The olive was peace; the world was, in that phrase, promised freedom and peace—'documenta libertatis et pacis'—'the charters of freedom and peace' wrote Dante in the last chapter of the *De Monarchia*. The care of these charters is the business of the Emperor; he is the heir of a long succession of princes loaded with that very care; miracles have gone to establish him, and high deeds, and the long contemplation of right; and more than all this—the direct submission to that imperial figure of Almighty God himself. For the last of all the chapters in the second book of the *De Monarchia* which go to build up that image brings as a testimony the authoritative judgement on our Lord. The Roman prince, Dante is saying, exercises temporal justice; he has penal jurisdiction. How is this known? Because the whole human race sinned in one man, Adam; and the whole human race was to be punished in one man, Christ. This punishment was a just punishment in so far as it was pronounced, in Christ, on the whole human race; but it would not have been a just sentence (nor therefore a just punishment) unless it had been pronounced by a power which had jurisdiction over the human race. Therefore Caiaphas (ignorantly) sent Christ to Pilate, and therefore Herod (ignorantly) sent Christ back to Pilate; that is, to Tiberius Caesar, 'cujus vicarius erat Pilatus'. In the *Paradiso* (VI-VII) the

The De Monarchia *and the Exile*

same idea is expressed, by the mouths of Justinian and Beatrice. The great canto in which the Emperor—'Cesare fui, e son Giustiniano'; 'Caesar I was, and am Justinian'—declares the image of the Emperor, as if he too said: 'Yes, look well; we are, we are indeed the Emperor'—includes this claim in its rehearsal: that it properly and gloriously carried out the judgement of God. Beatrice, 'with such a smile as would make a burning man happy,' dilates upon it: 'this penalty of the Cross never (if it is measured by the assumed nature) bit anyone so justly, though never so unjustly if the assuming Person is considered. God and the Jews were pleased by one and the same death—Ch' a Dio ed ai Giudei piacque una morte.'

This is not the place to enter on a dispute on the doctrine. The main point is that the image of earthly justice (which, by definition, is all with which the Emperor is concerned) is here raised to its highest capacity; he is that which, in its divine commission, properly condemns the nature of man in Christ for its temporal sin. He is therefore the guardian of everlasting law; he also is, in that sense, arch-natural, and not only Christ, but Beatrice, and the lady of the window, and Dante, are subject to him. With the loss of monarchy, we have lost the idea of the image being in a single person; we have to say 'the State', or (better) 'the Republic'. This will serve very well, so long as all that we mean by our best imagination of the Republic contains all the best of the Imperial image; only that image is more, rather than less, than the general best of our imagination. Dante certainly had known a Republic also, however inadequate; he had known Florence. When he appealed to the Emperor against Florence he was appealing to the arch-natural against the natural. It is not to be supposed that he found any joy in it. O misera, misera, patria mia!

But there was another authentic image, as mighty as, and, in some sense, more final than, Beatrice or Virgil or the Emperor —the image of the Pope. That image was given, as the images of the Emperor and Virgil were given; it was not revealed as Beatrice was. It was part of Dante's ordinary awareness from childhood, and no disturbing shock of new experience. It is nevertheless not much referred to—I doubt if it is at all referred to—in those books which deal with the Beatrician discovery, the

The De Monarchia and the Exile

Vita and the *Convivio*, and is introduced into the *De Monarchia* only to be defined and limited. But the last treatise of that book, and the whole of the allusions in the *Commedia*, show how intense for Dante its validity, so limited, was. 'The form of the Church', he writes (Chap. XV) 'is nothing else than the life of Christ, understood as much in words as in deeds.' 'Forma autem ecclesiae nihil aliud est quam vita Christi . . . Vita enim ipsius idea fuit et exemplar militantis Ecclesiae, praesertim pastorum, maxime summi.' 'For his life was the idea and example of the Church militant, especially of the pastors (i.e. the priests), and mostly of the chief pastor.' Christ renounced all temporal rule; therefore so must the Church, and so therefore the Pope. 'Formale igitur est Ecclesiae, illud idem dicere, illud idem sentire'; 'it is therefore the formal principle of the Church to say that very thing and to feel that very thing.' Man has two ends—temporal blessedness and eternal blessedness. The first he reaches by the practice of the moral and intellectual virtues; the second, by the practice of the theological. The first is shown by reason; the second, revealed by the Holy Spirit. But these man would abandon, were he not restrained and directed, by the Emperor towards his temporal blessedness, by the Pope towards his eternal. One authority—to which faith and obedience are due—moves in both.

Something of all this had been already seen in the completeness of the feminine image, as it had been worked out in the philosophical analysis. The girl had come like the True Light. The eleven fruits of nobility answer to the moral virtues (and correspond in the active life to the intellectual in the contemplative life). They are the marks of the soul-in-largesse, perfect in her temporal blessedness; which consists, as Dante now defines it, 'in operatione propriae virtutis,' 'in the operation of his proper power.' This operation would be the fulfilling of his function; his function is his vocation, and he follows it by this proper operation.[1] But there had been something more. She had not only been

[1] It is worth remarking that Dante says this corresponds to, or is imaged by, the terrestrial paradise: 'per terrestrium Paradisum figuratur.' This idea is renewed in the *Commedia*; it is in that operation of proper power that Dante again meets Beatrice, and more passionately asserts the validity of Beatrice. He is, in fact, then precisely doing what the incidents of the poem describe.

The De Monarchia *and the Exile*

so natural that the very earth and all habits of our mortal life are not more so; she had also been so arch-natural that she had thrown light on the Faith itself. Faith began, and after faith the hope of that which we already foresee, and from that the activity of love . . . fede . . . speranza . . . carità. These are the theological virtues which lead to eternal life. In this degree therefore of that sacred Order to which Lancelot and Guido of Montefeltro belonged, the soul is—at least in vision—at the centre. 'God is intelligible light', said Saint Thomas; that invisible light is absorbed by and re-emanates from the visible girl; its rays are directed on either hand by the great shapes of the Emperor and the Pope (say, by the Republic and the Church); they meet again in God who ordained all; indeed, all the images are moving sweetly and strongly into God, with whom this union is, as it were, by that painting of 'our effigy', 'nostra effigie', which appeared at the close of the *Commedia* in the Second Circle of 'lume riflesso', 'reflected light'. Or if, abandoning the image of the circle Love had used in the *Vita*, we turn again to the four meanings, then they are now the Beatrician, the imperial, the papal, and the divine. They are all in the soul, so that the soul itself is not so much at the centre of their circle, but itself a circle which includes them all. This again is, in some sense, at least in vision, the union of the centre and the circumference, for there is no part of the circumference of the circle on which the soul moves which is not in relation through one or other of those Powers, or perhaps through all, with the centre. 'I am the centre of a circle to which all parts of the circumference are equal, but with you——'

No; it was not yet so. This was the great pattern. But things were unlike it. Beatrice was dead. That was the least of the difficulties, for the experience of her was fixed; she of the window had confirmed it; and he was very well set to write of that total Beatrice 'what had not yet been written of any woman'. That image at least was always valid. But as if the image of a sacrilegious Beatrice had risen in his heart (just as afterwards in the *Inferno* the image of the false Geryon was to float up out of the deeper abyss), the other two great shapes became false before his eyes. He saw apostasy; and if I propose again an apostate Beatrice, it is because his real experience was more than that and not less. Florence had banished her most loyal son, in her preference of

The De Monarchia *and the Exile*

vice to virtue; but, what was worse, she had set herself against the divine image of the Emperor. 'You', he wrote to the 'scelestissimis Florentinis', 'turning from the bondage of liberty, have raged against the glory of the Roman prince, the king of the world and the minister of God . . . O concord of evil! . . . An overwhelming cupidity has made you prisoners of the law of sin, and forbidden you to obey those most sacred laws which copy the image of natural justice (justitiae naturalis . . . imaginem); obedience to which, if joyful, if free, proves to be not only no slavery, but to anyone whose intuition is perspicacious, is itself obviously the highest liberty. For what else is liberty but the free passage of the will into action, which the laws hasten for those who accept them generously (mansuerunt—cf. the mansuetude of the eleven notes of the noble life)?'

Florence had betrayed natural justice; the Pope had betrayed supernatural justice. Florence and the Pope were alike greedy of money and rule. The life of Christ which was the 'forma' of the Church was betrayed and deformed. The Emperor (Henry of Luxembourg) himself delayed his coming, and when he came, in 1310, nothing went well. Dante seems to have seen him in person, and retained hope. In 1312 the Emperor was crowned in Rome; he then laid siege to Florence; during the siege he fell ill; on 24 August 1313 he died. The Imperial army retired uselessly from Italy. Two or three years afterwards Dante wrote to a friend in Florence. It is the statement of the opposite of Beatrice, the sigh which, loosed from Love-in-grief, did not now rise to behold the glory, but consented to the separation on earth of the inseparate, and endured the breach 'in unity itself'. It should therefore be given in itself; it is the ninth of the Letters.

'I have had your letter—you will know with what reverence and affection I received it—and I am indeed grateful to see, from very careful reading, how much my repatriation means to you. You put me under the deepest obligation; it rarely happens that exiles are able to find friends. I proceed to answer it; and if the answer is not what certain cowards might wish, I beg you, in all affection, to consider it carefully before you come to an opinion on it.

'I understand, from the letters of your nephew and mine and of a number of friends, that a decree recently passed in Florence

The De Monarchia *and the Exile*

on this matter of the pardoning of the exiles declares that if I choose to pay a certain amount of money, and to go through the ceremonies of submission, I may be reconciled and return immediately. These two things, Father, are as ridiculous as they are ill-considered, I mean, ill-considered on the part of those who wrote to me about them, for your own letter, which was much more cautiously and thoughtfully phrased, said nothing about them.

'This then is the gracious recall by which Dante Alighieri may be brought back to his native land, after enduring almost fifteen years of exile! this is what an innocence of which everyone knows has deserved! This is what the sweat and labour of unceasing study has deserved! Is a man somewhat familiar with philosophy likely to abandon himself to such humiliation? as any Cioli or other infamous creature might do, allowing himself to be bound and presented as an offering. Shall a preacher of justice, a victim of injustice, pay money to those who have injured him, exactly as if they had been his benefactors?

'That, Father, is not the way to return to my country. But if any other way can be found, by you or (after you) by anyone, which will not be derogatory to Dante's reputation and honour, I shall not be slow to accept it. If I cannot enter Florence by such a path, I will not enter Florence. What then? cannot I look everywhere on the mirror of the sun and the stars? Can I not everywhere under heaven mirror the sweetest truths, without first returning to my city, making myself inglorious and ignominious in the sight of the people of Florence? I shall not want for bread.'

VII

THE MAKING OF THE *COMMEDIA*

Some, so defeated, have abandoned the Way of Affirmation. Their defeat has been the occasion of their discovery of their true vocation; they have rejected Images. Raymond Lully and Ignatius Loyola are two who did so. Loyola indeed established an outward Order of Rejection in place of a more secret Order of Affirmation, which might have been as truly named 'of Jesus'. Dante, however, did not turn from his original vows. He was deprived of any direct action except one single action, but that (it is to be supposed) was the single action he was called on to take, the design of his existence, the function of his power. He was left free, if he chose, to write the *Divina Commedia*. He did so choose.

He was left therefore to follow, by his own particular duty, the Way of Affirmation of Images. It is easy to say that he compensated himself for the loss of Beatrice and of his native city by imagining an even fairer Beatrice and a much nobler City. It is a tender, ironic, and consoling view. It is consoling because it shows us that, though we cannot write like Dante, yet we shall not be taken in by Dante. It is also consoling because it relieves us from the necessity of supposing that Dante may be relevant to us. The Beatrice of the *Commedia* is a compensation, and the Beatrice of the *Vita* is dead; thus neither of them has any real relation to our own love-affairs or our own moments of adoration. Sir Thomas Browne wrote that he loved to lose himself in an 'O altitudo!' Confronted with any 'altitudo' there are several things we may do about it—ignore it, explain it away, explore it, or lose ourselves in it. Of these Dante chose the third.

It is, no doubt, ironical that the death of Beatrice and the loss of Florence led him to a re-assertion of their intermingled validity. But it was so; it is a mere fact. Irony is therefore only the means and not the end. We can only be finally ironical about the *Commedia* by flatly denying that the re-assertion has any validity

The Making of the Commedia

at all. Irony is a good servant but—not so much a bad as a foolish master; it should be, in life as in letters, only a transitory technique. The challenge in the earthly Paradise (and it will be remembered that the earthly Paradise 'figures' a man's exercise of his proper power) is hurled at the ironists: 'Yes, look well; We are, We are indeed Beatrice.' The only answer, other than Dante's, is a flat denial.

The ironists, nevertheless, are on the whole a more respectable company than the spiritualizers; I do not mean the allegorists. The allegorists are those who, at the point of the *Commedia*, deny altogether the mortal identity of Beatrice, and turn her wholly into Theology or Divine Grace or what not. Her smiles are, for them, always metaphorical; her anger is abstract and not feminine; her teasing—but for them she does not tease. She is unblooded and exalted, but at least she remains defined. In the spiritualizers, however, she becomes so dim that she is, in fact, nothing but a kind of vapour of the soul, a mist that goes up out of the ground of the heart. Since it is obvious that very few young lovers are going to be interested in that, there is nothing in the two later parts of the *Commedia* for them to be interested in; and they are therefore left with the *Inferno* in which, after the first two or three cantos, she does not appear. The same kind of miserable spiritualizing has taken place in another myth, with Galahad the High Prince, the mystery of whose fatherhood in Lancelot has been forgotten. Admittedly, the *Paradiso*, being the high close of Romanticism, is not easy going for beginners in Romanticism. But to spiritualize Beatrice away from earth into a pseudo-Romanticism is, in criticism, very like mortal sin. It will be suggested presently that the *Paradiso* would be, for unfallen natures, the normal development of human romantic love; and being so, must remain even for our fallen natures a matter of perpetual study. The 'glorious and holy flesh' is a part of its consummation; it is included in the painting of 'nostra effigie' in the reflected light of the Second Circle at the grand poetic close. The passage through the Paradises is the true passage and history of Love—impossible to men and women because of sin, but comprehensible to the 'nobile intelletto', the intellect of the noble life, and even in a sense, after repentance, possible to it. It is the simple and arch-natural process of any two lovers—for-

The Making of the Commedia

tunate if they obey, infinitely unfortunate if they continue to disobey.

Dante had long since conceived the kind of poem the *Commedia* was to be; he had said so in the *Vita*. It was to say about a woman 'such things as have not yet been written'. These things were to be true, according to the later definition of his own verse as being a record of the dictation of Love. The kind of thing had been hinted at everywhere in the *Vita*, specially in the canzone 'Donne, ch' avete intelletto d' amore', which was re-asserted in the *Commedia*. There God was imagined to say of Dante that 'he shall say in hell to the evil-born: "I have seen the hope of the blessed"!' This need not be pressed so far as to suggest that Dante already had the whole poem charted in his head. But we know that Milton had the thought of *Paradise Lost* with him for years; we know that Wordsworth brooded for years over the great poem to which the *Prelude* was to be a prelude; and we know, by the *Convivio* (however we interpret it), that Dante brooded for years over the same subject which the *Vita* had been and the *Commedia* was to be. The actual method was probably, at the time of that original conception, not yet known, though it may have been. But the poem was to concern the total Beatrice; it was also to concern religion; it was to be accurate, and it was to be new.

There is, in the *Purgatorio*, a description of the carvings on the wall of the first terrace. The *Purgatorio* is full of the arts. They are there for a purpose; they are, after that first incident in which Dante's own poem is the cause of a delay, to speed the soul towards heaven. It seems likely that Dante (with all the medievals) thought that this was what the arts were chiefly for, though the incident of the censors of the *Vita*, and the history of the study of the *Commedia*, does not suggest that the arts are going to be much thanked by the official ministers of heaven for their assistance. But the point here is that these carvings (*Purg.* X) are themselves arch-natural; they 'put Nature itself to shame'. The Annunciation is there so sculptured that the images of the Virgin and the Angel seem to be actually speaking. This intensity is like the accuracy which Dante spoke of in his own verse. It is the moment of the thing happening.

This intensity does not prevent complexity. In the letter dedicating the *Paradiso* to 'the magnificent and most victorious

The Making of the Commedia

lord, the lord Can Grande della Scala, Vicar-General of the most holy principality of Caesar in the city of Verona and town of Vicenza', we are reminded again of the four meanings which this poem has. It is improbable that Dante, it is certain that few of his readers, have been able to read the poem with all four meanings in their minds at once, or indeed sequentially. Nothing less than this is in the full demand, and anyone who has a strong belief in poetry may believe that it is justified, since poetry is apt to hold much more than even the poets know. This continual relevance and co-ordination is the most unpredictable and incomprehensible thing about great verse. It gives occasion for all the interpretations, and it gives some excuse (though quite insufficient) to each interpreter when he claims, as he is apt to do, that his own interpretation is singularly valid. It might not be a bad thing if we accustomed ourselves to thinking in terms of Dante's four headings—granted that their implicit content would be less rigid in our day than in his. This would apply only to great 'allegorical' poetry, but then there is (outside lyrics) hardly any great poetry which is not 'allegorical'. It is this realization which has released *Paradise Lost*, and may release the *Prelude*, to us as of profound relevance to our affairs, whether we rationally accept the God of the one or the Nature of the other or not.

The identity of the thing happening in all its various categories is Dante's subject; and the thing happening is the release and progress of the soul. This is told in three parts, which again are in two ways divisible into two. They may be considered as three equal books, describing three several states. Or the first and second, the *Inferno* and *Purgatorio*, may be taken together as a prelude, and the *Paradiso* seen as a complete whole in itself. Or the *Inferno* may be taken separately as a complete whole, alternative to the other two parts taken together. Each of these methods causes a slight alteration in our vision; the stresses, ever so lightly, vary. All the three methods however should lead to the fourth, that which sees the *Paradiso* as inclusive of the other two. The *Inferno* cannot, so, be cut off from the *Paradiso*, nor at all should be; we make nonsense of the first and impoverish the second if we so cut it off. Much less can they be separated romantically. The sense which underlies the communication of love and courtesy to Dante in the *Vita* implies that unfortunately he was

The Making of the Commedia

not always in possession of love and courtesy. These states are arch-natural certainly, in the sense that the knowledge of them does not depend (as is sometimes blasphemously asserted) upon our knowledge of their opposites. We are able to know good without knowing evil; I mean, that our nature is of that kind, though unhappily it has been so twisted that in fact we do not. The existence of Beatrice therefore is a danger to her lover; the *Vita* is more concerned with the vision than with the danger, but the danger is there, the danger of disobedience to the heavenly vision—of discourtesy, of sullenness, of greed, of postponement and delay, of infidelity masquerading as fidelity. Even our motives will not altogether save us; they become hypocritical too easily, as Dante discovered with a shock during his first encounters with the Lady of the Window; our deeds must count for something in the whole. It is something to be sure of the deed; our courteous Lord will deign to redeem the motive. It is of lovers whose motives and deeds have been alike redeemed that the *Paradiso* is full, but the empyrean which surrounds all surrounds also hell; it is because of the empyrean that hell is there at all. The *Vita* itself might well have written on its title-page 'Per me si va nella città dolente'—'through me is the way to the sorrowful city.'

The vision of which the poem is an account was set by Dante at Eastertide in the year 1300. The *Vita* records that it had, in fact, happened much earlier, unless we are to suppose that in the later year he had some confirmation of it. But there is no need for this; the dating is a part of the poem. There were reasons enough; it was the turn of the century; it was the year of the Papal Jubilee. It was still a time of unfulfilled hopes; the Emperor had not yet come into Italy, and when he did all might be recovered. The poem might therefore sway level between possibilities; it might hope, temporally, as well as despair. A minor point is perhaps worth noting. We are so used to thinking of the Dante of the *Commedia* as a disappointed man and an exile, owing to our extra-poetic knowledge of the time at which the poem was written, that we miss the other recollection that in the poem this is not so at all. In 1300 Dante was what might be called a successful man. He was thirty-five years old; he had a poetic reputation; he was that year elected as one of the priors; he was

The Making of the Commedia

taking a notable part in the business of the city. It is held by some that the first eight cantos of the *Commedia* were written before the exile. If so, then they were written precisely when he was a successful man. The point is of some small importance for our appreciation of the meaning of the metaphor of the dark wood at the opening. It is the practical man, the politician, the husband and father, the scholar and poet (the terms had not for the Middle Ages the kind of specialized remoteness that we give them)—it is such a man who is blinded and lost. This is the danger of the Way of Affirmations, and it is hardly to be doubted that Dante put it there deliberately. He was lost in a wild tangled growth of affirmations; his very vocation, too unwisely followed, had misled him. 'Tanto è amara, che poco è più morte—So bitter is it that death is hardly more' (*Inferno*, I, 7).

This is the image which the vision first presented; it is perhaps permissible, and even becoming, to ask one more question. We know very well what Dante was like; can we guess at all what Beatrice was like? what kind of girl had walked in Florence? what kind of woman had sprung from heaven? or was to be carried in the double-natured Gryphon's car? or taught her lover truths as much by her voice as her words? Little, yet a little. Of her height, nothing; we may perhaps take her for nothing out of the common either way. Of her colour—dark probably, as a Florentine would be likely to be, and of a noble pallor, as the *Vita* says, a pallor which Dante also calls 'color d' amore', the colour of love; she and the Lady of the Window were both apt to pale yet more under the stress of passion. Her eyes were greenish; it was from 'emeralds' that Love first shot his arrows at Dante. She was apt to be gay, but wisely; a coruscation of laughter lived in her eyes and mouth. Her voice (Virgil said) was 'suave et piano—gentle and low'; he chose to describe it so, and not as firm or clear. She was full of courtesies, and of *amicitia*; the praise which honoured her for being generally loved chose to honour her for that and not for seclusion. She was capable of high passion; the *Paradiso* is full of it; what it is also full of is its restraint. She had that great femininity which demanded of her lover what her lover demanded of himself; in Florence and in the earthly paradise she required his function perfectly fulfilled. But she puts herself to the same test; in the heavenly paradise she will be for him what

The Making of the Commedia

he needs. She explains sunspots? but he wished it; she recounts the origin of angels? but again he wished it; and all these things she simply knew: why not explain them, changing and charging the explanations with the deep smile of passion? She was eighteen; she was thirty-four; her age in the poem is both, and eternal.

This was Beatrice in the poem of Beatrice.

VIII

THE *INFERNO*

> Now entertain conjecture of a time
> When creeping murmur and the poring dark
> Fill the wide vessel of the universe...

The image of a wood has appeared often enough in English verse. It has indeed appeared so often that it has gathered a good deal of verse into itself; so that it has become a great forest where, with long leagues of changing green between them, strange episodes of high poetry have place. Thus in one part there are the lovers of a midsummer night, or by day a duke and his followers, and in another men behind branches so that the wood seems moving, and in another a girl separated from her two lordly young brothers, and in another a poet listening to a nightingale but rather dreaming richly of the grand art than there exploring it, and there are other inhabitants, belonging even more closely to the wood, dryads, fairies, an enchanter's rout. The forest itself has different names in different tongues—Westermain, Arden, Birnam, Broceliande; and in places there are separate trees named, such as that on the outskirts against which a young Northern poet saw a spectral wanderer leaning, or, in the unexplored centre of which only rumours reach even poetry, Igdrasil of one myth, or the Trees of Knowledge and Life of another. So that indeed the whole earth seems to become this one enormous forest, and our longest and most stable civilizations are only clearings in the midst of it.

The use of such an extended image is to allow the verse of those various 'parts of the wood' to point distantly towards each other, without the danger of too hasty comparisons. The 'amplitude of mind' which Wordsworth ascribed to the Imagination is thus communicated. We become aware that so much as we know of poetry is not all; a happier generation may discover an even more intense life in the relation of one part of it to another, but it will not serve ours to rush in with false ingenuities. We must wait yet; the unifying of our imaginations is an arduous

The Inferno

business, and national committees will not help, not even academic committees, let alone those which some think more suitable—men of the world, business men, politicians, journalists. The academics may petrify in the forest, but as a general rule the others have not even seen the forest. Yet perhaps before we can unify the world, we shall have to unify the poetic imagination of the world; and the best way towards that is, first, to be acquainted with some part of the forest, and then slowly to push on towards other parts. He who could, at the end of a hard life, have done something towards the study of the living forest in European verse alone, might have fulfilled his function, and deserved well of the Republic—or of the Emperor.

There is, in that forest, as deep as any poet has yet penetrated towards the centre, one especially wild part; worse than anything known in verse even by Spenser or Milton. There is a valley, of great trees and tangled shrubs, 'selvaggia e aspra e forte—savage and rough and strong' where no path can be kept; the true path (through the forest or to the centre of the forest—it is perhaps the same thing, in Westermain or Broceliande) does not lead through it, but side paths do, less and less easy, more and more dark. A man, on his journey through the strange growths of the forest, may inattentively turn aside down those paths; perhaps many men do, and perhaps some die there, for the sense of the valley is like death itself. One man indeed, finding himself in it, said in so many words that no mortal ever came from it alive—'che non lasciò già mai persona viva.' The man was **Dante Alighieri**; he was thirty-five years old—'nel mezzo del cammin di nostra vita.' He had himself been full of an interior slumber when he was misled by the deceits of the forest, and there —in such a dangerous gloom—he 're-found himself—mi ritrovai.'

Some translations give only 'I found myself in a . . . wood'. But the original is more intense—'I came to myself again.' He is suddenly re-aware of himself in this misery, and the misery is so great that he would not willingly recall it now, except to tell of other things, of the good that is hidden in the wild maze. At the end of the valley the ground rises before him into a high hill. The dawn is already lightening the height. It is, as we learn afterwards, a hill which is mysteriously called 'è principio e cagion di tutta gioia—the source and occasion of all joy'

The Inferno

(*Inf.* I, 78). There is a sense of dream deepening into nightmare over the whole of this opening of the *Commedia*; the sensation is familiar enough—one is caught in a twisted helplessness, with some lovely place of escape just near and open, and then some hindrance, perhaps some horror, interferes. What here interferes, as Dante, after resting a little, begins to mount the slope, is, first of all, a beast like a leopard, dappled, light, and swift. It does not attack him but it wanders in front of him, so that he cannot get by. In seven lines Dante gathers 'that beast with the gay skin' into a union with a universal freshness of beauty—'The time was early morning, and the sun was rising, with those stars which were with it when the Divine Love first bade those lovelinesses move, so that the hour of the time and the sweet season moved me to good hope of escape from the gay-skinned beast' (*Inf.* I, 37–43). His heart is high, therefore, and hope has returned when he suddenly discerns two other creatures—a lion so hungry and fierce that the very air seems shaken with fear, coming terribly against him, and a lean she-wolf.

These three beasts are habitually interpreted as lechery, pride, and covetousness; so no doubt they are. But they are something more. They are the powers of the three periods of life which Dante called Adolescence, Youth (or Manhood), and Age. In the *Convivio* he had spoken of the adolescent who 'would not be able to follow the right way in the wandering wood of this life, if his elders did not show it him'. He had been shown, and had not followed; now he has suddenly come to himself in a region (more austere even than any in the *Vita*) from which there is indeed no return. Before him he sees the sun-lit slope of a hill, the timeless hill of the good, and the images of all the three periods of perilous life drive him back. The greatest invention of all three is the She-wolf. This is Age, lean with infinite craving, who has brought sorrow to many, and so frightens Dante that he loses hope of the height; he turns and runs back; his little life is haunted and hunted away into the terrible wood—'like one who has willingly taken his gains, and when time brings loss, he weeps and laments,' so he, driven back, step by step, 'la dove 'l sol tace—to where the sun is silent' (I, 60).

It is important to grasp this very great image—the man emerging from a death-like perdition; the sun over the hill; the

The Inferno

gay swift leopard of lechery and youth, yet somehow related to all the first things and those very stars which are, throughout, the hints and glories of perfection; the furious and hungry lion of the mature energy of manhood; and then *she*—the use of the English pronoun recalls all those other *shes*, but now horrid—craving, always craving, and driving the man back into his tangled and treacherous and dark past, the sun silent and the Way of Affirmation wholly lost; only the savage and (as it were) vegetable affirmations themselves growing chaotic without and within him. It is impossible for us to imagine an adequate poetic emergence from that image, but Dante could—as the man hurries away from that awful craving into the very past that made the craving, he sees before him a dim figure, almost a ghost, lonely in the great wilderness. Dante cries out to it for help, 'whether you be shade or true man—od ombra od uomo certo,' and it answers him in a voice that seems thick through its long silence: 'No man; I was once a man; my parents were Lombards and both were of Mantuan land. I was born under Julius, though late; I lived at Rome under the good Augustus, in the time of false and deceitful gods. I was a poet———' and so he proceeds to the name of Troy. 'Are you then that Virgil—quel Virgilio . . .' (I, 65-79) but the point is that, so lost is the place, even all that Virgil is and means is spectral and thick-speaking; all poetry, all philosophy, all human institutions, all greatness of man—'od ombra, od uomo certo? Non uomo, uomo già fui.'

There is over the fear in that moment a kind of sacred awe, which the sense of the Wolf itself cannot disperse—that 'stupor' which Dante said we ought to feel before such high things as the meeting of great poets. In this wilderness, Dante has come to himself alone, outside the City, without derivation, and now suddenly he is able to name derivation again, and does—'Tu se' lo mio maestro e 'l mio autore' (I, 85), a line to which Milton's is the only correspondent in English, and worthily so—

> My author and disposer, what thou bidd'st
> Unargued I obey.

This is practically what Dante says, and the fact that he can so say it, and glory in it, might have helped to redeem Milton's Eve also from the charge of imbecility which has been long and perversely

The Inferno

laid on her. Eve and Dante, in their passion of love and adoration before Adam and Virgil, speak so because they know their derivations and their 'authorities'. They recognize truth; say, rather, they speak facts and their own rapture in the facts. In the *Paradiso* it is all so; there the great derivations are praised on all sides.

This is a convenient place to say something of the recurrent question of Virgil being shut out of heaven. It must, I think, be admitted that that exclusion does, to our differently thinking minds, a little jar—in spite of our Lord's comment on St. John the Precursor. We are intensely conscious of the personal Virgil. It should however be recognized that, so far from Dante being compelled against his poetic will to keep Virgil theologically out of heaven, Dante as a poet simply could not afford to let him in. The poetry is not in the least reluctantly acceding to a theological doctrine; it is taking every advantage of the doctrine; in a sense, we may say that, if the doctrine had not been there for Dante, then Dante would have had to invent it. To think otherwise is to miss the real point of Virgil. The figure of Beatrice alone is enough to show that Dante set no limit to the great orderly development of natural things; the eyes of Beatrice are always human. But as there is an infinite development, so there must also be an infinite division. 'This also is thou, neither is this Thou.' Neither the Affirmations nor the Rejections are allowed to forget either half of that maxim. Virgil, the image of so much, is also the image of the necessary separation—or at least willingness towards separation—from the dearest thing. The consciousness of the sighs which trouble the air of Limbo is the consciousness of our sighs when we are expected to abandon all—for ever; and what seems to us the terrible phrase of Beatrice when she says to Virgil himself 'I am made such that your misery does not touch me' (II, 92) means a division which has to be endured. But this necessary Rejection must here be justified in its particulars. Virgil is poetry, and the greatest of European poets knew the limitation of poetry. Poetry may be as 'spiritual' as its rash devotees are in the habit of calling it. In so far as it is 'spiritual' it is of the nature of those visions and locutions from which the wise are warned to be detached. Poetry cannot possess charity; it cannot be humble. It is therefore justly presented in Virgil, who precisely lacked baptism; that is, by the theological decision of the

The Inferno

time, the capacity for infinite charity and infinite humility.[1] So of Virgil as philosophy, and Virgil as human learning; nay, of Virgil as the Institution itself. It is a part of the poem that Virgil should lack grace; did he not, he would be too like Beatrice herself. The *Aeneid* has *pietas* and not *caritas*; so must its author have here.

Yet the image of his coming is exact. Beatrice has to ask him to go; she cannot command him, though she puts her trust in his 'fair speech'. Religion itself cannot order poetry about; the grand art is wholly autonomous. 'The voice of Virgil is his own.' Its chief business may be to indicate and honour the Emperor (as in the *Aeneid*) or to 'remove those in this life from misery and bring them to happiness' (as in the *Commedia*); it will do so however on its own terms. We should have been fortunate if the ministers of religion and poetry had always spoken to each other with such courtesy as these. Virgil, speaking to Beatrice, has almost a lover's dramatization: 'Lady . . . if I had already done what you asked, I should have been slow in doing it!' (II, 80). And though, for poetic reasons rather than purely theological, Virgil could not find a place in the *Paradiso*, yet it is just worth noting that, at the very close of the *Paradiso*, something not altogether unlike Virgil does, in fact, appear—a man of 'age', glorious and courteous, who also comes at the request of Beatrice. It is St. Bernard. Virgil could hardly, without (in spite of the Fourth Eclogue) ceasing to be Virgil, have addressed himself with passion to the glory of the Virgin-Mother. But this is necessary; it is she into whose eyes the eyes of Beatrice are transmuted. Therefore, once more, Virgil must not be there; he must not play a second part and the first part he cannot play; but something which is not Beatrice, something which is instead of Virgil, something which in the total mystery fulfils the function Virgil fulfilled in the imperial, is there. That last masculine appearance in the poem, by its very office, recalls the first masculine appearance.

It is not necessary to believe that Dante wholly succeeded in his task of reconciling us to the exclusion; his own poetry has made that too poignant. It is necessary to believe that the ex-

---

[1] The point of the definition has been discussed in R. W. Chambers's *Man's Unconquerable Mind*. He allows for baptism by desire, but he shows that Dante probably did not know of it.

The Inferno

clusion was demanded not so much by theology as by poetry, and that those who too monotonously lament the personal Virgil's exclusion have not cared to understand the more technical problems of the grand art.

In the talk between the poets Virgil, in a highly Virgilian way, declares that the she-wolf is to be driven back to hell by one who is to come. This is generally supposed to be Can Grande della Scala, 'the imperial Vicar', and must anyhow have some political allusion. So far as Dante is concerned, this does not help and will not save him. There is only one way for him; it is to behold the principle of the universe, in its three great modes. He must see (i) 'the ancient spirits who in pain bewail the second death', (ii) 'those who are contented in the fire', (iii) 'the blessed peoples'. 'And I answered: "Poet . . . by the God you did not know . . . lead on." ' (I, 112–36). The Rejection is thus entwined with the Affirmation: 'Poetry, by the God you cannot know, lead on!'—yet, for the Way itself, the Affirmation is repeated: 'tu duca, tu signore, e tu maestro—you the leader, you the lord, and you the master!' (II, 140).

Under that imperial banner, in that fair speech, they come presently to a great gate. The dark inscription over it is: 'Through me is the way into the city of woe, into eternal pain, among the lost people. Justice moved my high Creator; Divine Power, supreme Wisdom, primal Love made me. Before me were no things created but the eternal, and I eternally endure. Abandon all hope, ye who enter' (III, 1–9). The abandonment of all hope 'lasciate ogni speranza'—is immediately after balanced by Virgil's command to the perplexed Dante—'lasciare ogni sospetto' (III, 14)—to abandon all distrust. This choice is the significant moment of free-will. If there is God, if there is free-will, then man is able to choose the opposite of God. Power, Wisdom, Love, gave man free-will; therefore Power, Wisdom, Love, created the gate of hell, and the possibility of hell. We shall see later the place in hell where this evil choice is re-exhibited in its full obstinacy. For if men are to be able to reason, they must be able not to reason; and it is therefore here that Virgil pronounces that frightful description—

le genti dolorosa
c' hanno perduto il ben dell' intelletto,—

The Inferno

'the miserable race who have lost the good of intellect' (III, 17–18). And as he speaks he lays his hand on Dante's—the hand that wrote the *Aeneid* on the hand that wrote the *Commedia*—'con lieto volto, with a joyous countenance from which I took comfort' (III, 20). Joy!

Joy. It is permissible, in weakness, to call Dante inhuman—or perhaps superhuman. It is not, however, permissible to read the *Inferno* without understanding how Dante meant it to be read. He himself is as frightened as we are. It is a small comfort to some of us to find Dante so presenting himself. He is always willing to appeal to Virgil to save him; and he will even write down quite simply that he would willingly have joined the three Florentines under the shower of fire—'but I should have burnt and baked myself, so fear overcame my goodwill' (XVI, 49–50). It is the face of Virgil which, through that arch, looks joyously into and over hell. This face of joy is a very different thing from a certain base pleasure which at one point Dante disgustingly begins to feel and is rebuked for feeling. It is the power of a master of the Way of Affirmation over those who pervert the Way—the power of a white magician (such as Virgil was supposed to be) over the dwellers on the threshold and beyond. Dante had been lost in the wood, but he had not entered this gate; here are those who have, by their own will and by the will of God immutably assenting to theirs. The wild and savage forest of chaotic vegetable affirmations has been fossilized into the fixed pattern of perverted voluntary affirmations. The circles of hell contain what is left of the images after the good of intellect has been deliberately drawn away.

The long silence, the vast silence, of the forest had only three sounds—the voices of the two poets and the sound of Dante's feet. Now 'the secret things—segrete cose' begin to sound. Silence is broken. As they pass the arch, they come into an air 'senza tempo tinto—tinted without time', dark and unchanging. They are at the first grasp by the imagination of the meaning of 'for ever' and 'never'. When we use these words, however bitter the sense, it is certain that our consciousness of the sense will ease; it does ease. In hell it does not ease; the consciousness of 'for ever' itself lasts for ever; the consciousness of never is itself never lightened. All that happens here is 'senza tempo tinto'—tinted for ever by that for everness. To apprehend this, as

The Inferno

far as we can, is a condition of any poetic apprehension of the poem. The perversion of an image involves precisely an unchanging image, infinitely unchanging. The tumult that breaks on the two poets, coming from the vast silence without, is a tumult which rushes for ever through that air for ever black (III, 22-30). It is not, however, at present the tumult of the perverted. The open country, so to call it, within the verge, is full of a crowd whose cries, howls, hoarse voices, and 'the sound of hands'—that sound coming directly after Virgil's hand has fallen soundlessly on Dante's—blast the dark air with lament not for evil choice but for no choice. These are the entirely futile; they have wished neither for God nor for anything else; now they envy everything. Their imaginations refused to affirm or reject; therefore now, stung by wasps and hornets, they run for ever after an everwhirling standard. 'Do not let us speak of them', says Virgil: 'guarda e passa—look and pass' (III, 51). This place is flung to them casually, scornfully, and worms live on their blood and tears.

Beyond them is the River Acheron, the first of those rivers which flow through all the *Commedia*. Acheron is a river of separation, as (at the end of the *Purgatorio*) Eunoe is a river of inclusion. Here is the first of the Organisms of Hell, those driving instruments by which Necessity now expresses itself. All the crowd of souls who wait on the bank are those who have willingly insisted on the necessity of their own wishes. They now blaspheme

> Iddio e lor parenti,
> l' umana specie e 'l luogo e 'l tempo e 'l seme
> di lor semenza e di lor nascimenti;

'God and their parents, human kind, the place and the time, the seed of their engendering and of their birth' (III, 103-5); all the order and necessity of human life. Blaspheme as they may, Necessity is terribly upon them: an old man, with white hair, and with flame about his eyes, comes in a boat, wielding his oar and shouting. He protests against the appearance of Dante, and Virgil utters for the first time that great invocation of Necessity which he is to use again—

> Thus it is willed
> Where will and power are one; ask thou no more (III, 95-6).

The Inferno

The whole multitude of souls, 'lassa e nuda—weary and naked', thronging there, throw themselves into the boat, 'ad una ad una—one by one.' The crowd becomes particular; each is recollected; the indefinite number becomes units—'ad una ad una.' Why so hasty to pass? 'la tema si volge in disio'. Their fear is changed to a horrid desire of that which still remains hateful; this is their finality. 'No good soul ever passes here,' never experiences this infernal conflict. The good have passed that conflict long since; once perhaps they disliked what they desired, but they gave themselves to that order and necessity which these others here blaspheme; to God, to mankind, to their own engendering and birth, and to the place and the time; therefore their own necessity is now one with that. 'But with these it is not so.' The saying of Love in the early dream is now the sentence of Judgement in a vision. The earth shakes; wind and red lightning strike the sorrowful land. Dante faints from sheer terror; only Virgil, his stern joy already paling with pietà—pity, *pietas*—looks onward across Acheron.

As the thunder crashes, perhaps of that same lightning-flash, perhaps of some later—and yet neither, for Dante, when he had recovered and found himself on the other side of Acheron, discovered what it was; it was 'the thunder of endless wailings'. It comes up from the abyss on the edge of which he is; and this also means that it arises from the interior abyss. The whole poem is, in general, the analysis of one soul as well as the description of many. But the way into that descending pit has not yet been begun. There is a circle still of pause (or, say, suspense) round that funnel which is Hell before the journey proper opens. We are still in the circles, as one might call them, of the Suspended Imagination: the place where the mean creatures are who would not choose or the noble who were not offered choice. Dante has seen the first; he is now brought to the second—into the Limbo, where the great pagans are; he uses the word 'suspense'—'che in quel limbo eran sospesi—who were held, suspense, in that limbo' (IV, 45). The Affirmations and Rejections of the Romantic Way have not yet begun. Indeed, historically, they had not; before Dante, there had been no great poetic presentation of this Way. Virgil knew the City, but Beatrice he did not know; there could be no reconciliation, much less any reflection of identity,

The Inferno

between Dido and Rome. The responsibilities of that Way therefore cannot be there for any of these great ones, especially since their work knew nothing of the Incarnation. How could Plato, who in the famous close of the *Symposium* left all matter behind in his own plotted Way, be taken into the matter of the Christian Paradise? No; we could only save their personal souls by making nonsense of their personal work; this Dante refused to do. We have more tenderness for them, but Dante had more honour.

It is neither possible nor desirable here to treat the whole *Inferno* in such detail as these last few pages have involved; let them be excused. It must be sufficient to indicate the general line of the movement through damnation, and to delay slightly on certain points. One might say that the literal meaning of the poem here covers four 'allegorical' meanings, (i) the Way of Romantic love, (ii) the Way of Romanticism in general, (iii) the Way of the City, (iv) the Way of the soul at all times. These cannot, of course, be neatly separated; it is always one Way in four categories. Dante, more or less explicitly, alludes sometimes to one category and sometimes to another, but there are few moments which have not, contained in them, the sense of all.

Hell proper begins after the Limbo of the suspended Imagination. It consists of four chief divisions, (i) the circles of the Incontinent, (ii) the tombs of the heretics, (iii) the circles of the Violent, (iv) the circles of the Fraudulent or Malicious. After leaving the 'noble castle' of the great pagans, they pass Minos who sentences souls, or rather who confirms their own sentence; since, wail as they will, they desire to be where they must be. Him also Virgil subdues with the same sacred words—'Thus it is willed Where will and power are one,' and they come to the circle where the lecherous are tossed on a storm. This is the place of what is probably the most famous episode in the whole *Commedia*, the episode of Paolo and Francesca—which is always quoted as an example of Dante's tenderness. So, no doubt, it is, but it is not here for that reason, nor even for the more important reason of poetically lightening the monotonous gloom of hell. It has a much more important place; it presents the first tender, passionate, and half-excusable consent of the soul to sin.

Up to this point (*Inf.* V) the Imagination has been in suspense; it has not chosen—whether from a shameful shrinking from

The Inferno

choice into a spiritual cosiness, or from its not being confronted with this religious choice. It is now shown as choosing, and the choice is made as plausible as it possibly can be. Francesca's description of how she and Paolo read together, how in that reading their eyes sometimes met and their colour changed, how they came to the moment when Lancelot kissed Guinevere; how

> questi, che mai da me non fia diviso,
> la bocca mi baciò tutto tremante—

'ne who shall never be divided from me kissed my mouth all trembling; the book was a pander, and he who wrote it; that day we read no more': Francesca's description of Love itself, with a certain reminiscence of Dante's own poem, 'Love and the gentle heart', for she says: 'Love which quickly knows itself in the gentle heart . . . Love which excuses no loved one from loving . . . Love does not yet abandon me'—all this heightens comprehension until Dante himself sighs to think 'how many sweet thoughts, how great a desire, brought them to this dolorous state'. What indeed was the sin? It was a forbidden love? yes, but Dante (in the place he gives it in the *Commedia*) does not leave it at that. He so manages the very description, he so heightens the excuse, that the excuse reveals itself as precisely the sin. The old name for lechery was *luxuria*; *lussuria* is the word Virgil uses of this circle, and it is *lussuria*, luxury, indulgence, self-yielding, which is the sin, and the opening out of hell. The persistent parleying with the occasion of sin, the sweet prolonged laziness of love, is the first surrender of the soul to hell—small but certain. The formal sin here is the adultery of the two lovers; the poetic sin is their shrinking from the adult love demanded of them, and their refusal of the opportunity of glory. Hell, in Dante, is in the shape of a funnel, and a funnel is exactly what hell is; and this moment of the lovers' yielding is the imagination swept around the inner edge of the funnel. Here all is still good except the very good itself; all is still valuable except value itself; 'il ben dell' intelletto' quivers and a little disintegrates.

The adultery here is only the outer mark; the sin is a sin possible to all lovers, married or unmarried, adulterous or marital. It is a sin especially dangerous to Romantics, so much

The Inferno

so that its essence has often been taken to be a mark of Romanticism. But this, if we allow Dante and Wordsworth to be true Romantics, it hardly is; it is much more the sign of the pseudo-Romantic—in life even more than in letters. At the Francescan moment the delay and the deceit have only begun; therefore their punishment—say, their choice—has in it all the good they chose as well as all the evil. Their love is as changeless as the storm. A consolation lingers with them through the infinite 'for ever'. So in the poem; and could the soft delaying indulgence of the soul so delay perpetually, the imagination and the will might be almost content to lose heaven for *that*.

It cannot; it has entered hell. It has, as the two poets, following their own way of discovery, so well see, to lose gradually what good was still left to it. In the Francescan moment each of the lovers had delight in the image of the other, and both of them had a mutual delight in their love. Their mutual *lussuria* indulged this. But *lussuria* cannot in fact stop there; the mutual indulgence is bound too soon to become two separate single indulgences. It is true that *lussuria* is to be distinguished from the *sollagia* of the *Convivio*. *Sollagia*, with all the rest of Pleasantness, is a moral duty—to oneself as to the other; eros itself is in that sense not only permissible but enjoined. It is part of our 'honourable estate'—of nobility—to amuse and be amused; the *Convivio* is in that sense a commentary on the words used in the marriage-rite according to the use of the Church of England. But when the *sollagia* dominate, they become *lussuria*; they set up in the human organism a hunger for them which, from being mutual, becomes single. An appetite for the use of the Image prevails; this is Gluttony and this is the next circle of hell (VI).

The souls there lie under a foul and heavy rain, and below the claws of an Organism of hell, Cerberus, who deafeningly barks and sharply tears them for ever. They lie turning restlessly from side to side to shield themselves as they may. The stinking earth is more difficult lying than Francesca's bed, though if anyone were to discern a sexual interpretation in this circle, I do not know that he need be contradicted. Dante was writing about sex as well as the rest. This is the result of prolonged incontinence, incontinence of mind as well as of body; gluttony of delicacies as

The Inferno

of vulgarities, of quality as of quantity. The fatal development of sin in the soul might all be read in terms of gluttony as well as of lechery. Over-indulgence, culpable delay, the beginning of perversion, is the same with whatever kind of flesh. Or mind or spirit.

It is the same also with the Image of the City. In this circle is the first of those conversations concerning Florence which are sprinkled through the *Commedia*. So far from Dante putting only his personal enemies into the *Inferno*, he frequently put those into it of whom he thought highly. He names here certain Florentines whom he calls 'men of worth', 'men who set their minds on goodness', and though later he finds them in other circles of hell, yet it is not from his enmity but to his agony that they are there. Here the 'glutton' to whom Dante is speaking blames Florence for *invidia* or envy. The early concentration on solace has envy for its end, has obstinacy and violence and malice, and at last total treachery to all.

Beyond Cerberus and the gluttons lie the first signs of this. Luxury has become gluttony, and must now again change; what was once mutual was split into separateness, and now those separatenesses are hostile. Of the heavy rain on the gluttons Dante says: 'regola e qualità mai non l' è nuova—its law and quality are never new' (VI, 9). The surprise of hell—say, in this present life, the surprise of sin—lies in two things only: first, that it does not change, that it can go on being so monotonously the same; second, that other and worse sins so certainly appear —worse in the sense, for example, of the continual and sensitive loss of charity. This sensitiveness may in the end vanish, but in these first stages the poem itself by slow degrees insists on it—as far at least as the two muddy hands that stretch out to clutch the boat in which the sacred poets cross the marsh of *accidie*. This sensitiveness again is not unlike a quite different sensitiveness— the sense of guilt which arises in the soul with the growth of charity. It is when Dante has been purged from separate sins that he is most open to the reproach of Beatrice. So that, either way, in this business of the affirmation, a lack of charity in us is likely to strike at our minds; but whether it is sin or purification depends entirely on which we choose it to be.

There arises here, after the full indulgence of our own

The Inferno

lussuria, a resentment towards any *lussuria* which others enjoy —first when it is of a different kind, afterwards when it is of the same kind. The misers and spendthrifts are seen everlastingly butting great stones against each other; the one side shriek: 'Why hoard?', the other: 'Why squander?' It is no wonder that the guardian of this circle is Plutus—the ancient god of wealth, a bloated figure clucking out meaningless sounds. All hell repeats itself; this is futility again, but a futility more hateful because more full of hate. A separation from others has become a resentment at others. No-one of them is recognizable, nor does Virgil permit Dante the effort. 'Ill-giving and ill-keeping has taken the bright world from them and brought them to this affray; which what it is, I will not beautify with words. See, my son, the short mockery of the goods Luck gives to men——' (VII, 58–62).

And then, over the dull stupidity of that brawl about ill-used gold, the golden voice of Virgil breaks into one of his loveliest orations. 'What is this Luck?' Dante asks him. Luck, or Fortune —Fortune rather than Luck, but because we habitually use the shorter and more vulgar word it may be used here to stress the meaning—Luck then was a familiar figure of the Middle Ages; and whatever we call her the idea is and must be popular among all ages of men. 'What then is Luck?' Dante asks, and Virgil answers: 'He whose wisdom transcends all created the heavens and gave them there those who should lead them, so that each part shines to each part, and equally distributes light. So also he ordained for the splendours of this world a general minister and leader who should in due time change the holding of its vain wealth from race to race, from blood to blood, much more than human wit can prevent, so that one race comes to government and one to weakness according to her judgement which is as hidden as the snake within the grass. Your wisdom cannot strive with her; for she foresees and judges and maintains her kingdom as the other gods do theirs. Her combinations have no pause; she is quickened by Necessity, so fast do men in turn follow each other. This is she who is reviled by those who ought to praise her, but instead they blame her with bitter voices. But she is in bliss and does not hear; she with all the other primal and joyous beings revolves her sphere and tastes her blessedness.—Now let

The Inferno

us descend towards greater misery;[1] already each star sinks that was rising when I set out, and it is forbidden to stay too long' (VII, 70–99).

This praise of blessed Luck is, it may be thought, an extreme Romantic position; it is also, inevitably, the orthodox Christian position. It refers here to earthly possessions, but it is clearly, in a wider sense, applicable to all chances—to the coming of Beatrice and the exile from Florence. This great and blessed personification is itself a first taste in hell of the final Paradise; all the talk about 'hard luck' and 'bad luck' is, primarily, nonsense. Fortune is one of those first heavenly creatures and does not know of these revilings. It is not without some relation to those heavenly beings that Virgil here speaks again immediately of the stars—the scintillations of hope and beauty, the hints of perfection. The stars are descending; it is already Holy Saturday; greater evils are still to be seen. By a rough track the poets reach the foot of the descending slope. A marsh spreads before them; it is that called Styx, and in the Stygian bog are naked creatures covered with mud, striking, kicking, biting, and tearing each other. Here the erring soul has passed from what was, at worst, a kind of common hostility against a common hostility to a sheer anarchic anger. Every other creature is its foe; its resentment springs against all. This is called Anger, and so it is, but what we know as anger is really a part of this anarchy rather than this of what we call anger. But do all souls, sinking farther and farther into that loosed depth of indulgence, so rage against companionable men? No; there are others, in whom the indulged moment has reached a different—end? say, a temporary end, or an end for those who are not haunted and hunted deeper by the she-wolf into the place where sun and stars are known only within the range of the voice of Virgil. Hatred may turn outwards or inwards; in this swamp lie all—those who look outward seen on the surface raging; those who look inward . . . 'Beneath are those whose sighs make the water bubble, as, wherever you look, you may see. Fixed in the slime, they say: "We were sullen once in the sweet air where the sun brings gladness, for we bore a

[1] But what Virgil says is 'pietà', which suggests not only wretchedness but pity, and not only pity but that *pietas* against which all hell is an unnatural offence.

The Inferno

sluggish smoke in our hearts; now we lie sullenly in the black mire." This is the hymn they gurgle in their throats, for they are not able to utter whole words' (VII, 117–26).

The poets move along the edge of the swamp, looking out over the bitter battle above and the bitter bubbles rising from below. This is the end of the first division of hell, and of the first, and least, perversion of the 'visionary power' that off-sprang from Beatrice, the power of Almighty Love. It may be convenient briefly to consider the alteration.

The Beatrician moment is a moment of revelation and communicated conversion by means of a girl. This, as the *Vita* and the *Commedia* show, and as the *Commedia* is again presently to make clear, present the lover with a way of effort towards nobility and sanctity; say, of salvation—it is the simpler word. But he need not follow it; Beatrice is therefore a moment of choice. It is a choice between action and no action, intellect and no intellect, energy and no energy, romanticism and pseudo-romanticism. There is a brief time when the Imagination—the power of grasping images and exploring distances of meaning—remains suspended in a contemplation. We use the word 'intellect', but what is usually meant by 'intellect' is rather a part of this thing than this of it; it is not a matter of worldly education, but of a sensitive apprehension and spiritual knowledge. That Imagination in action becomes faith, the quality by which the truths within the image are actualized within us. But the temptation to turn aside is immediate, swift, subtle, and very sweet. It is only to linger in the moment, to desire to be lost passionately and permanently in the moment, to live only for the recurrence of the moment. Recurrence there may be; the Lady of the Window exhibited it. But, if anything, it must be protested against and postponed rather than encouraged; or if that is a doubtful saying, still at least a something other is our concern. Dante was in a coma, 'pieno di sonno—full of sleep' when he abandoned the true way; Paolo and Francesca are, beyond rising, drowned in their passion. The strange tempting little paths lead aside; even a gaiety is in them, for this, all the first part of hell, is the land of the Leopard. The Leopard is pleasantly dappled, dark and bright, though in the end it will become the She-wolf, if life lasts, and if life does not last, then still it will be the She-wolf, for her insatiable craving is immortal hell; her nature is summed in the instant when the souls who have lost intellect leap to their doom: ' 'la tema si volge in disio—fear is turned to desire.' Beatrice has become Francesca. It is still, on this earth, possible to change and turn back; the hell of the poem is the Imagination and will shown fixed for ever in each state, but here (as the *Purgatorio* shows) it is not so. But if there is no turn, then Beatrice or Dante, Francesco or Paolo—say, the lover—say, the soul—sinks deeper in indulgence, and becomes gluttonous of its satisfaction (spiritual or carnal—or both). It is incontinent to its function; it treats its function as created for it. The priests seen among the misers serve for exact symbols. It has, by now, lost courtesy; it begins to resent others, especially at first those others who behave differently, but presently that resentment grows into either an active hate or a passive sullenness. Beatrice, in the poem, loved Dante and rushed to save and serve Dante. But an apostate Beatrice, like an apostate Dante, giving full way to all the angers which life holds, will hate Dante; this is incontinence at full. The angers of sex are but a part of it; the thing is deeper and crueller even than they. Young adoration may for a little hold those living angers down, but this will not always serve; they must be converted and (in Dante's later word) transhumanized to heaven, or they will be, as far as may be, dehumanized in hell. When the poets take boat across the swamp—a boat rowed by another of those greedy organisms crying out a welcome—there rises beside them out of the stagnant water a muddy figure. It asks: 'Who are you, coming before your time?' 'If I come', Dante answers, 'I do not stay; but who are you, who are so foul?' 'You see I am one who weeps.' 'Stay there then, accursed spirit, with the weeping and the sorrow; filthy as you are, I know you.' The muddy creature stretches out hands once beautiful to grasp the boat; Virgil thrusts him off. The other damned attack him, and he even furiously bites at himself (VIII, 31–63).

It is a Florentine, one of those to whom Dante thought the ruin of the city was due. It is Florence against Florence. But also —muddy, foul, ghastly—it is the apostate Beatrice and the apostate Dante in their stagnation. For the damned not only see this, but are this; they not only are this, but they see this—in a

The Inferno

brief foresight on earth and an infinite realization in hell. The muddy beastliness clutches at the boat; 'yes, you know us; we are Beatrice.'

The poets land. We are at a very great alteration, implied previously, but here stated in a particular image. They have seen, as the boat drove forward, a glow in the dark air, and the shape of burning mosques. Now they see before them moats and iron walls, gates and many looking down on them, fallen spirits, demons, the 'grave cittadini—the grave citizens', in Virgil's phrase, of this City named Dis. They call to Virgil to enter; 'you shall stay here, but he shall return alone along his foolish path; let him try, if he can.' Few moments in the *Inferno* have such plain fear as this, for Dante and for us, of his being left to retrace alone his way through hell. While they parley, and await the coming of divine help, the Furies appear above the wall, calling to Medusa to join them. Virgil cries to Dante to turn his back and cover his eyes—Virgil's hands are laid over Dante's hands; if he sees Medusa, there is no going back. And then

> O voi, ch' avete gl' intelletti sani,
> mirate la dottrina, che s' asconde
> sotto il velame degli versi strani.

—'O you whose intellects are whole, mark the doctrine, which conceals itself under the veil of the strange verses.' The verses are strange, but all things are of a similar strangeness—the iron walls of Dis, the insolence of the devils, the petrifying power of Medusa (from which a turned head and a double thickness of poetry hardly save Dante), all lead to what lies within the City. The poets—'sicuri appresso le parole sante—secure after the sacred words' (of the angelic messenger; perhaps also of high poetry) enter at last. Around them are many burning sepulchres, their lids raised. 'Master, who are these?' 'These are the heresiarchs with all their followers', Virgil answers, and adds: 'and much more than you would believe, the tombs are laden' (VIII–IX).

It is an obdurate barrier—iron without, fire within, which only direct intervention has broken for the poets; this is the City and circle of heretics. It is necessary to remember what Dante meant by heresy. He meant an obduracy of the mind; a spiritual state

The Inferno

which defied, consciously, a power 'to which trust and obedience are due'; an intellectual obstinacy. A heretic, strictly, was a man who knew what he was doing; he accepted the Church, but at the same time he preferred his own judgement to that of the Church. This would seem to be impossible, except that it is apt to happen in all of us after our manner. One might say that incontinence is now justifying itself; inconsistency has now rooted in the mind. A heretic, strictly, was a man whose integrity of mind had disintegrated; he justified error and evil to himself, and propagated the justification. The temptation to it is a Medusa's head, for it petrifies. It is an incredible state—yes? yet 'much more than you would believe, the tombs lie laden'. This is apt to be the doom of the false Romantic. The Beatrician doctrine has its own dangers there also; it is very necessary that it should be subdued to that clear communion of intelligences which is the City.

The chief sinner to whom Dante speaks here is Farinata, a Florentine, an Epicurean, and an enemy of Dante's party in Florence. With our modern views of party-politics, at worst, or with our English views of party-politics, at best, it is a little difficult for us to remember that Dante thought his own political opponents metaphysically and morally *wrong*. He was also so touched by the habits of the Middle Ages (which he, of course, did not think were the Middle Ages; he thought he was a modern) that he believed it to be less important that men should think for themselves than that they should think rightly. We later moderns, on the whole, believe that men had better think for themselves even if they think wrongly. There is much to be said on both sides; this is not the place to argue it. Farinata is there because he thought wrongly, and justified his wrong thought. But he is also there, poetically, that his great despite, even of hell, may accentuate this circle of the obdurate. He has been much admired. Some admiration indeed is due to the superb figure—to his endurance and courage. Yet it is, after all, a second-best. There is a greatness in his behaviour in hell, but there is nothing great in his deliberate insistence on going to hell. It is far enough, this dark pride, from the blessedness of holy Luck.

This is now the quality of hell—arrogant in Farinata, weak in

The Inferno

others, but always this obstinacy. It is eternity without the quality of eternity, the Now of heaven without heaven. Something of this quality strikes backward through the incontinent above. 'That gate which is denied to none', said Virgil of the entrance; and of the sinners: 'no hope . . . nor any small lessening of pain'; and Francesca of Paolo: 'he who never again shall be parted from me.' And an element in the dreadful loss of intellect is hinted here by Farinata, when he says of the knowledge of the future held in hell: 'We see things at a distance . . . when they approach or are taking place, our intellect is vain . . . all our knowledge dies when the future closes its gate' (X, 100–108). When earthly time ceases there will be nothing to know—nothing but the sin of the past and that sin in the present. 'Charity never faileth; but whether there be prophecies they shall fail, whether there be tongues, they shall cease; whether there be knowledge it shall vanish away.' Charity has already failed here; presently prophecies and tongues and knowledge are to cease too.

Farinata then is the opening image of the deeper hell. That farther depth is divided into two pits, of which the second again is double. The immediate Way goes through the circles of the violent; below are the fraudulent or malicious; below again are the traitors. Violence is less deep because it is regarded as an animal sin; fraud more deep, because it is rational—more significant of a deliberate damnation of the whole being. The violent are more like the Lion, the fraudulent and malicious more like the She-wolf. There is a progress even here. We are not always able to be violent; Beatrice and Dante may hate, or even only desire their own particular gains, and violence may not serve or they may be afraid to use it. The image of the City shows it; in our own police-controlled cities violence is often inconvenient, so that when we are greedy or malicious, we are generally driven back on the longer and slower process of deceit, conscious or unconscious, deliberately unconscious. We take advantage of the heresy in our blood; we encourage and petrify it: 'much more than you think the tombs lie laden'—much more than we think the great deceptions multiply in us. Even to write such a sentence, even to read it, may be such a deception. The Popes whom Dante condemned must often, like Paolo, have indulged themselves in the *lussuria* of sermons, orations, dis-

The Inferno

cussions, and theological works on the good. It is sometimes the office of Beatrice to point the deception in her lover out to him; little gratitude need she expect, and much danger to herself she runs, in doing it.

The poets pass over the boiling river of blood where the violent against their neighbours are immersed; through the wood of the suicides, where those who have wasted their possessions are hunted by dogs, and those who have wasted their lives are changed to trees. We have, of course, in the progress of the poem, to accept Dante's judgement on the general hierarchy of sin. You may, or may not, think hypocrites worse than seducers, or coiners than hypocrites, but (inside the poem) you cannot argue about it, and you cannot disagree or you lose the poem. It is more possible to disagree, not so much intellectually as emotionally, about the punishments—almost to feel an occasional sense of relief when, far below the field of the fiery rain, we find the seducers of women only lashed at intervals by devils, or even when beyond them, flatterers are—dare one say, merely?—plunged in human excrement. That is more loathsome, but not perhaps so painful? It is, however, not much more than a momentary relief, for the longer imagination contradicts it. (1) In the first place, all these punishments, all these retributions, which are in some sense the sin itself, have about them the quality of infinity, in which quality there is but one change—the increased sense of it which must come when these souls are reunited to their bodies. This infinite quality equalizes the torments; degree vanishes in unending duration. I am not sure how far it might be argued that the recollection, which the poem imposes but does not stress, that all that is here seen is spirit increases the sense of symbolism; something is happening which is *like* this, which can only be expressed *as* this, which may (when the body is here) *be* this, but is at present only a more remote, though even more intense, fact. In that case the whole of hell is hidden though exposed: we see through a glass darkly. It may be said that Dante thought of a physical hell, and no doubt that is so, but he also thought of a spiritual. The corporal vitality of the diagram, on his own showing, is not yet here, and the spiritual reality is a fixed truth, yet infinitely recessive to the understanding.

The Inferno

(ii) Another point in these hierarchized woes is that each class is hierarchized within itself; the worst of incontinence may be worse than the better of Fraud. The progress is not merely a descent from bad to worse, though no doubt it is that in general; there are, as it were, recoveries towards the height. There is, in the deepening horror, an occasional lightening of the horror. It never grows absolutely less, but it seems for a moment to be relatively less. This is the effect of that semi-easing of the infliction; but the ease ends before we are aware, the pain (the invoked pain) shrieks again more bitterly, the grand evils throng. There is indeed another point which is only fully disclosed at the end—the very appearance of lightening is sometimes deceit. The ice at the close may seem less horrible than some of the earlier evils; it is, in fact, as we may see, more so.

(iii) But lastly there is, as the poem proceeds, a kind of qualitative difference in the damned; it is brought about in the simplest way—there is, after a point, no-one in hell whom Dante personally pities. There is no Francesca, no Brunetto, in the second or third pit; Geryon has carried the poets beyond any personal tenderness. Those who have said (half-falsely) that Dante only put into hell people whom he disliked, have not always seen that what is true in their comment was a *poetic* necessity. There must be no *refrigeria* below; the poetry could not allow it. The nearest to it is the sight of Jason and the voice of Ulysses, but Jason and Ulysses are not loved as Brunetto had been; at most, they were admired: and the poetry designed also in another way that great change in soul—the loss of tenderness was the negative change, but the positive is the coarsening of all. There is no Farinata; there is only the sinner 'making figs' at heaven; no Francesca but Ugolino munching his enemy's head. There is even the terrible moment when Dante himself lingers, and all but enjoys hell.

It is perhaps true to say that in these circles of the Violent the reader is peculiarly conscious of a sense of sterility (XII-XVI). The bloody river, the dreary wood, the harsh sand, which compose them, to some extent are there as symbols of unfruitfulness. This is true also of the iron walls and the hard grey rock of the rest of hell, but it is here accentuated by the discussion between the poets about the third circle, where under a rain of dropping

The Inferno

fire the sinful souls lie or sit or wander on burning sand, the violent 'against Nature, God, and Art'. Here are blasphemers, homosexuals, and usurers. One modern commentator says that 'the argument about usury and the classification of this with sodomy, so strange and repellent to us, is a notable example of the scholastic reasoning imposed on Dante by the leaders of thought in his time'. It is, on the contrary, lucently suitable; indeed, of the two, the homosexualist is (as Dante thought) less culpable. Blasphemy, usury, sodomy, are all a turning against the order and means of life. What sodomy is in regard to Beatrice, usury is in regard to the City. There moves, in and through Beatrice and the City, a natural and supernatural vitality; to work against either is to work for the death of the soul. Paolo and Francesca are, in the City, those who are without regard for the City; Farinata is the pride of the citizen in his house or his party held more passionately close than the City; the usurers make private profit out of the City. The infernal progress is as exact here as in any other of the meanings.

There is one incident in this circle which presents a thing frequently in Dante's thought—the incident of Brunetto Latini. Brunetto had been Dante's own teacher; he sees him here running on the sand: 'Siete voi qui, Ser Brunetto?—are you here, Ser Brunetto?' (XV, 30). Dante speaks of and to him as he speaks of and to no-one else in hell; Brunetto is indeed the nearest to the shape of a damned Beatrice.

> Chè in la mente m' è fitta, ed or mi accora,
>   la cara e buona imagine paterna
>   di voi, quando nel mondo ad ora ad ora
> m' insegnavate come l' uom s' eterna;
>   e quant' io l' abbia in grado, mentre io vivo
>   convien che nella mia lingua si scerna.
>   (XV, 82–7)

'The dear, kind, paternal image of you is fixed in my mind and goes now to my heart, when hour by hour in the world you taught me how man makes himself eternal, and whilst I live it is proper that my tongue should show how great is my gratitude.' Possibly in the final depth of hell, such courtesy, like all courtesy, would be forbidden, but only there. Whatever Brunetto—say,

The Inferno

whatever Beatrice—has been brought to, there is owed to him and to her that freedom of admiration and respect. Our sources may be both dammed and damned, but we must acknowledge the derivation. It is the explanation of Dante's attitude towards even the criminal Popes. Boniface VIII is in hell, but all heaven shudders at the outrage done to his office in his person. The office and function is always to be honoured; much more those from whose functions we ourselves have lived and learnt to live; much more those whom we loved. 'While I live, it is right I should show my debt.' To ask what Dante would have said to Brunetto, had he found him in the final all but dehumanized ice, is to go beyond decency; only the raising of the question shows, in its suggestion of agony, how deep both passions went with him. There are some things Dante spared himself and us. But only there, if there, can derivation be forgotten. Elsewhere, for ever and ever, it must be remembered, willingly praised, and ardently published before earth and heaven. Any who have been at all our source and derivation deserve, for ever and ever, no less; such a loyalty is necessary to the life of the City, and he who forgets it sins himself against Nature and deserves for ever to run, far from the City, on the harsh sand under the unabsolving fire.

The poets come to a new depth—and we to an odd incident. They look over the edge. 'Io aveva una corda intorno cinta', says Dante suddenly, 'I had a cord girt about me',

> e con essa pensai alcuna volta
> prender la lonza alla pelle dipinta . . .

'and with it I had thought at another time to catch the Leopard of the painted skin' (XVI, 106–8). He has said nothing of this previously; there was not a hint of it when we were, in the poem, meeting the Leopard. It is true that poets do behave so; their inventions are sudden. Shakespeare did a similar thing; we had heard nothing of the handkerchief in *Othello* until he needed and chose to make it of such intense importance. Dante now takes off the girdle, rolls it up, and passes it over. Virgil throws it into the abyss. Presently there floats up another of those organisms of hell, one who is called by Virgil 'he who defiles the whole world'. It has a benign face, as of a just man—the rest is serpent, with two

The Inferno

shaggy paws and arms. Its body is brightly coloured—painted diversely; the tail, as it ends, still reaches into the abyss—the 'vano', the void—with a forked and poisonous point like a scorpion's. This is Geryon, or Fraud. But why is Fraud summoned up by the girdle that was to bind the Leopard?

Dante does not explain. We have only the coincidence of the Leopard and the parti-coloured Image of Fraud. The bright coat is common to both. The Leopard was not only lechery; it was also the gay beauty of youth—it comes with dawn and spring. It has seemed to Dante a hopeful sign, and (now we are told) he had a girdle which could catch it. But it did not; what it now does is to bring up the treachery of a similar fairness and brightness, which pollutes the whole world. It is perhaps the real deceit of the Leopard, the falsehood in that early romanticism, the fraud within the gaiety, the deliberate perversity within the natural behaviour. In this sense Dante has indeed now caught the Leopard—or, at least, caught this essence of it. The union of the two organisms is the exhibition of the romanticism of youth as what it must become in Dis, an infernalized romanticism, a fraudulent pseudo-romanticism, appearing at the moment when the lowest places of hell begin to be opened, the circles of deepening Malice. The moment of Paolo and Francesca has deepened to this. Beatrice herself has now become this. But not Beatrice alone, Geryon has the face 'of a just man'; all the City is here infernalized. The place of the heretics has been passed; obduracy has been passed; now the full evil comes, the universalized and infernalized person of Fraud, the Leopard hiding the Wolf.

In that play which Shakespeare opened with a renunciation of the stars and of nature, and carried on into the world's cannibalism, Cordelia says: 'Shall we not see These daughters and these sisters?' In Dante we do. As, on the back of Geryon, the poets are carried slowly down, a horrible roaring is heard; they see fire; and by 'li gran mali—the great evils' which become visible on all sides, Dante discovers how they are wheeling and descending. There is to be only one more such descent, and that is to the last ice and the freezing of hell into hell. The poets dismount; they turn to the left; they move forward. There is on their right a vast open space in which are ten concentric and enormous moats, their rocky divisions joined by bridges. In these moats are

The Inferno

punished ten different kinds of malicious deceit—all those who have obstinately practised for their personal gain. The spiritual principle is still individual; it is the individual soul who is here drawn down the perverted Way of Affirmation. It is, of course, true that no single soul commits all these sins, nor does Dante say so. But there is a sense in which his single soul, following Virgil, creates for us an opposite vision of a single shade, without Virgil, clambering, stupidly, obstinately, and painfully, from ridge to ridge of deepening evil. The progress of that perversion is seen in many incidents, but it is true essentially of each; there is no place yet where the weary spirit can stop. The earlier plagues still torment it, and drive it on to more. The accidents multiply, but the substance (could we use the word of hell) includes more.

The first two moats are of seducers, panders, and flatterers; those who, one way or another, mingled coin with flesh and flesh with coin—'there are no women here to coin, pander!' (XVIII, 66) a devil shouts to one. Their hearts were 'avaro'—the old miserly fault now grown so as to be capable of any guilt. There is one moment which ranks with the Beatrician and Francescan for significance. The Flatterers, in their ditch, are immersed in the filth of human excrement. Flattery is precisely the unfruitful excrement of mankind; its evil is that it asserts falsely what can be asserted truly. Kings are flattered because they are kings, the desired because he or she is desired, but meaning is lost, accuracy is lost, and accuracy is fruitfulness—it is the first law of the spiritual life. It is consequently especially important that accuracy should be maintained in all romantic matters, and it seems as if Dante had deliberately set here as a warning an image of falsity. 'Look at that dirty and dishevelled strumpet, who is scratching herself with her filthy nails, and is sometimes cowering and sometimes standing up. That is Thaïs who when her paramour asked: "Do you thank me very greatly?" answered "Nay, marvellously". And let our gaze be satiated with this.' What is there in this story (taken from Cicero out of Terence) to make Thaïs the saturation of their eyes? It is precisely the word Thaïs used—*meravigliose*, wonderfully, miraculously (XVIII, 135). It is what Dante had continually said in the *Vita*: 'I am infinitely grateful.' The word itself is either spiritual truth or else verbal excrement. Thaïs is in its filth and for ever scratches there.

The Inferno

This is, I think, the last of the images of sex in hell. The first (but its cause and value are not apprehended in the *Commedia* till much later) is the image of the intercession of Beatrice in the second canto. This is at once the climax of the *Vita* and the beginning of the *Paradiso*. The *Vita* had analysed the Beatrician moment into heart, brain, and liver. The way of the *Inferno*, of the perversion of images, is in effect the abandonment of the heart for the liver, and the consequent loss of the brain. This loss is variously universalized, but (of its own sex-kind) two images stand out—the Francescan, with its tender but unwise surrender —the surrender of intellect to the disordered sensualism of the moment; and the Thaïan—'she scratches herself with filthy nails, and is restlessly crouching or standing alternately.' The three great phrases of the beginning of love in the *Vita* are here concluded in hell; the great spirit of the heart is still, trembling, compelled to say: 'Behold, a God stronger than I who comes and overpowers me'; the mind has lost its vision—'its beatitude has ceased to appear to it'; and the 'natural' spirit is indeed weeping and saying that 'henceforth it will be for ever *impeditus*, hindered, dragged down'. The frank harlots are far above, blown on a monotonous wind; the flatterer, the fraudulent in love, the pseudo-romantic, is far below, plunged in monotonous filth.

Either by accident or deliberation, but let us believe by deliberation, the image of the harlot-for-profit is reproduced in the next canto, the ditch of the simoniacs; but there it is no longer the woman, but the Pope, the chief minister of that divine Femininity which is the Church or the City, who is withdrawn into the ineluctable vengeance of the City. The canto opens with an invocation of Simon Magus and his folk—'e voi . . . adulterate —they adulterate,' they commit adultery by the same kind of falsity as Thaïs. They sell 'le cose di Dio—the things of God'. Here the livid rock is pierced by round holes, from each of which emerge the calves and feet of a sinner, and on the soles of the feet so exposed flame moves, from heels to toes. Dante is allowed to speak to one who is Nicholas III. Nicholas, not being able to see the face of whoever speaks to him, supposes Dante to be Boniface VIII, his successor in the Papacy, in sin, and in punishment. Boniface (according to the imaginary date of the poem) was then alive, and that very year holding his Jubilee. It is

The Inferno

therefore this image of the great spectacular triumph of the fraudulent Pontiff which is here invoked, and its intensity of sinful splendour is related to the other allusions to that Pontiff in the *Commedia*—in the *Purgatorio* (XX, 85-90) and in the *Paradiso* (XXVII, 19-39). The three may be taken together as the combined shape of the fact of this kind of fraudulence. There is a gainful pseudo-romanticism in the offices of Pastoral as well as of Romantic Theology. In hell is the individual punishment of Boniface. In Purgatory we are shown how the same Boniface is attacked by the soldiers of the King of France—because of the King's avarice. Boniface is maltreated because of—say, by—the very sin which he commits. And this renewal of the passion of Christ in Christ's Vicar is shown in Purgatory perhaps because it is precisely *not* purgatorial to Boniface himself. The passion of Christ, the President of the City, is useless to him, even though in some sense he re-enacts it as a resentful victim; and the reason is shown in the *Paradiso*, for there Boniface is hinted as re-enacting it again, but this time as subject and not as object. The whole of heaven contemplating the sin he commits, changes colour, and Beatrice changes colour. The high and true doctrine, both as the City and as the Lady—or say rather, the City and the Lady intellectualized into doctrine—have still this co-inherence with their perversion—that they are compelled to blush at it; Beatrice herself crimsons, 'per l' altrui fallanza—through another's shame.' The moment when the whole universe seems to laugh with joy is the moment when it flames red with the consciousness of that mystical corruption—and 'I believe that such an eclipse was in heaven when the Supreme Power suffered'. Boniface, in this combination of images—the public thing, and each man in his public function—both inflicts and endures the Passion; but he gains nothing by his endurance for his will is set to inflict. We are, by this union, brought back to the single element of the choice; it is what Boniface *wills* that decides his fate. It is the will in general which is stated to be the subject of the *Commedia*. To stand in Malebolge above the holes is to see what the wills of the simoniacs truly are. Dante, thinking of it, cries out on the gift of Constantine to the Papacy—thus the evil began; it was, as it were, the kiss of Francesca. Geryon has had his way with both. Beatrice is, as a woman, Thaïs; in the City, Boniface; she herself,

The Inferno

both as a woman and as Theology, blushes at the sight. The doctrine of grace has either way become a scandal; yet even to the vessel of the scandal, because it was the office of the glory, some *pietas* is due. Thaïs never was, but Francesca was—and Dante fainted at the thought; Boniface was, and Nicholas, and even in hell Dante restrains his words out of reverence 'for the high Keys'. It is the lesson of Brunetto. They who turned them for us once are not, even in the lowest corruption, to be wholly unreverenced.

Virgil has carried Dante to the side of Nicholas, and carries him back; the ancient Form to the newer Form. They look down now into the next ditch, and there is a kind of change. Here are the sorcerers and diviners, who walk with their heads twisted backwards (XX), so that they have to walk backwards, 'for to look before them is denied': twisted sight to twisted sight. It might indeed be maintained that this is the inevitable result of the moment of Thaïs and Boniface; and that, as fiery sepulchres are the mark of obstinate heretics, so the twisted organism is the result of the twisting of the glory—for the glory is not something bestowed on the organism; it and the organism are one, though in hell the measure of the glory is the measure of the darkness. Now, however, there is a new measurement, or rather the measurement of hell which has always been present to the yet-un-lost soul is now stressed and final. Dante weeps, not now for any personal discovery in hell, but from sheer misery at the physical contortion of the human form. The twisted figures themselves are weeping; the tears inordinately and, as it were, obscenely 'bathe the buttocks at the cleft' (XX, 23–4). Dante's tears, directly falling from pure human pity, parallel in their proper channel those other tears. All is gone awry; all is perverted —and so much so that his pity has here no place.

'Are you too, like the other fools? Here pity lives when it is dead indeed! Who is more guilty than he who is brought into suffering by the divine judgement?' This is Virgil's question; if it seems harsh, one must remember that, in the scheme of the poem, Virgil demands of Dante no more than he allows himself for his own fate. 'Pity' is in the Italian 'pietà', and has therefore something about it of 'piety', of the natural as well as the supernatural *pietas*. It can hardly be by accident that Dante's last

The Inferno

moment of pious reverence among the damned preceded this august sentence. Up to now he has been called to reprobate, but also allowed, at times, to weep, to faint, to condole, to honour, to respect. All that is past. It is true that Dante yields to it once or twice, as in the incident of his kinsman Geri dell Bello—but it is only a by-thought and is not stressed. Pity is to become like the hard grey rock itself; nay, it *is* that, for the divine Compassion itself is now only known as rock. We have to imagine ourselves into that state where sin is, more and more terribly, merely sin. The punishments are, more and more clearly, simply the sin itself. This is the steady exploration of the great Romantic vision betrayed: the damned, one may say, have passed beyond anything that can be humanly understood.

We have passed three of the ten circles of perversion; the remaining ditches are seven, this of the distortion of the physical shape, and six more. They are

(5) the Barrators, plunged in boiling pitch and watched by demons.
(6) the Hypocrites, walking under cloaks of lead.
(7) the Robbers, stung by serpents and transmuted into serpents.
(8) The False Counsellors, running and each wrapped in flame.
(9) the Sowers of Discord, cleft by a demon with a sword.
(10) the Tricksters, Forgers, and Quacks of every kind—dissemblers, liars, coiners—diseased and disgusting.

Through all these circles there is hardly any noble moment—except indeed when Ulysses speaks from his flame in the eighth moat. Hell itself, but for that moment, has become more obscene. Thus we may compare the trench of the Barrators with those other places above where the Angry lay in the Marsh and the Violent in the River of Blood. The Angry were not guarded; the Violent were guarded by Centaurs with arrows. But these deceivers are watched by devils with long hooks who tear and mangle the wretches they guard—spawn of Dis and of the human heart, who live only in those profound trenches. There are the perverted images of heaven taking vengeance on the perverters of the images of earth. One flings a new-arrived sinner into the pitch, and as he rises, doubled up with the agony, he hears the

The Inferno

cry: 'here pilfer secretly—if you can!' It is spoken by devils, and yet it has an ambiguous beauty about it. The vengeance of morality is here the only cause of beauty; but the cause and the effect are both there; the grotesque becomes a classic proportion. Dante crowds horror on horror, and the only 'enjoyment' of it is the sense of that proper vengeance. It is that which readers must compel themselves to enjoy, and that alone; any other—the aesthetic? almost, I fear, the aesthetic—is condemned by Dante in the last trench of Malebolge. But that is forced and reforced on us; as in the vignette of the sinners lying on the edge of the pitch—like frogs with their muzzles just above the boiling level, and quick to hide under it when the devils come near; two of the devils themselves, quarrelling over a hooked sinner, fall into the pitch—'O tu che leggi, udirai nuovo ludo—now, reader, hear of new sport': why sport? because hell endures hell, delight in the pitch falls into the pitch, justice of the pitch into justice of the pitch.

The same theme is carried on in the seventh moat, where the thieves are, tormented by serpents, and so tormented that their bodies are stolen from them. 'I saw', Dante says, 'the ballast (of this moat) change and interchange—mutare e trasmutare.' A serpent stings a man, and he takes fire and burns to ashes, and immediately rises again out of his ashes; a serpent fastens itself all on a man, and the two become hideously united; a serpent transfixes a man, and the two are changed, man to serpent and serpent to man. That the sinners are so often Florentines accentuates the perversion of the City; indeed, to enter into the *Commedia* it is necessary to become a Florentine, so far at least that we may use the name of Florence or the name of our own city or country as all but identical. This sort of thing is going on in Florence and (on Dante's showing) this sort of thing is going on in England. The word Florence itself has four meanings—Dante's own particular city, and any city, and the universal Empire, and the Divine City. Malebolge is made up of the guilds of those who sin against it; the trenches are for ever separated, and so are the guilds. The supreme achievement of hell is to make interchange impossible. Heretics and hypocrites, flatterers and simoniacs, thieves and evil counsellors, schismatics and falsifiers—these are they with whom the moats of Malebolge are full. That which began with the concealed kiss of Francesca now spreads and pollutes the whole world.

One episode should be mentioned because of the *Convivio*. There Guido of Montefeltro had been named with Lancelot as one of those noble persons who retired into a religious order; it was, in fact, the Franciscan. The *Commedia* prolongs and complicates the story with damnation. Using the same simile he had used in the *Convivio*, Dante causes Guido's voice, issuing from the flame of evil-counsel in which he is wholly wrapped, to say that he had come to that age when a man should lower his sails and gather in the ropes, and with repentance and confession turned friar—'and—O misery!—it would have served me.' 'But', cries the quivering flame, 'the prince of the new Pharisees' —the Pope Boniface—was making war on Christians, and desired to take Palestrina, 'and he asked counsel, but I was silent, and he said, "I have power to lock and unlock heaven: I absolve thee." So I counselled him; and when I was dead Francis came for me, but one of the black cherubim said: "Do not cheat me . . . a man cannot be absolved if he does not repent, nor can repentance and will exist at once—the contradiction does not allow it." And he took me, saying: "You perhaps did not think I was a logician."' Even within that last sacred Order of secret hearts, the danger exists, and it is by the mouth of the Pontiff that the temptation to ruin the Divine City comes.

They come to the last ditch of Malebolge. A stench goes up from it, and great lamentation. It is full of a kind of absolute corruption—disease of all kinds 'as if all the hospitals of Val di Chiana, and of the Maremma and of Sardinia' in the hottest Italian summer were crowded together (XXIX, 46–9). The inhabitants of that iron country crawl and lie and shift and lean on each other, scratching, biting, howling. It is an 'oscure valle', like the 'selva oscura' of the opening. The dimness of the first wood hid the darkness of this trench; it was near such depths that Dante found himself astray, and this is, in truth, the truth of such straying. There is no soul here that did not so wander; it is in relation to both that Virgil says, speaking of Dante to one of the lost: 'my purpose is to show him Hell.' The errors of middle-age are compared now with this finality. The smoke of disease goes up above the sick and the running mad, 'arrabiate ombre'; this is

The Inferno

the physical horror of the insatiate cravings of the Wolf. The cravings lie moaning or run round biting like Myrrha who was once something to do with sense and sex, who counterfeited some other in an incestuous lust. The last three of whom Dante speaks in Malebolge are two smoking with fever and one swollen with dropsy—Potiphar's wife and Sinon who betrayed Troy and Adam of Brescia who falsified the currency—love and the City are again seen in outraged perversity; and Sinon and Adam quarrel, as if the cravings of the Wolf quarrelled. This is still understandable; it is almost the last understandable thing in hell. They fling insults and (as much as they may) blows: this is the talk of humanity in hell. And Dante for a little delays to enjoy it—the vengeance, the justice? no, the obscenity; the divine austerity? no, the indecent abuse: 'ad ascoltarli er' io del tutto fisso'—'I was all set to go on listening to them when——'? Virgil speaks: 'Go on looking. A little more, and we shall quarrel' (XXX, 130–2). It is the second moment when he is bidden *not* look; the first was for fear of the Gorgon, this is something less and yet lower—vulgar, in the pejorative sense, though Virgil does not say 'vulgar' but 'bassa', low, as he had spoken of this 'low hell'. It is like the moment of the craven Imagination in suspense, like the delay of the soul over some indelicacy. He turns at once on the rebuke; but still the moment remains, almost like the first faint beginning of indulged curiosity, like the first faint attraction of hell introduced into this lowest depth of hell. Dante blushes, though not so fiercely as he is to do at the height of Purgatory; his manners, not his soul, repent. He has been praised for his delicacy, but he himself remembers the moment when he failed from gentlehood. The horrid disputes between the Fever and the Dropsy are not for men to hear. Virgil excuses him, but also, in the last line of the canto, Virgil rebukes not only Dante but all those who prefer the *Inferno* to the *Paradiso*—'chè voler ciò udire è bassa voglia—to wish to hear so is a vulgar desire.'

Without any word, after that phrase of courteous scorn, the two go on, away from the diseased trench; it is twilight; and suddenly through the twilight there breaks on them, louder than thunder, the sound of a great horn. It is the horn of the Giants who stand, half embedded in the rock round the opening of the last pit—Nimrod yelling and blowing his horn and Ephialtes and

The Inferno

Antaeus; it is Antaeus who takes them and lowers them to the bottom of the abyss. It is now the bottom of hell, a place 'onde l' parlare è duro—whereof to speak is hard' (XXXII, 14), and it is as hard, or harder, to understand.

There is a complete change. There is a great cold, and there is (it seems) here only one sound—the chattering of teeth in the cold, which comes to Dante like the noise of storks. Otherwise, the silence of the beginning of the poem falls again; there it was less, here it is more, than all the noise of hell. A voice—it is Virgil's, but Dante does not say Virgil, only 'it was said to me', as if to emphasize this new and unrecognizable state—says 'Take care how you go, so that your feet do not tread on the heads of the sad and weary Brothers'. A dreadful monastery stretches before and below them—the great lake of ice. This is the alternative Order to the secret Order of all adult lovers. The silence (but for the chatter) and the cold propose to us the final difference; this is the Order of Traitors. It is simple damnation itself—relieved once only, and then by a human hate. The ice is in four circles, but not marked except by the more complete immersion of the spirits in the ice—Caina, Antenora, Ptolomea, Judecca; the immense inward of the cold. Dante scatters phrases on the *difference* of the place. It is treachery, but it is also—and in the same sense—cruelty; the traitor is cruel. The degrees of cruelty are—treachery to family; treachery to country; treachery to guests; treachery to lords and benefactors. There is no word here of private vision; private vision is a very important thing, but it is not, for all its greatness, ultimate; all that is ultimate is duty and the proper order, the right co-inherence, of things. Beatrice is an illumination by grace, but one could do without Beatrice; one cannot do without the City. Beatrice is here, as it were, but a guest. The final treachery to her (and all she is) might mean, as is often the case in 'this Ptolomea', that the treacherous soul would fall into the ice before the man was dead and a devil take his room; this is the 'vantaggio—privilege', of that circle, for guests, physical or spiritual, are invited, and he or she who betrays an invited guest is so changed that even courtesy to him is impossible; and Dante behaves so. It is the hardest of all things in hell to believe, but Dante had said that the bottom of hell is a hard place to speak of; it should not surprise us to find it so. When 'l' anima

The Inferno

trade—when the soul betrays' (XXXIII, 129)—this is what happens.

The story of Ugolino is told here. It is here, no doubt, for many reasons; but one of them is to introduce the sin *as it happens*. Horrible as it is—and Dante makes it horrible—it is yet the thing happening on earth. The union of the evil happening here with the evil fixed there is a piece of great art, and also of spiritual contrast. This is what you chose to do? this is what you chose to think? well, this is what it *is*; there are no changes now. It was a warm, comfortable enjoyable sin? it is sin—that is, neither comfortable nor enjoyable nor warm. Spiritual or physical, the guest was invited and betrayed. The traitors lie 'all turned up'; the frost congeals their tears; 'the very weeping does not allow them to weep.' But here there is a feeling as of a wind: 'My master, what is the cause of this? is not all heat quenched?' 'You shall soon be where your eyes shall answer you.' A little farther, and——

The wind is blowing; the iron-grey cliffs are behind; all round is the ice, and within it are souls now completely enclosed. The fallen spirit has now passed along the whole Way. It began with that moment of its suspended imagination in the Limbo, before, passing gently to its first consent, it yielded to the tender and poignant Francescan embrace; it descended a little farther to the indulgence of its own private appetites, no longer touched by a mutuality of love, and then to the inevitable hatred of other indulgences. It had yielded then to anger, and anger kept it—a hatred not only of other indulgences but of things themselves, a discontent with the sun, a withdrawal from the world of others to its own gurglings and bubblings. After this it becomes obstinate; in the first circle of Dis, it denies its own proper integrity, which is precisely an acknowledgement of something greater and other than itself; it becomes, intellectually and morally, obdurately heretical. That obduracy is violent at first; but it cannot always succeed so, and it becomes deceitful; it sinks into that which pollutes the whole world; it must make its own profit from the world, which in how many ways it proceeds to do. So inevitably it falls into those places where it is burned and mangled and diseased through and through, and its surroundings and companions are like it, only (to it) dreadfully worse, for their strength, which is like the strength of the universe against it, is

The Inferno

supreme over it, and must always pain it, and it is sometimes transmuted into them and sometimes not, but either way it has no power, and the stench of its willed disease smokes to the mighty roof so far above. So, in the end, it becomes wholly false; it invokes treachery and cruelty; it has nothing to do but betray —only presently there is nothing to betray. The imagination of that state wanders in the dim cold; it sees the soul—the indistinguishable soul—lying along, unable to weep; pain prevents grief and remorse sorrow. The soul is in that hell perhaps before death, for an infernal spirit inhabits its body, so much, here and there, now and then, is it one with separate and inflexible hell. No-one speaks; no-one hears; all sense but of the cold ceases; instead of speech is the wind.

Is there more? one thing more. 'Vexilla regis prodeunt inferni —the banners of the king of hell come forth': look. It shall see, finally, what it has willed and chosen. It knew this all along; in heaven there is' no deceit. All along its way of perversion of one image after another, its punishment, step by step, accompanied it. It was promised this at last, if it chose, and here it is. The cruel wind drives Dante to take refuge behind Virgil, as behind all this earth can give of culture and nobility and high design. Virgil is the only shelter, and Virgil is but a 'grotta', a grotto, a little shed; the word diminishes Virgil himself in the bleakness. Dante sees beneath him, beneath the ice, showing through the ice like straws in glass, the rest of the damned, some prone, some erect, some reversed, some bent, head to feet, like bows. In the distance is a dim erection, like a turning windmill seen by night or in a thick fog. They are moving towards it; and suddenly Virgil steps aside and checks Dante. 'Lo, Dis—and the place where you must be armed with courage.' All Dante can say of this experience is (XXXIV, 25-7):

> Io non morii, e non rimasi vivo:
> pensa oramai per te, s' hai fior d' ingegno,
> qual io divenni, d'uno e d' altro privo.

'I did not die; I did not remain alive; think for yourself, if you have enough intelligence, what I then became, deprived of death and life.' He can see it now—that which monotonously resents and rebels, that which despairs. The Emperor—Dante uses the

The Inferno

word with its full meaning of perversion—of the sorrowful kingdom is fixed in the ice from the mid-breast down. Above are the three heads—in front the red, the left black, the right livid with white and yellow. He gazes, and weeps great tears from all his eyes; he beats his six wings, and the wind from them keeps all Cocytus frozen and the cruel traitors within it: he crunches and claws three sinners with teeth and talons—Judas, whose head is in one mouth, Brutus and Cassius whose heads hang from the others. These are the three who cruelly betrayed Christ and Caesar, God and the Emperor.

Milton imagined Satan, but an active Satan; this is beyond it, this is passive except for its longing. Shakespeare imagined treachery; this is treachery raised to an infinite cannibalism. Treachery gnaws treachery, and so inevitably. It is the imagination of the freezing of every conception, an experience of which neither death nor life can know, and which is yet quite certain, if it is willed. This is the end of the Way that began with the girl in Florence or London or anywhere, the end of the young people and poets in the City, the end of the Leopard at daybreak and Francesca's kiss when she lifted her eyes from the book, of Brunetto's teaching and of the Pontiffs of the Holy See. The Leopard became Geryon, and Geryon has become this: say, Dante has become Judas, and the power that champs him is what was once Beatrice and Florence. The City is every way betrayed. 'But night rises; it is time to depart; all has been seen'—

> Ma la notte risurge, ed oramai
> è da partir, che tutto avem veduto.

IX

THE *PURGATORIO*

But if——? If the true Romantic Way had been followed? if intellect and the Images affirmed? if the Imagination, for a little suspended in choice, had then determined to actualize within itself the thing seen outside itself? if it had willed to become faith? Dante Alighieri so much supposed that it might that he devoted time and toil to the poetic discovery of the Way. He thought that to be his function, and that he had been created for that function. We can derive aesthetic pleasure from the poem without ourselves deciding if that Way is possible or not. But we shall hardly grow adult without deciding. The reader who never (consciously or unconsciously) even asked himself that question, while depending on his enjoyment of the verse, would have been supposed by Dante eventually to reach the first zone of futility, running after an ever-running standard and stung by hornets into blood and tears. He was, possibly, wrong; he was, possibly, right.

The *Commedia* continues; it also begins again. Dante is where he would have been at the beginning if he had come to the Mountain by the direct road. It is true we now find the Mountain, with its surrounding country, to be an island, so that Dante's original nearness must have been part of the disordered nightmare before he met Virgil. The phrase, however, that he used to describe it is a phrase almost of Beatrice; he called her, often enough, something like—for those young days—'the cause and occasion of all joy.' It, like so much else in the theme, is common; most lovers have, one time or other, called the adored 'the cause and occasion of all joy', and meant it. In that sense Beatrice and the Mountain are one.

Between the shaggy haunches of Satan and the frozen crusts, climbing and clinging to the matted hair of despair, the poets begin their journey out of hell—'da tanto male', from such a great evil. Virgil himself is exhausted when at last he sets Dante through a cleft in a rock on the floor of a rocky cell. From there they ascend by following, against its course, the channel of a stream. The stream is Lethe; they move against it—towards

The Purgatorio

recollection therefore; and that path, so followed, brings them at last through a round opening to the renewed sight of 'the beautiful things which heaven carries'—that is, the stars. These hints of perfection, not yet explorable, are above. Venus, 'the lovely planet which strengthens towards love' is shining in the east—'making the east laugh.' New stars—four of them—only once before seen by man, when he was in Paradise, are in the west. The dead air is left behind; promise of delight is everywhere; dead poetry can begin again to speak.

> Ma qui la morta poesì resurga,
> O sante Muse, poichè vostro sono.

Sin has been fully apprehended; 'all is seen.' This is a new movement—the discovery of the quality of eternity. The quality of eternity is discoverable by man only by two capacities—'repentance and faith.' These, in action on the Way of the Affirmation of Images, mean the purging of the Images; or, more strictly, of the mind that sees the Images. Those Images are not properly seen until the stars are reached—which are in some sense they. But the mount of recollection and of reconciliation is on earth always before the soul that wills. It must cease to know the Images as *it* chooses; it must know them as they are; that is, as God chose them to be; that is, it must (in its degree) know them as God knows them in their union with him. Its duty, therefore, is to put off all evil knowledge and to put on all good; this, heavenly, it chooses here to do.

Virgil is still the leading mind. It might have been thought that Beatrice would now take charge, but it is not so; and there are good poetic reasons. The first is that we had better not have too much of Beatrice. The poetic problem of dealing with Beatrice in the heavens is going to be difficult enough; we must not become accustomed to her too soon. The second is that it had in a sense been done. The discussion of Beatrice (or, more accurately, of her and of the Lady of the Window) in the *Convivio* is much like this journey; for her to lead through the *Purgatorio* would have been too much of a repetition. Thirdly, the re-establishment of her full supernatural validity is to be kept for Dante's purified mind. It is when he can see the Images clearly that he is to see her again; his 'antica fiamma—ancient fire', the early flame of love, is to

The Purgatorio

burn towards her 'seconda bellezza—her second beauty', the 'isplendor di viva luce eterna'. She is to be again what she was before—the first of the eternal images. Virgil shall yield his office then, but not till then. The fourth reason was mentioned above; it is that Beatrice is herself the mountain. She is, as so many of her sisters have been to their lovers, the means by which purification takes place. It is no insult to marriage, or any other form of adoration, any other sequence upon *stupor*, to say so. Beatrice is 'dead'; it is by a process of purgation that she may re-appear, here or hereafter, or even the Beatricianness in some further theophany. But to make her at once the Shower and the Shown in this purification would be improper; she can only be that, in her degree, in Paradise.

The arrangement of Purgatory is not the exact opposite of Hell —though it is so in general—and that because Hell is not the mere opposite of Heaven. Heaven is the absolute thing; Purgatory, the approach to it, is in proper relation to it; but the improper relation of Hell is twisted. All the sins indeed are a twisting of the virtues; and except for the sins we should merely enjoy those virtuous states of being which are only not normal because sin has made them abnormal. The great fundamental distinction is other. It was said of God that 'his necessity is in Himself', and this is the only necessity. Hell is the place of those spirits who wish to have their necessity in themselves. But Purgatory is the growing realization that there is no necessity in us, except indeed that of being united with the primal and only Necessity. 'If there were not a God, it would be necessary to invent Him', said Voltaire; alas, that only He could adequately meet even that Necessity. The only illusion is that there is in us a necessity to demand something other than He; the only disillusion is to find it is not so, and that our only necessity is love. This Piccarda formulates at the beginning of the *Paradiso*; the *Purgatorio* is the way to it. Yet, though we say so formally, there is in us, since the Fall, a kind of necessity of sin, and repentance is by no means so necessary. The unfairness of existence is precisely in this—unless indeed we shared in the Fall and were ourselves personally responsible for the first sin. Even Christ's own mysterious submission to injustice on our behalf does not seem quite to do away with the injustice; we did not ask to be tempted; we do not want,

The Purgatorio

in that sense, to sin. He wishes us to be tempted? very well, but then do not let him blame us. And yet in the first vision of the glory we were, perhaps, reconciled, and not as guiltless but as guilty; then indeed, for a moment, we lived from another root. Romantic Love at once sensitively exposes our guilt, and makes it both tolerable and intolerable. The passage of Purgatory is a passage to justice; in sin the universe is always unfair.

By the three days' journey then through Hell, by the consideration of the surrender to the Leopard, the Lion, and the Wolf—to Francesca, Farinata, and Satan—by this the Imagination returns to the beginning of the ascent.

> Imagination having been our theme,
> So also hath that spiritual Love,
> For they are each in each and cannot stand
> Dividually.

The stars—of Beatrice, of Wordsworth's Nature, of Milton's early and bright virtues and angels, of Shakespeare's young activities, and of all the rest—are re-beheld; now they are to be climbed to up the mountain, 'the cause and occasion of all joy.' 'The primal duties shine aloft like stars'—like Venus and the unknown four, once seen by Adam and Eve, 'the first people,' the first Nature of man. It is supposed generally that these four stars are the four cardinal virtues—prudence, courage, justice, temperance. These were the virtues known to—and yet not known to—the 'prima gente'; what need then had those heavenly creatures of *names*? But they are also the stars of nobility and of the City, the beauties of *pietas* and *civilitas*. The light of these five stars of heaven—of virtue and of the Southern Sky—suddenly illumines an old man standing near to the poets.

The poetic image here presented is closely related to the last poetic image of that state which has been left behind. Brutus and Cassius had killed Caesar by treachery; Cato had killed himself rather than submit to Caesar. The first two are in hell; the second is outside hell, and (as far as may be) within the City. Virgil himself who sang Caesar and the Empire praises Cato who fought them. The new and true City, of which the Empire on earth is an image, is a place of liberty, and Cato had died for liberty. The old man then is Cato, and it is noticeable that he is in a similar

The Purgatorio

state to that of Virgil; clear air and goodness about him as about them; but he has a single privilege as against a single disadvantage. He sees the angels and the arriving souls; but he has with him none of his companions and peers of Rome. There follows one of Dante's harder sayings. Virgil invokes Cato's aid—by the lady who descended from heaven and by Cato's own wife Marcia, who still remembers him with love. Cato answers that 'now she lives beyond the evil stream, she cannot move me any more, by that law which was made when I came forth from thence'. Presumably he was brought out from Limbo when Purgatory, as Purgatory, was established; that is, at the Resurrection; it was then that the law which removed Cato from Marcia was made, for Marcia was not to him a means of grace as the lady from heaven was to her lover. It is a harsh symbolism humanly, and yet august; what matters in all love is that which moves to heaven. This rejection of all else, it must be admitted, is cruel and yet, for that poem, convincing.

Cato, however, does as 'the lady from heaven' bade; perhaps the harshness was necessary that there should be no false spirituality about the obedience. He directs the poets; he bids that Dante shall be cleansed and re-girt with a reed of the island instead of the girdle that had been flung away to bring up Geryon. Virgil does so; and Dante is girt 'as pleased the other'.[1] This, I think, is the first note of a theme which is to be taken up continually until in the end it dominates all but one other, and is indeed made one with that. It is the in-othering of men, which is to be mingled with their in-Godding. Here it is simple enough; it is doing what someone else says; it is obedience. There has, of course, been obedience before; Dante has been obedient to Virgil throughout, and all the host of hell, like it or like it not, have been obedient to That 'where Will and Power are one'.

It is morning now as it was morning when the Leopard appeared; there slides across the sea a ship of felicity. There are in it the souls who are determined to undergo redemption; they are singing *In exitu Israel*, and in one general movement they leap from the ship to the beach. The movement is common, as is the song; their individuality is here understood better in the whole organic body. The psalms sung in Purgatory are part of the

[1] The Temple edition has 'as pleased Another', which is even loftier, if the Italian will bear it.

The Purgatorio

Church's ritual, but here it is better to say that the ritual is part of them. Dante is not in an open-air church; the roofed churches of earth are so roofed, as it were, to preserve in them something of this vernal air. It is in accord with the morning, spring, and Easter, that one of the souls who now crowd round the poets recognizes Dante and Dante him; it is his friend Casella who had set some of Dante's poems to music. Casella had died before 1300 when Dante was thirty-five, so that there is about the meeting a sense if not necessarily of youth, at least not of age. Dante begs him to sing one of the 'songs of love'—'amoroso canto'. Casella consents, and begins on one of Dante's own—the second canzone in the third book of the *Convivio*, the poem that defines the Lady and Philosophy. That song—in the interchange of words and music, of Dante and Casella; speaking of the Lady as of Beatrice and of Philosophy as of Virgil—is the fit beginning of the union. The vision and the intellect are here renewed, and they are to be put to action. This is the true romanticism, the purification by which the Leopard is to be disposed to mount among the stars which were rising when he first came out.

But action is indeed at hand. As a proof of this truth—say, of exploration, even of divine exploration, by the grace of divine things; that is, of natural things, for it cannot too often be urged that here there is no dichotomy, or if, it is only of the soul rejecting certain things in order that it may affirm others, but all, though perhaps difficult, is as natural as Beatrice in Florence or Dante writing verse or Casella making music—well, as a proof of this true exploration of the nature of things, Cato speaks. Casella is singing and all, Dante, Virgil, the holy and human souls, are listening in joy; there is a kind of lingering. The imagination has been suspended while the poets moved on the island, but now it lingers, it delays merely on the beauty. All the fair false schools that rear themselves on the notion that Beauty is Truth—uninvestigated Beauty and undiscovered Truth—are rebuked in that delay, a kind (even here!) of that delay which was Francesca. The moment is near being a pander of beauty; so to say—'Galeotto was the song and the singer.' The canzone is that in which, speaking of the Lady, Dante had said that 'her aspect . . . aids our faith', and that she 'made humble all the self-willed'. He had said also in it that he would for the time

The Purgatorio

dismiss anything that his intellect could not understand, and that is here suitable; these are not the dreadful people who have lost 'the good of intellect'. And suddenly, on any of those words, or on some other as noble, the stern Roman voice breaks in; it is for such moments the soldier of liberty is here. 'Che è ciò, spiriti lenti?' (The phrase, to an English reader, recalls Marlowe, and the moment when he desires an opposite delay—'*Lente, lente currite, noctis equi.*') 'What is this, slow spirits? what negligence? what standing?' as it were, what hanging about? 'Run to the mountain to strip off the slough that prevents God being clear—manifested—to you!' The trance of beauty is broken; they fly like pigeons. Could Paolo and Francesca have so fled, their redemption might have been assured! so delicate, so momentary, so decisive, are the real crises in love.

Virgil himself—fortunately it was a Roman who bade him; one could almost believe that Cato is there, poetically, for that very purpose; in order that no spirit, no angel, no-one other than a Roman should rebuke Virgil; it is true that Cato was no poet and was probably never tempted to delay in order to listen to poetry, but that is how it should be—even the grand art and its practitioners must be ordered by propriety and the needs of the hour—Virgil himself has moved quickly away. He subdues his haste; he recovers his natural dignity, but for a moment we have seen Virgil startled. It is from such moments that we should occasionally regard a poem; it will not do to think of Virgil as apt to be flustered, but even he for once can forget. The difference between him and Dante is that the Florentine is delayed by the obscenity of hell, the Roman only by the song of love in the island of purgatory; yet for that his self-reproach is as deep as Dante's had been, and Dante says, as Virgil had said, 'how little the fault!' But Virgil had said it aloud, and Dante does not; there are degrees in such things; it is not for Dante—Christian and capable of beatitude though he may be—to console Virgil. This certainly is one of the preludes to the in-othering, to observe everywhere a proper courtesy. The great may have their faults; but our business is to remember their greatness and not to cheapen it. Relation of one soul to another, in joy, has again begun; derivation is again to be happy.

There was no such relation in hell, or only what Virgil here

The Purgatorio

remembers, for in speaking to Dante he thinks of 'Aristotle and Plato and many others'—with the only touch of final grief allowed in Purgatory. He had shown a joyous face on entering hell; the eternal justice pleased him then though here he grieves at it, and either way it is accepted. They are not yet at the gate of purgatory proper, and in the approach, there are one or two points to be noticed. The first is the number of occasions on which the souls show surprise at Dante's casting a shadow. The repetition forces the fact on us, and reminds us that he does so only here, in all the journey, for hell is too murky and heaven too bright. This climb is most like earth, and we are so reminded of it; as the Lady Julian said: 'our life here is penance.' This, we being what we are, our life at best must be, but even so it may be joy. So here alone Dante is conscious of weariness, and here alone he sleeps. Though he was three days in hell, he could not sleep there. When he first complains of being tired Virgil, in a profound phrase, tells him that the path is hard at first but afterwards easier; when the climb is as easy 'as going down stream in a boat', then he shall rest. It is only when he has less need of repose that he shall find it; that is, proper repose belongs to power; it is, perhaps, in itself another kind of joy, and not only a necessary means of refreshment. Yet at night he does sleep, and this too is peculiar to purgatory; there is a kind of interspace of power. In hell there had been no such beat of rhythm; all there was monotonous mirk, but here the movement is ordered. Time itself is blessed, as with the spirits whom they meet at first, and who have either died excommunicate or have postponed repentance till death, till almost too late. The first kind linger thirty times the length of the ban; the second as long as their lives lasted. Those who delayed have to delay, but the invention urges on the reader their desire towards the purging. They are left, so long, with their images unpurged—disconsolate in that sustained state, they endure patiently their old procrastination.

There is one thing that helps them, and shortens the time; the air of the island quivers with their tender sighs for that help. Their need is repeated again and again, for it is the assertion not only of a need but of a principle of the City. It is the prayers of others. They stay there, 'if the decree is not shortened by holy prayers.' 'Here there is great advance through those yonder.'

The Purgatorio

'Unless prayer help me, rising from a heart in grace.' The preliminary to ascent in love is this intercession, intermediation, movement and action in love; and this is true both of romantic love and of love in the City. Instead of delay while admiring its beauty, or delay while listening to beautiful words about it, marvellous definitions of it, here is the developing thing. Prayers are more than poems. The grand sensuousness is not to hold us; the distances of the vision are to be explored.

> Now more than ever seems it rich to die,
> To cease upon the midnight with no pain . . .

No; not now; rather, 'Every kindness to others is a little death.' 'Che è ciò, spiriti lenti?' why do you not act? The prayer of all those shades who had not acted is that others shall—for them; of those who had not prayed enough that others shall—for them; that they may reach their holiness the sooner. It is a commanded longing. And will they? 'O my light,' Dante asks Virgil, 'did you not in one place deny that prayer would alter the decrees of heaven?' Virgil answers that the decree of heaven is not changed because it is in a moment satisfied. Prayer presupposes a willingness of love towards him prayed for—perhaps towards God; at least, there is simply the intention of love. But in such a matter, Virgil adds, 'do not settle unless she tells you who is the light between truth and intellect. *Non so s' intendi; io dico di Beatrice.* I do not know if you understand me; I speak of Beatrice; you shall see her above, at the top of this mountain—*ridere e felice*, laughing and happy.' 'I said, Lord, let us go quicker . . .'

Truth is the thing existing; intellect is the thing known. What joins these?—not now the verse and voice of Virgil, but experience. Beatrice, laughing and happy, is truth experienced in all ways. Virgil's phrase is an epigram of the *Vita* and the *Convivio*. This is what the Florentine Beatrice was, as Dante very well remembers. 'Lord, let us go quicker.' But that experience may happen in many ways, by the verse of Virgil even, by a vision of the City, by Wordsworth's Nature (it was he who spoke of 'the feeling intellect' and defined the manner of apprehension of Beatrice), by so many men and women. She did well, presently, to use the plural, who was herself but a single Image.[1] It is all

[1] It must be admitted that in some texts she uses only the singular.

The Purgatorio

the Images who, exhibiting to the purified soul at the height, their actual perfect validity, say: 'ben sem, ben sem Beatrice.'

It is as against this community—of prayer and of the Images—that directly afterwards there follows one of Dante's great denunciations of Italy and the cities of Italy. Italy is 'non donna di provincie, ma bordello'—no lady of provinces, but of a brothel, a place of single pleasures, and pleasures without any hint of images of love, or if, only perverted. 'E l' un l' altro si rode'—'one gnaws another'; it is the same word that was used in hell as a comparison for Ugolino—'si rose.' Everything there is out of joint, for all creatures have forgotten their function. The Pope and the Emperor both neglect their offices; the Montagues and Capulets are in wretchedness and fear. These are among the names he mentions, and as a consequence *Romeo and Juliet* becomes a little darker, for the play itself—there and for us—is a sudden vignette of that all-Italy upon which Dante is invoking the judgement and pity of God. Rome is weeping and in Florence 'many refuse the common burden', and laws and money and offices and customs are continually changed. 'See yourself,' Dante writes to his own City, 'you are like a sick woman who cannot find any rest on her soft bed, but turns continually to ease her pain.' There is a hint of Thaïs, she who scratched and stood and crouched; the steadiness of vocation in love has been utterly abandoned.

The first night is falling; the four stars are low and instead of them in the heaven above the three fiery lights shine. In the fourfold interpretation, these have a fourfold value; they are stars; they are ladies; they are virtues; they are modes of being. The poets go for the night to a dell in the mountain, where there are the souls of just princes—or at any rate repentant; those who remained aware of function and vocation, so that love was still green. It is a green valley here, and full of the smell of flowers which are so blended that their mingled odour is unknown to men. George Fox had a similar vision—'All things were new, and all the creation gave forth another smell unto me than before, beyond what words can utter.' It is, however, in this valley that there enters the last appearance of hell. As 'the little sun' sinks, two angels, as green as the valley in plumes and coverture—that colour too of a 'new-born-ness'—drop down with flaming but blunted swords. They come 'because of the serpents', and at the

The Purgatorio

words Dante is chilled and presses close to Virgil. Suddenly they see the enemy—*una biscia, la mala striscia*, 'a snake', 'the vile streak', sliding through grass and flowers, every now and then turning its head and licking its own back, as a beast that sleeks *itself*. And then the angels are in motion, and at the very sound of their wings the serpent slides away. It has served its purpose; for a moment all thoughts have gone back to the round aperture behind which is hell, and the deep tunnel, and the hatred and perversion beyond. The valley is for a moment like the Leopard (and indeed it is colour-dappled so), and this sliding venom like the evil of the Leopard, but the evil is not in the colour and the gaiety; it is only in the possibility of Geryon. In all human experience is that streak, but this island is to salvation what Dis was to damnation; it is obstinacy, decision, the submission to a common orthodoxy of all nature, as the burning tombs were heresy against all nature. In that security Dante sleeps and dreams. His dream comes at the hour near morning when 'the mind, less held by thoughts, is in its visions almost divinitized'. He sees a golden eagle, and he himself on Mount Ida where Ganymede was—perhaps

> in a vale of Ida, lovelier
> Than all the valleys of Ionian hills . . .
> The gorges, opening wide apart, reveal
> Troas, and Ilion's columned citadel,
> The crown of Troas.

The quotation is permissible because it is precisely Troy that is recalled through the gorges of the dream. Ganymede was the son of Tros, from whom Aeneas sprang. It is the eagle of Jove and Troy who now catches up Dante and bears him up to a place of fire, and they both burn together, though those golden plumes are renewed in the heat but Dante is scorched by the visionary flame. The actual place of fire is at the height of the mountain; beyond it is Paradise and Beatrice, 'ridere e felice.' The dream, in this sense, is a premonition of the union of those two great Images—Beatrice and the City, for the eagle is the City—Troy or Rome, Florence or London or New York, but all renewed in Zion—the shape of which bears him in vision to her, as she is to expound Zion to him. The principle of all is the fire, until the fire becomes the light.

The dream has, in fact, been a dream of what has been

The Purgatorio

happening. He wakes, to find himself on another part of the mountain; the sun is already two hours high; he is looking out on the sea; and he and Virgil are alone. Above them is the rampart of Purgatory itself, and the cleft of the entrance. He has been carried here, Virgil tells him, by Lucy. 'Venna una donna' —Dante was not afraid of those words; he did not sentimentalize but neither did he minimize the power of the masculine-feminine relationship; of gender rather than of sex. This lady has been the eagle of whom he dreamed, Lucy, the midmost of the three heavenly ladies who see to his safety—Beatrice and Lucy and Mary the absolute God-bearer. Lucy is 'the foe of all cruelty', the cruelty which is treachery to the true Images, the cruelty which is the ice. Her eyes have shown Virgil the entrance-cleft; then she and sleep at once departed. Anyone else (except Shakespeare) would have made Beatrice do it; but no—something less personal must be here; that intensely personal is only to be restored beyond the place of the fire.

The eagle which is here presented is an image of its greater Type in the fifth heaven of the *Paradiso*, the eagle of Jupiter, who speaks there of the Divine Justice: there the City is aware of its unity and can in its own speech say 'I' and 'My', though as men understand it, it is 'We' and 'Our'. That curious and human fact can be discussed in its proper place: here it is sufficient to say that the eagle of the approach is more like the expression of human justice. It sums up the ascent; by that achievement the community enters Paradise. It is like the Gospel of the Precursor preceding our Lord. There is in that justice and need for justice a certain equality; as there is in romantic love. There is, no doubt, a hierarchy too—and that perpetually shifting. It is the recognition of the change in the hierarchies—now one rank above another according to one mode, now reversed according to another—which prevents it becoming fixed and tyrannical. It is perhaps a lack in the divine Milton that he did not stress this. Dante does it by his so many intensely imagined persons, and by the declaration of equality in heaven—and perhaps a little by Beatrice. She is the superior—in the poem; but it is Dante's poem, and Dante chose that she should be.

> If one slight column counterweighs
> The ocean, 'tis the Maker's law—

The Purgatorio

but also it is the introduction of a balance; the hierarchy and the Republic are one.

The actual gate—the gate 'che 'l malo amor dell' anima disusa', 'which the soul's evil love disuses'—is reached, and its angelic guard. The angel is undoubtedly the Church and confession and so on; but the description of the three steps suggests, in relation to the Way of the Images, something more. They are, in fact, a summary of the true Affirmation. First, there is the white marble, so clear that Dante sees his own image exactly in the smooth clearness; then the dark purple stone, rough and burnt and split each way; then, porphyry, as red as spouting blood. These are the three degrees of all fidelity to the Images. The first love—say, the Beatrician—is seen first in its full appearance—its clarity and glory. It is seen—or rather not seen— in the state of dark contradiction and schism. The third step is the union of the vital self, the union in the blood. It is after that moment that there is no looking back; any who do so remain outside—were always outside. The union in the life is indestructible; it is why that life must be purged of all perversities. The angel of the gate is clad in the colour of ashes or dry earth; he holds two keys. The angel says of them: 'When one of these keys does not turn rightly, the passage does not open. One is more dear; but the other requires art and ingenuity before it will unlock, for it is this which undoes the lock. I hold them from Peter, who bade me err rather in opening than in shutting, if only the souls fall at my feet' (IX, 121–9). All this is asserted to be of the sacrament of penance, and so, no doubt, it is. But it has another allusiveness. The keys are also the methods of Rejection and Affirmation. Rejection is a silver key, which is 'more dear'; Affirmation is a golden key, more difficult to use. Yet both are necessary, for any life. The order of purging is according to the seven sins of the formal tradition of the Church. The Church is not a way for the soul to escape hell but to become heaven; it is virtues rather than sins which we must remember. A song is heard mingling with the sound of the opening of the gate; it is the *Te Deum*. Verse now is one with the ascent; there is no delay in it. By the side of the ascent are great carvings of holy and angelic deeds—pagan, Jewish, and Christian. The supreme Image is there as on other terraces, the Image of the God-bearer—here

The Purgatorio

as at the Annunciation; ivi era immaginata quella Che ad aprir l' alto amor volse la chiave—she was imaged there who turned the key to the highest love.' At the beginning of the way of the in-othering, and at last of the in-Godding, is the image of the great and unique in-Godding and the in-fleshing, 'figlia del tuo figlio,' the great maxim of exchange.

Such an exchange, however, needs material to work in. One of the carvings is of Trajan about to set out with his army and delayed by a poor woman asking for justice. He promises it 'when I return'. 'And if, lord, you do not return?' 'He who will be in my place will do it.' 'What use will another's goodness be to you if you set aside yours in oblivion?' Justice and pity overcome him; he fulfils his duty. Substitution of one for another is not to ease but to elucidate duties, and the proper duties of an office, of vocation, are not to be postponed. The glorious duties of office are to be postponed till after the duller; this is the humility of the imperial function, and of all functions—especially those of government. Such speech, Dante says, is not found among us. This is humility, and it is humility which is sought on this terrace. Dante sees coming towards him strange forms . . . not persons . . . yet persons; towers of stone, but of stone borne on the bowed shoulders of penitents. As he sees them, Dante seems to feel a like discomfort; he knew very well what was his own danger. It is of interest that the examples on which he here chiefly delays are those of art. There is no room on this terrace for the 'artistic temperament'; no place for the neglect of decent manners, let alone of morals (but they are one). Oderisi, an Italian artist, here speaks of his 'lack of courtesy' while he lived; he would not there have praised another at his own expense, so greatly did he wish to excel—rather perhaps to be thought to excel, for it is fame, or common report, to which he refers. Fame? Virgil's own fame was then but thirteen hundred years old, and is now only nineteen hundred. 'Cimabue thought to hold the field, and now Giotto hath the cry . . . one Guido in poetry, and then a second, and perhaps some other who shall excel both.' The third poet is generally supposed to be Dante himself; the potential claim and the potential sin are both there. Dante, like Milton, knew what the dangers of pride were, because he lay open to them. He is obscurely warned, by the labouring spirit, of the image of ruin

The Purgatorio

which is, in 1300, still to come; but it is because of the spiritual danger rather than the physical banishment. He is told how one there, for the sake of a friend who had been taken prisoner, stood as a beggar in Siena, 'putting shame aside,' yet 'causing himself to tremble in every limb'. The prophecy is of Dante's own dependence on others, of the 'steep stair' and 'bitter bread' of exile. He is to interpret of himself 'the putting shame aside'; he is to take that holy luck humbly and in love; he is to become in disgrace outside his own city as courteous and full of largesse as he once was within the city, by means of Beatrice and supernatural grace.

The proud spirits, as they go, sing the Lord's Prayer: 'Our Father, which art in heaven, not circumscribed, but through the greater love thou hast for thy first works on high; praised be thy name and thy worth by every creature, as it is proper to give thee thanks for thy sweet effluence. Let come to us the peace of thy kingdom, for if it come not we cannot reach it for all our effort. As thy angels sacrifice towards thee their will, singing *Hosanna*, so may men theirs. Give us this day our daily manna, without which he who most struggles to advance goes backward through this rough wilderness. And as we forgive everyone what evil we have suffered, do thou in loving-kindness forgive us, and regard not our deserving. Put not our virtue, which gives way so lightly, to trial with the ancient enemy, but deliver us from him who incites it. The last prayer, dear Lord, we do not make for ourselves, since there is no need, but for those who remained behind us.'

The prayer is not for them, yet they say 'us'; the explanation is certainly for Dante and the reader. Christian readers, at least, might bear the great identification of the pronoun in mind. It is the last point in that terrace. The purification is over. The affirmation of the Images has been at least so far cleared that one's own image is not seen as more important than any; so far, at least, equality has been established. Art, for what it is worth, is to be considered only in itself; noble birth and places of power give no superiority to the soul; therefore as between man and man there is no false shame. The burdens that weigh us down are the burdens of ourselves; they last 'tanto che a Dio si sadisfaccia—until God is satisfied'. It is so expressed here, but later, on the highest terrace, we find that is not the whole truth, for

The Purgatorio

we find that God is satisfied when we are satisfied. The souls in purgatory, says Statius there, ascend when they desire to ascend; they *will* the ascent always, but the desire is turned to the torment as once to the sin; when its desire finds itself free, the will too is free. Thus the divine justice works. But as the desire is set towards such clarity, so it is also towards taking and giving all advantages of love. The proud are praying for those on earth, and those on earth for them, that 'mondo e lievi', 'pure and light', they may enter the complete freedom of all the affirmed images, and of the Unimaged and the All-Imaged.

The angel of the second terrace comes to meet them; they emerge on it. A clarification of truth, which is equality and humility, leaves still much behaviour in truth to be rectified, and the second terrace is that of Envy. One may see and yet envy. Magnanimity is not so apt to do so; Dante does not himself much expect to spend long here. 'My eyes have not much offended with envious looks; the fear of the torment below is greater, and the load there is heavy on me.' The envious, clothed in haircloth, lie on the bare terrace against the cliff; the sun shines on them, but they do not see it, for their eyes are sewn up with wires though the tears burst through. They made themselves dark once; why? they did not take pleasure in others' pleasures or rejoice in others' joy. To think oneself superior is stupid; to regret good in or for others is foul. High exchange is blinded; and the sun of the commonwealth is not seen. Guido del Duca says that he hated to see a man make merry: 'I became livid.' Envy may become hatred; it may indeed lead to that other blindness of hell, where the frozen eyes of the traitors to hosts and guests prevent tears in Ptolomea. Envy is treachery to mankind. 'O human race!' del Duca exclaims,

'perchè poni 'l core
là 'v' è mestier di consorto divieto?—

why set your hearts where partnership cannot be?' why be opposed to that consort of hearts?' (XIV, 86–7).

Dante, brooding over the saying, asks Virgil about it. It is, so to speak, too easy; Virgil has a kind of tender loftiness in his answer. 'You—all of you—are always thinking of those things which are diminished by sharing. But above, the more there are

The Purgatorio

to say *ours*, the more of good and the more of love each has and knows.' 'How can the good itself be greater for each when many share it? how greater than if few?' 'Because the more the love, the greater the good; the larger the number of those who comprehend each other,[1] the more love, e come specchio l' uno all' altro rende—and each like a mirror renders it back to the other.' And the great master of reason adds once more: 'And if my words do not appease your hunger, you shall see Beatrice; she will deliver you from this and all longing' (XV, 46–78). So, no doubt, she will; but then so, no doubt, she had. The more the love in Florence (or elsewhere) the greater the good. It was precisely envy which could not exist when the girl was seen in Florence. Could he envy Beatrice? could he, under the vision of Beatrice, envy others? 'If anyone had asked me a question, I could only have answered, Love.' This is exactly what Virgil has now done, though Dante has not, at the moment, grasped it, any more than he has the relation of that love to his being a beggar in the marketplace. It is these things also which are *grave*, serious, grievous, to him, as the dazzling sight of the angel of the third terrace is, but both that and they are to be delight. Ardour is still the demand.

During this talk they have come into the third state of purification, and as Dante moves he seems to see in a vision images of gentleness and pardon. The God-bearer appears finding her Son —'many people in a temple and a woman at the entrance saying with the sweet murmur of a mother: "Little son, why have you done this to us? See, your father and I have been looking for you with tears."' It is a kind of ecstasy of gentleness, and when this vision and the others are done Dante sees little by little rising against the beams of the late sun—it is already evening—a black smoke which fills the whole terrace. As it sweeps round them it is worse to his senses than any earthly night or even than the darkness of hell itself. It is possible that this is accurate in the sense that the holy ones are more acutely aware of it than those in hell; their sensitiveness is greater, for they are nearer perfection. Nothing can be seen. Dante clings to Virgil's shoulder; now, as it were, he blindly follows pure intelligence, for this is the terrace

[1] 'e più vi s' ama'. The *Temple* is as above. But Mr. John D. Sinclair in his translation reads 'the more souls . . . enamoured'. Enamoured is 'in-love'; it is the cause and condition of comprehension.

of anger, of violent rage: 'these', says Virgil, 'are solving—loosening—the knot of anger.' The tightness of anger is dissolved by that ecstasy of gentleness; voices in the darkness begin all their prayers with *Agnus Dei*. The word 'Lamb' has perhaps lost some of its force; certainly it has lost the idea of the vitality of tenderness. In that darkness the poem allows but one voice to speak to Dante, that of Marco Lombardo, and the speech is metaphysical—on the nature of cause and choice, though from metaphysics it passes on to politics. The anguish of the world is due to that lack of reciprocity which has been so often rebuked; the Pope attempts to seize secular rule, and there are no longer the two proper suns of government—but while he speaks the smoke is thinning; brightness is shining through it; Marco plunges again into the smoke; the others emerge.

The angel of the Fourth Purification is unseen and unbesought; he hides himself in his own light; only as they turn to the new ascent, Dante hears him say *Beati pacifici*, and feels his wings over him. It is almost night; they have just time to reach the terrace when the stars show all round them. Dante asks of the terrace; it is that of Sloth. He begs Virgil to go on talking. Virgil complies—he delivers the great discourse on Love.

It is night on the fourth of the curving terraces, high above the sea. The stars are full out, known and unknown. Dante is halfway up the mountain, he lies and listens—'in the midway of this our arch-natural life.' The voice of the thing that is Virgil is speaking, the voice of the master of wisdom, of poetry and the mortal City. It is half through the poem; half the whole is seen and said: hell where grace is not known but as a punishment; purgatory where grace and punishment are two manners of one fact. There is a small fantastic pleasure in the fact that the poets are compelled to delay precisely on the terrace where they are purified from delay, unless (but I doubt it) Dante pointed again the moral of the danger of listening only.

> 'Nè creator nè creatura mai',
>   cominciò ei, 'figliuol, fu senza amore,
>   o naturale o d' animo; e tu 'l sai.'

'Neither creator nor creature, little son, was ever without love'—he began. What then is this love? it is the cause of all actions,

The Purgatorio

whether good or bad. The perception, Virgil explains, receives an impression from real objects, and this is developed within until it is contemplated by the mind, and the mind takes delight in the image. That is love. It is either natural or rational. This natural love is always good. But the rational may err. How does the rational work? The mind enters into desire, which is a spiritual act, nor does it cease from that act until the object which it loves gives it adequate joy. But love, at that point of entrance into desire, needs the strength which counsels, and ought to control assent. It is at this point that the question of good or bad enters. For all things must be loved in order and after their proper kind and with (as one may say) the proper form—the manner and ceremony that belongs to it. The primal good itself must be first preferred; then the secondary goods must be loved in measure, and with their due concern. No love can, fundamentally, hate that which loves; it cannot hate itself, nor since the creature's self-existence depends on and lives by the Creator, can any creaturely love hate that Creator. This must certainly be set against those circles of the *Inferno* in which the damned seem to hate both God and themselves, but (*a*) Virgil is speaking of natural and not final supernatural states; and (*b*) it is the rational choice of which he is talking, and in hell the rational choice no longer exists; there are 'the people who have lost the good of intellect'—choice has been swallowed up in desire. It is perhaps true that even on earth it sometimes seems as if it was only an illusion of choice that existed; we do not believe in our own freedom. There is only one state in which Dante could have allowed anything like this; it is when the soul is in hell and a devil lives in its place.

The words 'diletto' and 'cagion'—'cagion di mal diletto'—take us back to the opening of the whole poem. 'Why', the unknown Virgil had asked there, 'do you not climb that mountain of delight, the beginning and occasion of all joy?—

> il dilettoso monte
> ch' è principio e cagion di tutta gioia?'

It is clearer now what that Mount is; it is the purgatorial ascent of love; the nature from which Dante was triply driven back by the beasts, especially by the rabid She-wolf, the chaotic cravings for secondary things. These three beasts are abstractly defined here

The Purgatorio

(XVII, 102): 'against the Creator his creature works.' But how, if the creature cannot hate his Creator? and cannot hate himself? Indirectly, by the hurt of a neighbour, the harming of an image or images given to one for due love. In that community which exists in its proper glory only by the great equality of all within it—the equality defined by the Dominical phrase: 'do unto others as you would . . .'—in that City there are three chief means of hate. The first rises from the desire to excel by the suppression of one's neighbour, and therefore longs to see others deposed from their proper greatness. This is rather the hate arising from pride than mere pride, but then such hate must rise. For if I am superior, how should not others be inferior? And then the second fault—when one longs *not* to share, when one is fearful of losing something—'podere, grazia, onore e fama—power, grace, honour, reputation'—*something*, so that one loves others not to rise: 'he is so saddened by the very thought that he loves the contrary— onde s' attrista sì che 'l contrario ama.' These two kinds of desire have not been actively injured, but the third kind of hater has; men have done him wrong; the justice of this world (perhaps) has been outraged; some sort of vengeance is justifiable? no; for him who inflicts it there is the harsh smoke, worse than hell. He has become 'hungry for vengeance—della vendetta ghiotto' (the word 'vendetta' is to recur), and he works for the other's harm. 'This tri-formed love is mourned below'—on the three terraces; perhaps with some hint of that even lower and darker place where such things are perpetually mourned.

Yet even if these 'great evils' are avoided, the soul is not yet made perfect in love. Love besides proper direction needs proper speed: here, on this terrace where they talk, the slothfulness of love is purged by compelled haste. And besides proper speed it needs proper direction. To avoid harm is not, in itself, sufficient. There is the good which is not felicity, not the good essence, not the fruit and root of all good; the desolation of this, and its correction, occupies the three cornices above—as Dante shall see. Those err who think that all love is in itself worthy of praise, even though the object itself is good. The grand image of Beatrice does not by itself justify the kind of love offered her; the lover himself must see to that. This is his choice; it is 'the faculty which holds the threshold of assent'. Every love raised by any

The Purgatorio

image is, to that degree, necessity; but 'la podestate' is in the lover—the power to control it. This is the beginning of the great union of necessity and 'that noble virtue which Beatrice intends by free-will'—

>La nobile virtù Beatrice intende
>per lo libero arbitrio.

Love and will are one. 'Look', Virgil ends, 'that you keep this well in mind, if she disposes herself to speak to you about it' (XVII, 91–XVIII, 75).

It is midnight as that clear voice ceases; the moon is so full that it is a bucket full of fire, and the stars seem thin beside it. Dante, his questions satisfied, is drowsy, when there comes bursting round him a racing throng of souls. Goodwill and just love drive them: 'haste, haste!' they cry, 'haste!' 'Mary ran with haste to the hills. Caesar made all speed to Spain.' The God-bearer and the Emperor supply the two invoked images; the Church and the Republic drive after them. Virgil calls to know where the next opening lies, and the poets, bidden to follow behind the urgent spirits, only hear a few sentences from one of them before already all of them are far beyond hearing. The two last rebuke those who once delayed—in the Church and the Empire: those Israelites who died in the wilderness because of lack of devotion, and those Trojans who did not follow Aeneas to Rome because of lack of devotion. But as the crowd disappear, the thoughts in Dante's mind become vague and rambling; he sleeps and dreams.

The dream is of a woman, deformed throughout, with crooked feet and maimed hands, squinting and stuttering. Dante 'la mirava'—stares at her; and this gaze seems to straighten and strengthen her; she finds true speech; and her 'pallid face colours with love'. It is perhaps a coincidence, though I do not believe it, that this woman in a dream is pale, like Beatrice and the Lady of the Window. She is a dream, and a dream arising in Dante's sleep on the terrace of Sloth. Dim remembrances stir in him; she sings. She sings of herself: 'Io son . . . io son dolce Sirena—I am, I am the sweet Siren.' Would it be to consider too curiously to compare the single 'Io son' with the coming plural of Beatrice— 'ben sem, ben sem'? Perhaps not; the whole purgation of the mountain is of love; that is, of making the singular the plural.

The Purgatorio

But if Sloth overtakes Love, Beatrice is lost in the Siren, the romantic Image in the pseudo-romantic mirage. She comes in mid-purgatory (but naturally only in a dream) as Geryon came in mid-hell. She has been called the image of Sensual Pleasure, but this (it would seem) need not be the whole significance. She is as much—let us say—Ideal Gratification; all the sighs that lament the imperfection of a man's actual mistress, the verses that sweetly moan over *her* failure to live up to *his* dreams (or the other way round), the self-condolences, the 'disillusions'—all these are the Siren's song. She takes flesh and colour and music within the night-reveries of laziness; she is, then—what? what we want; and that is? we do not rightly know, but certainly a Siren and a song. 'I am she who beguiles the sailors in mid-ocean, so much pleasure they have who listen to me; I turned Ulysses from his path with my song; and any who dwells with me rarely departs, so wholly do I satisfy him.' Caesar and the God-bearer did not know her, but both Popes and Emperors have dwelled with her. Suddenly, in the dream, 'una donna apparve santa e presta—a lady, holy and alert, appeared'; Lucy, perhaps; at least 'una donna', who calls to Virgil, and Virgil, like all intelligence and all great art, seizes the Siren and tears her clothes away, and there is smoke issuing from her belly, and Dante awakes at the stench. There had been another such stench below, in the moat where Thaïs crouched in human excrement; and Thaïs and the Siren are not dissimilar, only perhaps the Siren is more deadly, for she is vitalized within out of the night of Sloth by the mere attention of the soul. Dante wakes; Virgil is speaking. 'I have called you three times at least; come' (XIX, 1–36).

Of the three sins that remain the nearest in kind and in enjoyment to Sloth and the Siren is Avarice; it is most content with an inner satisfaction of dream. The two others, Intemperance and Lechery—and here we are following hell in reverse—need increasing attention to something objectively other. In that sense the in-othering is now a continuous process. From the Siren to the appearance of Beatrice, the power of the real other becomes more defined. The Siren is wholly within; Avarice almost wholly —gold is inorganic; Gluttony and Drunkenness less—food and wine are, or were, organic; Lechery still less—a real externalness and a real distinction are necessary there; and then Beatrice is

The Purgatorio

absolutely without. So that part of the purification is the real recovery of the exterior image; which when it is done, there are but Lethe and Eunoe to drink, absolution of all evil, renewal of all good, and the soul is disposed for the stars. Avaricious souls cannot mount; they lie on the ground—that is all, and yet that one of them with whom Dante first holds talk says 'è nulla pena il monte ha più amara—the mountain holds no pain more bitter'. It is, I think, true to say that in proportion as one becomes better acquainted (but how poorly!) with the whole imagination of the *Commedia*, so the pains of the *Purgatorio* become more sharp than the pains of the *Inferno*. Those certainly have the awful quality of no-quality. The hypocrites in their cloaks of lead who walk for ever round one of the moats of Malebolge have the sullen awfulness of 'for ever', but the proud under their burdens on the first terrace of the mountain have an age-long contrast with joy, because joy is already somehow mingled with them. It is the joy which, even to the imagination, makes sharp the agony. The *Inferno* is sickening and repulsive; it was meant to be. To blame Dante for making it so is to blame him for writing about hell at all; for hell is sickening and repulsive. It is his genius that he has made it so while at the same time making it fatally attractive—which also hell is, to us here. Mere repulsiveness will not serve; mere attractiveness must not serve; the poem must have both to an all but infinite degree. But the *Purgatorio* must have pain and joy, and so it has; and the more the *Paradiso* becomes real to us, the more the *Purgatorio* has both.

The fixedness of the avaricious, 'immobili e distesi—unmoving and outstretched,' concentrates both. The first soul is that of the Pope Adrian V; and here the effect of the public office has been to enlighten a sinner to his sin: 'when I was made the Roman Shepherd, I found how life cheats.' The next is Hugh Capet who denounces his dynasty, and the outrage which his descendant wrought on that same office when his men seized the person of the Pope Boniface. It is certainly the Papacy which is here spoken of, but in the sense of the poem it is also all public office. Any such office may help to redeem or to ruin its holder. The form of the Church, which (as the *De Monarchia* had thought) is the life of Christ, is living in its offices, whoever holds those offices; and so also with the Empire or the Republic. It is proper to be sensitive

The Purgatorio

to our offices; humility does not consist in despising them, though a great courtesy rules all. The Pope and the Emperor must be as courteous as Beatrice; the doctrine of largesse is in all.

The poets go on. Dante (he says) 'was condoling with the just vendetta—e condoliami alla giusta vendetta'. The phrase translated so may seem meaningless, but I am not quite convinced that anything else gets the implications. He is not merely 'grieving over'; he is 'condoling with'; he is, in some sense, suffering with —but with what? with a 'vendetta'. It is the vendetta of all justice with all injustice, of the proper Affirmation with the false affirmations. It is while he is so condoling that he suddenly feels the mountain shake beneath him, as if it were falling. A chill of terror seizes him; and at the same time he hears on all sides a great shout—'Gloria in excelsis Deo.' 'Something has happened, as it were in the very substance of purgatory, that is beyond their understanding, and seems to be of overwhelming significance. The sense here of a supernatural mystery reminds us inevitably of Virgil's reference to the other earthquake.'[1] That other earthquake, or rather the results of it, are seen in hell, in the steep passage between the fiery tombs of Dis and the river of blood. There the rocks are shattered, so that as Dante steps they move under his footing, and Virgil tells him this has not always been so, but it happened a little before the coming of Christ in the harrowing of hell: 'the deep and foul valley shook on all sides so that I thought the universe felt love, by which (some hold) the world has often been turned to chaos'—

> . . . che l' universo
> sentisse amor, per lo quai è chi creda
> più volte il mondo in caòs converso.

The scientific reference there is to the Greek philosophers; the religious to the substantial movement of Love which forms, destroys, and re-forms. But what is ruin in hell is freedom in purgatory; a soul has known its freedom and moves on to God. Soon it salutes the poets—itself a poet, Statius of Rome.

On the delicate and beautiful talk between the three, this is not the place to enlarge; only one line cannot be forgotten,

[1] *The Divine Comedy*. With Translation and Commentary by John D. Sinclair. 1939.

The Purgatorio

because it is, even in the *Commedia,* one of the greatest acknowledgements of derivation, and both by what it acknowledges and by how it acknowledges a princely largesse of spirit, a Paradisal courtesy:

> Per te poeta fui, per te cristiano,

says Statius to Virgil: 'through you I was a poet, through you a Christian' (XXII, 73). It is with such freedom that all acknowledgements should be made—and believed; only it does not help Virgil, and the personal pang returns; but here Dante agreed also with Saint Paul who spoke of preaching to others and himself being a castaway. That others have through us become poets and Christians does not make us Christians and poets; that we father salvation does not save us. Virgil's conclusion has a more terrible warning about it; many of whom it was said 'per te' may be in the Pit; what of Brunetto Latini? Or at least so Saint Paul and Dante wrote, and it is not wise to look further; otherwise—the mysteries of exchange and substitution are very deep, and it might be that, in the Mercy, the whole co-inherence of mankind will not be broken. The divine reciprocity is everywhere in love. 'Per te poeta . . . Per te cristiano'—we do not know how far that way of love and acknowledgement might go. At least our business, whenever we ourselves utter it, is to proclaim it sweetly, passionately, and for ever.

The three come past a tree, where fruit grows and clear water falls. There are but two terraces left, and this is the first. Drunkards and gluttons are here, whom the mere fragrance of the fruit and spray—l' odor ch'· esce del pomo e dello sprazzo'—makes almost like skeletons with craving and abstinence. Matter (by this intense and delicate invention) seems to be almost approaching its—dematerialization? never; say, its transmaterialization. Though indeed all these penances are for the soul alone; Purgatory alone, according to Dante, the body will never know, for in the consummation the bodies of the damned and of the blessed will, in their separate kinds, perfect them by the restoration of the whole identity, but the purging mountain will then be empty, and the angel and Cato will have gone to their own places. But all through the *Commedia* we forget that these are but images of bodies until then, and Dante (I think) does not

The Purgatorio

much trouble to remind us; so that here the material universe seems to be refining, but not losing itself.

Here Dante meets a friend of his youth, Forese Donati, with whom he had once exchanged abusive and indecent, but amicable, sonnets. There is a heavenly apology to Forese's wife, to whom Dante had been rude, for to her prayers is ascribed Forese's swift progress up the mountain: 'la Nella mia', says Forese. He uses one other word which is of high value, for, speaking of the sufferings, he says: 'Io dico pena e dovrei dir sollazzo—I say pain and should say solace' (XXIII, 72). The word 'sollazzo' rings back to the *Convivio*; where 'sollazia' were to be part of Pleasantness in love, and Pleasantness of Nobility; indeed, Pleasantness was one of the stars in Nobility: 'it is a heaven in which many different stars shine; in it shine the intellectual and moral virtues.' The metaphor arches from one book to the other; for now the poetry is approaching the stars; soon Dante will write 'puro e disposto a salire alle stelle—pure and disposed for mounting to the stars,' and that world of which stars and virtues and 'sollazia' are alike proposals will be there itself to be explored. But Forese's use of the word recalls something else; it recalls that, even here (even? often) 'sollazia' are not without what we call pain; a thousand lovers have known it in their delight—

> The stroke of death is as a lover's pinch
> Which hurts and is desired.

We need not burden those pleasures with any ponderous or pompous significance; they are what they are, so they be in degree joyous and good. But they might help us to less fear of other pains. The words pain and pleasure are as much an unfair dichotomy as body and soul. We must use them, yet we betray ourselves in using them. We have indeed too much lost 'il *ben* del' intelletto—the *good* of intellect'; we lie helplessly, and we are bound to untruth. 'Io dico pena e dovrei dir sollazzo.' The memory of the lesser solace might sometimes hearten us to the endurance of the uncomprehended greater.

But also it is on this terrace that Dante continues his reassertion of the validity of his past and of his poems. He speaks with one Bonagiunta of Lucca, who says to him: 'Tell me if I see him who brought forth the new rhymes, beginning with

The Purgatorio

Donne ch' avete intelletto d' amore.' They are in the great mountain air; the sharp fragrance of the fruited and watered tree is about them; Virgil and Statius are listening; beyond are Beatrice and the stars. Dante answers steadily: 'I am one who when Love —Amor—breathes in me, note it, and write as he dictates' (XXIV, 52–4). 'O frate—O brother,' the other says, 'now I see what kept [other poets] and me from that sweet new style— dolce stil nuovo—that I hear. I see how your pens follow the Dictator close, which was not so with ours; and he who sets himself to gaze farther sees no difference but this between one style and the other—dall' uno all' altro stilo.' And he is silent, being content.

It is worth while to remember, as Dante does not stay to do, a very few of the phrases of this here-justified poem. It was written for the *Vita*, not even for the *Convivio*. It was in that rush of revelation and love, so ordinary, so common, so unbelieved; only particularized in the Florentine by the poetic genius which (as he here says) drove him to record it; more accurately, but not in essence otherwise, than a thousand poets have tried to do, and a million, and more, of those who were not poets, in stumbling phrases and incredulous words, to their girls in streets and stations, passages and gardens. 'An angel in divine intellect cried out: "Sir, on earth a wonder is shown in act"—meraviglia dell' atto . . . there is one who in hell shall say to the evil-born: "I have seen the hope of the blessed"—la speranza de' beati . . . he who can bear to behold her becomes a noble thing or dies . . . Love says of her: "How can mortal thing be so lovely and so pure?"— si adorna e si pura . . . she is as much of goodness as Nature can make . . . she is desired in high heaven . . . Madonna è desiata in altro cielo . . . Say this, O song, only to the courteous—solo con donna o con uomo cortese.' And all is meant only for those who have intelligence in love; soon now that great intelligence is to be pageanted through the earthly Paradise itself, which is 'operatio proprius virtutis', the operation of a man's proper virtue, or poem, or function.

The early poem is thus, as it were, re-written. On the other hand, though we must, I think, accept this validity, it is also true that Bonagiunta and Dante are talking not of doctrine but of style; they are speaking of poems as poems. As the sollazia, poems

The Purgatorio

are to be considered in themselves. Each Image—solace or poem—is autonomous; it was given a life of its own, and an office; it owes final fealty to God, but if we are always introducing the idea of God we merely hamper our discussion. 'This also is He, neither is this He'—and not being may be discussed as though it was not. Statius and Virgil as they mounted to this terrace had been talking of poetry, and that talk, Dante says, 'made me poetically intelligent.' So, on the next and last terrace, the poet Guido Guinicelli speaks of the grand art. Things do not lose themselves as they draw near Paradise; the very prayers required are a proof: 'say a Paternoster for me', says Guido, 'to the point that we need who have no longer power to sin'—omitting, that is, the last clauses. But it is another whom he asks, and that for the sake of another. Co-inherence depends on individuality, as much as individuality on co-inherence: 'figlia del tuo figlio.'

The last terrace is reached. It is, formally, the purgation of lechery; fire breaks from the rock, and a wind from below the precipice drives it back toward the rock, so that the three poets move in single file along the edge. The sun is near setting; Dante's shadow falls on the fire. Voices sing and speak within: 'Summae Deus clementiae', 'I know not a man', and mingle with the praise of the God-bearer the praise of Artemis, and of many wives and husbands who lived 'chaste as virtue and matrimony command—casti come virtute e matrimonio impone', and of those also who kept high virginity; for the two great Ways of Affirmation and Rejection are here praised alike. So the spirits in the flame, passionately burning away all impurity in desires of flesh, cry of Dante: 'he seems not to be unreal flesh', and this perhaps, in spite of all the spiritualizers, is Dante's greatest praise and the greatest praise of his love—he and it were not unreal flesh. So also those who mourn for unholy kisses meet with true kisses. It was a lordly imagination that gave them that excelling grace—

> e baciarsi una con una,
> senza restar, contente a breve festa;

'one kissed the other, without delaying, content with the brief joy' (XXVI, 31-3). In such true and real kisses, the two great Ways become one. The terrace is, formally, that of the purging of lechery, but, informally, of every kind of indulgence and

The Purgatorio

deceit, of all lingering pseudo-truth, of all deliberate lack of intellect, of all which is not true to the great arch-natural order and life of man. The fire burns across the road; the road——

The fire burns across the road; below is the mountain and the path up the mountain. Long since the soul had beheld the Image that stirred it with reality, among the colours and sounds of Florence or among its own chaotic vegetable growths, and it had delayed a little in a stupor at the wonder, at the marvel seen in act. That momentary pause over, it had begun its purging of its own consciousness and therefore of its own deeds. It had realized, first, the burden of its own self-esteem which weighed on it, and had long paced under that burden—'lo gran disio dell' eccellenza —the great desire to excel,' always recollecting its freedom. But that too has its more subtle forms, and as the crude first weight of self-esteem is lightened, it found that it envied and hated others; love? so far from love that even the joy of others made it livid, and Almighty Love never looked from 'the balconies of its eyes'—but slowly it could mourn and weep and even force those balconies open, though even then it found the harsh smoke of anger apt to blow round them, worse (to its growing sensitiveness of spirit) than the smoke of hell itself. But if and when escape was found from that, it became agonizedly aware of the slowness of its own movement and the tardiness of its own desire, and yet now it could hear more closely its own reason, and all humane learning, and certain great poets, and mighty Institutions discoursing to it of arch-natural love, and of liberty and power, and even naming again in terms of promise the Image from which it had itself begun its way. It grew aware now of avarice, avarice of all kinds, or indeed equally of the careless spendthrift opposite of avarice, as something that seemed not merely to delay but wholly to immobilize it. Courtesy and largesse seemed utterly paralysed, so sensitive (but not to its own existence) had it grown, until at last it broke that old seal and was away into a hunger and a thirsting and a burning, at once its purification and its ardour— for? it did not yet see what, except for what the Pope and the Emperor and Virgil had taught it, and the divine Beatrice, ridere e felice, had once (unknowingly) revealed. But now the fire is right across the road, and Virgil utters once more the great, the recollected, name.

The Purgatorio

>   or vedi, figlio,
>   tra Beatrice e te è questo muro ...
>   Come?
>   volemci star di qua? ...
>   Gli occhi suoi già veder parmi.

'now see, my son, this wall is between Beatrice and you ... What! will you stay on this side ... It seems that I see her eyes already' (XXVII, 35–54).

In fact, the wall of fire is across the path, and Dante shrinks from it. Virgil once more, and for the last time, encourages him. 'Remember, remember ... if I guided you safely on Geryon, what shall I do now, nearer God?' if safely amid the deceit that polluted the world, how not safely so near to things as they truly are? Yet in that last divine courtesy of the great Roman poet, we have to allow the poem is, for itself, right; he cannot do more; poetry cannot do more, nor greatness, nor even Romanness; the Emperor himself cannot do more, nor (beyond this fire) the Pope. Dante plunges in; a voice beyond sings: 'Come, blessed of my Father'; the three emerge. The sun is almost set; a few steps, and it is already dark; they must, for the last time, sleep. Dante, for the last time, dreams: of Leah gathering flowers—what else is all action? and of Rachel looking in her glass—what else is all contemplation? for now the soul may justly take joy in herself and in love and beauty. When he wakes, they mount the last few rocky steps of the last ascent. Then Virgil turns and gazes at him.

'Son, you have seen the temporal and the eternal fire; you are come to a place where, of myself, I can discern nothing beyond. I have brought you here by knowledge and by art; now take your own pleasure for guide; you are come out from the steep and narrow roads. Look there, the sun shines on you; look, the grass, the flowers and bushes which earth here untilled brings forth. While those joyful and lovely eyes, whose tears brought me to you, are drawing near, sit or go as you will. Look no more to me for word or motion. Your own will now is free, true, and integral; it would be a fault not to act as it bids; I crown and mitre you over yourself—

>   io te sopra te corono e mitrio.'

X

THE RE-ASSERTION OF BEATRICE

It is the hour of Venus, the morning-star, 'the planet which heartens to love.' At the same hour the poets entered Purgatory. Dante moves on and enters a forest, as great as that in which he re-found himself at the beginning of the poem. It is a 'selva antica', an ancient wood (XXVIII, 23), but of a different nature—'la divina foresta, spessa e viva.' This is the Earthly Paradise, which is, as the *De Monarchia* had told us, the 'figure' of temporal blessedness and of man in his proper operation. The trees are calm and full of birds; a gentle breeze so stirs the leaves that the birds' songs and they make tone and undertone together. A small stream runs through the forest; it is clear even under the everlasting shade. On the other side of the brook he sees (as in his dream) a lady gathering flowers, to whom he speaks and she comes lightly towards him. Her name is afterwards found to be Matilda, and many suggestions of her identity have been offered. It would be pleasant to know, though it is hardly necessary to inquire. Beatrice, in the *Vita*, had gone surrounded by other girls, and Dante had been by no means unaware of them. It is sufficient to think of Matilda as we thought of Joan, Primavera, who resembled the Precursor. The Active Life and the Contemplative are here like women—almost like girls—together; and all the learning which Matilda first and Beatrice after pour out on Dante cannot make them other. Because that learning is high and strange to us, we continually suppose it to be high and strange to them—but it is not; it is but a part of their own archnatural world. We know, in fact, that Dante got it from Aristotle and Saint Thomas and the rest, and we instinctively think of those young and great ladies poring over folios, but it is not so—though (kept they their beauty) it would be no worse if it were; they know it simply, and this simple knowledge is very much part of Paradise and of the poem. Their minds certainly are as lovely as their bodies. Learned comments must not deprive us of that beauty; any more than the slow English translations must ruin

The Re-assertion of Beatrice

the quick Italian voice of Beatrice for us, let alone her accent of heaven. We usually begin with the learning and laboriously listen for the joy—but again it is not so; we must begin with the joy, of which the learning is a radiant and patterned part. It is thus, after all, in its degree, with all happy love. Did no one of the commentators ever hear the beloved joyously explaining to him something he did not know? We have looked everywhere for enlightenment on Dante except in our lives and our love-affairs. Matilda is—what she is called, 'bella donna', 'cantando come donna innamorata—singing like a lady enamoured,' moving 'like a nymph—come ninfe'. She and Dante go on a very little way; they are facing the east, when the lady turns to him: 'Look, brother, and listen!' (XXIX, 15).

What follows is said, in one sense, to come through the forest, but in another it seems to break out of the forest, out of the air and the trees, as if the forest on all sides gave up its secret. The modesty of the flower-gathering lady, of beauty in happy action, directs Dante's attention to contemplate the magnificence that everywhere opens; one might say, her own magnificence, for she and Dante and Beatrice are peers. A brightness sweeps through the wood:

>   una melodia dolce correva
>   per l' aer luminoso . . .

'a sweet melody ran through the shining air.' Dante's thoughts fly to Eve: thus—O thus!—things once were; and now the air is burning fire and the sound is all sweet song. Far off, there seem to be trees of gold, but as he and they move together, they are no longer trees but great candlesticks of gold. Dante glances back at Virgil, but Virgil himself is in as high a 'stupor' as he. It is another example of how far even the opening of the Paradises is above our common imagination that the mere imagination of this incident is, or certainly ought to be, difficult for us. Anyone who finds it easy to imagine the wisdom, goodness, and authority of Virgil in that 'stupor' has clearly never begun to imagine what Virgil is; he clearly supposes that Virgil is such a one as himself, that he is as good as Virgil. This is unlikely to be so. And if Virgil is greater, how much more great the Coming that astonishes Virgil. No; that astonishment ought to be to us

The Re-assertion of Beatrice

an awe, greater even than that with which we heard the two sacred poets talking in the other forest at the beginning of the *Commedia*. The affirmation of these poetic images demands a humility on our part; that would be, after all, if nothing else, at least good practice. The arts in the *Purgatorio* were to help men towards heaven, not necessarily by their moral advice (though we need not despise that) but by the opportunity they give them to use towards those lesser images something of the decency needed for the greater.

'The high things—alte cose' move slowly on; an exposition is at hand. The pageant which follows is not altogether easy for us, for our literary tastes are now different. But we need not start, as so many writers on Dante seem to start, by warning every reader away. It is (as we all know) the pageant of Beatrice, but of course Dante—in the poem—does not know that. All he knows is this slow exhibition of greatness. Yet the figures of greatness have a meaning for him; they are, even as he sees them, 'allegorical' to his mind. And it is perhaps worth remarking that, even in human life, the re-appearance of Beatrice is likely to be strange. Even physically, there is a moment at which a new highness appears in the adored—in so far, at least, as we have been faithful and intelligent; a forehead, a gesture, a word, will emerge suddenly from custom and 'the light of common day'. The counsel to 'watch and pray' implied that we might or might not see the unexpected. We are not to be always on tiptoe, but always to be prepared. At any moment a new strangeness of beauty may be there and gone; the activity of our minds must be ready for that contemplation. The pageant of this medieval Italian poet is not really as alien to our most intimate life as we choose to think.

The burning flames pass; after them, wise men, 'seniori' (as it were, all Virgils of another tradition), singing in a chorus:

> Benedetta tue
> nelle figlie d' Adamo, e benedette
> sieno in eterno le bellezze tue—

'blessed are you among Adam's daughters, and blessed your beauties for ever' (XXIX, 85–8). Mary? certainly Mary; certainly also another—the first Image. These are the books of the Old

The Re-assertion of Beatrice

Testament? rather, those books are notes of these adult intelligences, who are followed, out of the heart of the forest, by 'living creatures—animali', plumed and winged and eyed—the breathing heraldry of fact; and in their midst a car drawn by the Sacred Griffin. The Griffin is twy-natured; eagle and lion—the eagle *or*, the lion *argent* and *gules*. About the car seven ladies are dancing and singing—virtues? no doubt, virtues, but virtues living and breathing as women; and then more wise men, one like Saint Luke and Hippocrates, a doctor after the flesh, and another like Paul, martyred by the sword and having here the sword of the Spirit. These two are as co-relevant—say, co-inherent—as the two great Ways—in which indeed medicine is part of the Affirmation and the sword part of the Rejection. Four others are 'in umile paruta —appearing in humility', such as those who were chosen for the care of the faithful, and wrote the General Epistles to instruct the wisdom of the young Church; and last an old man, 'dormendo, con la faccia arguta—in a sleep (or trance), with a countenance keen-set.' Saint John of the Apocalypse then? yes, if Saint John is taken for a type of him; he would not be unlike Dante himself else, or certain others—all who, tranced to intellectual joy, retrieve the diagram of glory. The pageant moves and glows and wheels; a clap of thunder sounds, as if high direction spoke; all stays.

The car seems empty; those of the intellect, liberty, and power of heaven who have preceded it turn 'come a sua pace—as to their peace'. They call out 'Veni, sponsa, di Libano'; and at once on the car are a hundred 'ministers and messengers of eternal life—ministri e messaggier di vita eterna' (XXX, 18), who are tossing flowers and crying 'Benedictus qui venis'. The storm of flung flowers rises and falls, and in that cloud of beauty 'donna m' apparve—a lady appeared to me' . . . it is even permissible to let 'the flash of a smile' pass at that phrase, so often noted. . . . She wore some kind of dress 'di fiamma viva—of living flame', and over it a green mantle; white-veiled, olive-crowned, she paused there, and Dante——

The great pageant has been so, and more than so. We may not be able to stay its pace, but Dante could. He has heaped up references and allusions; he has involved doctrine and history and myth, and the central dogma of the twy-natured Christ

The Re-assertion of Beatrice

itself. He has concentrated meanings, and now the living figure for whom all the structure was meant is here. He had described his awe, his wonder, his perception of the preparation—and now how did he feel when the figure of the preparation showed? with what paradisal phrase could he meet it? It is Theology, divine grace, spiritual truth? he must say so? He did not say so. All his awareness rushed away and back; the splendour of the court of the Griffin lies, as it were, at a distance, for one instant all but forgotten. Long ago, shaken, fearful, in a 'stupor'—it is his word now—in *her* presence . . . in Florence once. . . . He cannot see her face, but he knows, as (they say) so many have known, the unmistakable; other women may have been mistaken for her, but never she for another; his spirit rushes back to Florence . . .

> E lo spirito mio . . .
> d' antico amor sentì la gran potenza

—'and my spirit . . . felt the great power of the old love' (XXX, 39). He remembers his boyhood—'puerizia'—and remembers her; he remembers those sweet and shaken moments 'alla sua presenza', and is shaken again. He turns round to Virgil, like a frightened child—and to delay with one's masculine friend for sheer lack of courage is not so strange; he begins to say to that dear wisdom: 'Every drop of blood in me is trembling; I know the signs of the ancient flame—conosco i segni dell' antica fiamma.'

It could not be more explicit; this is the Florentine woman or the phrases, at that crisis of high verse, are so symbolical as to be almost meaningless. This, at last, is what Beatrice was, but it was she who was and is this. 'The Images of Dante', wrote Coleridge, meaning the poetic images, but it is applicable to much more, 'are not only taken from obvious nature, and are all intelligible to all, but are ever conjoined with the universal feeling received from nature, and therefore affect the general feelings of all men' . . . antico amor . . . gran potenza . . . antica fiamma; at the height of Purgatory, as in the savage wood, as in the Florentine street, he talked the language of our common blood.

He turns to Virgil. Virgil is not there. Silently, between the first flame of the golden glory and the flower-torrented coming

The Re-assertion of Beatrice

of Beatrice, Virgil had gone. 'Virgil had left us bereft of himself, Virgil my most sweet father, Virgil to whom I gave myself for my salvation (salute)' (XXX, 49–51). The shock is too much; Dante, trembling and without any protection, breaks into tears. Virgil had not left him alone outside Dis; now he has. He had been a shed of safety on the ice; now he is not. There is no safety now. All that Virgil had been has vanished; all (to call it so) indirection of experience—the Institution, wisdom, learning, reason, poetry, everything which might support his humanity under the direct shock of humanity.

Virgil had perfectly fulfilled his function; with his last words he had 'crowned and mitred' that also, on the verge of the paradise of fulfilled function, and now he and it are gone together. The loneliness of Dante at this moment is almost terrible. Here at last are the voice and the eyes for which he had looked, and he is alone with them except for that strange new City which surrounds and contemplates the meeting.

> 'Dante, perchè Virgilio se ne vada,
> non pianger anco, non pianger ancora:
> chè pianger ti convien per altra spada.

Dante, because Virgil is gone, do not weep, do not yet weep; you shall weep more fittingly from another sword' (XXX, 55–7). 'Vidi la donna . . . drizzar gli occhi ver me—I saw the lady . . . direct her eyes towards me.

> "Guardaci ben: ben sem, ben sem Beatrice:
> come degnasti d' accedere al monte?
> non sapei tu che qui è l' uom felice?"—

Yes, look well; We are, We are, Beatrice. How is it you have deigned to draw near the mountain? did you not know that here man is happy?'

The terrific concentration of the last two lines has its effect on the first line. The irony (if it can be called that) gives colour. It adds to the pure consummate fact the least necessary touch of human emotion, almost of human anger. The important poetic question for us, with the *Paradiso* in view, is whether Beatrice can still remain human. It is Dante who has raised this question by his evocation of that old 'vita nuova' which he is in a moment

The Re-assertion of Beatrice

to name. By that evocation he gave himself the task of making the celestial Beatrice Florentine as well as the Florentine celestial. Through the whole great progress, from the beginning of the *Vita* till now, Beatrice has only rarely been seen in action; in the *Commedia* not at all. But yes; Virgil described it in the second canto of the *Inferno*, and we have here to recall that description. If the whole thing were on a different level, it might almost be said that the divine creature is here suffering from a re-action; she had saved Dante and now she rounds on him. It is, of course, not so; it would be wrong and rude to say so. But there is this truth in the falsity—that we must not separate her from either moment. She is still the woman who precipitated herself from heaven into Limbo for Dante's sake, and Dante remembers it if we forget it. She is the woman

> 'che soffristi per la mia salute
> in Inferno lasciar le tue vestige;—

who endured for my salvation to leave your footprints in hell' (*Par.* XXXI, 80–1). It was she who entreated Virgil, who wept to Virgil, for 'l' amico mio'.

> 'La tua magnificenza in me custodi—

'guard your magnificence in me' (*Par.* XXXI, 88), he prays to her afterwards, in a profound phrase consonant with all the vicarious life of heaven. It is this magnificence of passion which is now blazing. In Florence she had saluted and snubbed him; infinitely redeemed, her 'liberty and power' sweep into their double function of his salvation; that, either way, is her concern; after that she can look again into the Eternal Fountain. Our love is only for this conclusion, and our love is an intermission of this conclusion, even though the intermission is but another mode of this conclusion. 'This is not He, yet this also is He.'

To study Beatrice so is not to diminish her, or her lover. It is only to restore to her that love for Dante of which she has been too unjustly deprived. Whether the actual Beatrice had it is another matter, and one with which the reader is not in the least concerned. She has it in the poem. It is Dante's imagination only with which the reader is concerned. Even that poem was necessarily limited. It does not attempt to deal with the problem of

The Re-assertion of Beatrice

Beatrice's own salvation, and Dante's function there. Poem of marriage, or of any similar state of process, it may be in the single sense; it is not in the double, therefore it is not, in another sense, a poem of marriage at all. Any living state of such mutual fidelity, imposed and chosen, must include both functions, and much more. He would be unwise who chose always to carry himself towards a woman as Dante in the poem carries himself towards Beatrice. Beatrice as a sinner does not come in to the poem, for the reason that the Way of Affirmation is much the same for all—for her, in her turn, as for him. Dante's spiritual movement is the pattern of hers; reverse the names, and it holds. Set the two on the Way together, and the pattern becomes more darkly lovely, more full of interchange of function, than Dante said—not perhaps than he saw—but it still, morally and metaphysically, remains true. All the same, it might not be unwise to print a few extracts from Mr. Shaw's *Arms and the Man*—the Sergius and Raina scenes—in every edition of the *Commedia*. Geryon had an honest face, and Paolo and Francesca can be deluded into hell by a spiritual rhodomontade as well as by a kiss. In those cases Geryon follows close on the Leopard. Eros is often our salvation from a false agape, as agape is from tyrannical eros. Redemption is everywhere exchanged.

In the actual facts of life the Beatrice of any couple will probably see that the poetry of the *Commedia* is not overdone; it is part of her function. On the whole, the chances are that the actual Beatrice would have been both charming and intelligent about, but fundamentally indifferent to, the *Commedia*. It might easily have been her function. Can Grande della Scala perhaps did not observe how far Dante's life corresponded with his poetry. Beatrice would certainly have noticed; as, in fact, she here does. Dante made her do it in great poetry; there is none greater. But I doubt whether Dante was so ignorant of the way a real woman feels as most of the spiritualizers will have him.

The moment to which the long journey has been leading has arrived. The little breeze still stirs the 'everlasting shade— l' ombra perpetua' of the great forest, beyond whose verge the mountain, terrace by terrace, falls away. There, from the top of the steep ascent, of the stair in the rock, the curving path descends, and the last glance of the ascending spirit could take in

The Re-assertion of Beatrice

the fire billowing over the highest cornice, and, far below, the angry smoke that covers the third; towards the bottom is the gate where the first angelical watches, and beyond is the open country of an island, with that green vale where a small serpent of cruelty is still, for mere disappointment of its greed, allowed to slide at evening. The stream of the forest, dropping down the mountain, there flows on till it disappears in the ground; by that path under the ground the poets had re-issued 'a riveder le stelle—to rebehold the stars'. The sun is high now upon the mountain-side; by another day the souls on the sacred terraces find themselves nearer their final perfection. All the purifications are done for Dante, except, now, the proper acknowledgement. The sun does not pierce the forest, or if it does, here in the open space where the spiritual Rite is worked, then the brighter air and the flashing colours of the Mystery hide it. On the one side of the stream, the heraldic splendour waits, gathered round the noble incarnate beauty on the car among the small angelicals and their flowers; on the other is Dante, alone—except indeed for Statius, but Statius is forgotten for a time.

'Guardaci ben... How is it you have condescended to come here? are you ignorant that this is where men are happy?' It is almost as if that small malign serpent far below was held quivering by Beatrice's forked words. 'Come *degnasti* d' accedere...?' To call the word ironical is hardly sufficient; no adjective is sufficient. It is a description of what has been happening. Dante has had to be moved and persuaded and commanded and threatened before he would condescend to be happy; he has almost had to be scared into joy. The single word, in a sense, reverses the whole poem. It defines the state in which man ordinarily exists, call it pride or egotism or self-rootedness or whatever; it is, simply, the state from which man audaciously condescends to the good and to joy. It has taken not only the tears of Beatrice and the talk of Virgil, and all manner of vision of Images, to draw him from it, but still other things of which no word is yet said but the silent twy-natured Griffin is the only present hint. There are those who have refused to condescend—all those hidden within the earth below the Mount, and the chief who champs and weeps for ever in the central ice. Dante, one way and another, had spoken a good deal about that original

The Re-assertion of Beatrice

Image by which he was once confronted—praising and adoring and studying and explaining. But as for union, he had turned away down the side-paths of that savage forest with its wild vegetable growths and its loss of the 'self', so that in the end, when he recollected that self, he found all his life gathered against him in the fierce bestial shapes; and the she-wolf's cravings his only future.

He has been saved from that. But now he is confronted with the Image he chose. He is challenged by what he knew and professed that he knew—nothing more, but certainly that. Other powers surround it, but it alone accuses him. Others might spare him; it alone will not. When at that 'felice' he looks down in shame—so harshly pitiful is the voice of the long-since-accepted Image—he sees his own reflection in the brook, and hastily looks away. He cannot now bear the sight of himself. The tender angelicals see it and protest to Beatrice; the creatures of heaven cannot endure the bitterness of earth. 'Donna, perchè si lo stempre?—Lady, why do you put him to such shame?' (XXX, 96). Beatrice justifies herself; the poem is sufficiently courteous to her lover as to put her accusation in that form; she defends herself rather than attacks him. 'This man, not only by those powers which direct each seed to its proper end, but by a largesse of divine graces—larghezza di grazie divine—had such powers of possibility in his new life—vita nuova—that every good talent could have marvellously increased in him. . . . For a while I sustained him with my countenance; I showed him the eyes of my youth; I led him so, with me, in the right direction. As soon as I came to my second state and changed life, he left me and gave himself to others. When I rose from flesh to spirit, and beauty and virtue grew in me, I was less dear and less delightful to him. Then he turned to go by a false path, following untrue images of good—imagini di ben seguendo false—which never entirely fulfil any promise. The inspirations for which I prayed and with which, in dream and otherwise, I called him back were of no use; he cared nothing for them. He sank so low that all means for his salvation—alla salute sua—were exhausted, except showing him the race of the lost. I went for this to the gate of the dead, and my tears and prayers were carried to him who brought him hither. The high law of God would be broken if Lethe were

The Re-assertion of Beatrice

passed, and such food tasted without any touch of repentance to bring tears.' She turns on Dante. 'Say then, say, you who are beyond the sacred brook—is this true? You must join your confession to so much accusation . . .' and when Dante cannot answer: 'What are you thinking? Answer me; the water has not swept away the miserable memories.' He bursts into a 'Yes'; and she continues to speak to him directly, but now more gently: 'In those desires of me which brought you to a love of that good beyond which is no point for any aspiring, what ditches did you find, what chains, that could do away with the hope of going on? what allurement and what advantage was shown in the faces of the others, that you had to go wandering about in front of them?' He answers only: 'Present things, with their false pleasure, turned my steps as soon as your face was hidden.' She says again: 'If you had been speechless or had denied what you now confess, it would be none the less noted; it is known to such a judge. But when self-accusation bursts from the sinner, in our court the wheel turns against the edge—in nostra corte'—is it too fanciful to think the speech grows lighter?—'but that you may be more ashamed now and another time stronger against the Sirens, do not weep; listen:

> sì udirai come in contraria parte
> mover doveati mia carne sepolta—

and hear how my buried flesh ought to have moved you, as it were, to the opposite. Nothing in nature or art offered such delight to you as the loveliness of those limbs in which I was closed, and which are now scattered in earth; and if that highest delight failed you in my death, what other mortal thing should make you desire it? at the first arrow-touch of deceptive things, you should truly have risen to follow me who was then no more of that kind. Nothing should have held your wings down to wait for more shots—neither any girl nor any other emptiness of such short use. The fledgeling waits for two or three shafts; the eyes of the fledged see net spread and arrow shot in vain . . . Are you so sad through hearing? lift up your beard and be made more sad by looking.' He looks; she has turned towards the twy-natured being—she now more lovely than of old by as much as once she seemed lovelier than others.

The Re-assertion of Beatrice

This is the great dialogue. The sin of which Dante had been guilty is not clearly defined, and (except for curiosity of detail) does not much concern us. From the point of sanctity at which Beatrice is standing, any sin in all the *Inferno* and *Purgatorio* would be spoken of as she speaks. It is generally supposed by the commentators that one of two things is meant (*a*) an indulgence in *lussuria*, (*b*) an indulgence in false reason. There is a certain amount of evidence for (*a*), very little for (*b*). It is extremely improbable that there is any allusion to the Lady of the Window, unless we are to ignore the statement in the *Convivio*. Beatrice is not to be supposed to be vulgarly and extremely jealous. She could not, by definition, denounce any state where that other Lady was truly 'accompanied by Love'; indeed her present accusation is that Dante has not sufficiently attended to subjects 'accompanied by Love'. It is credible that at some moment, perhaps after the exile, Dante had intellectually abandoned his peculiar Dantean vocation, and persuaded himself that he had been deceived. It is credible, but it is not very probable. It is more probable that his renewal of the Image threw up all his infidelities—with a girl here, with learning there, with *lussuria* of one sort or another. The guilt which every lover must sooner or later feel towards the vision—and must justly feel—may here be named according as every lover must in his own case name it.

What is clear is that the whole validity of the original Beatrice is now re-asserted. It is here put first into the mouth of Beatrice herself. It is she who is made to speak of the God-willed function of her body—'le belle membre', to speak of the significance of 'mia carne sepolta'. If, as has been suggested, her death is equivalent to the withdrawal of the first light, then these phrases also have a similar and special meaning. It is in that withdrawal that the fidelity to the knowledge is to be sustained. 'I sustained him by my countenance', says Beatrice, but the countenance is reciprocally to be sustained.

> 'E se 'l sommo piacer sì ti fallio
> per la mia morte, qual cosa mortale
> dovea poi trarre te nel suo disio?—

If the highest delight fails you by my death, what mortal thing ought to have drawn you into desire?' (XXXI, 52–4). It is this

The Re-assertion of Beatrice

which is the message and admonition of the 'fair members', the shining limbs, the soul visible in mouth and eyes, the courtesies, the largesse. Authority demands 'trust and obedience'; without trust and obedience, authority cannot act.

But that beauty, named so often, is to be still more deeply shown. The friend of Beatrice—we may give Matilda the name—draws Dante through the brook. The brook is Lethe; Lethe is forgetfulness—forgetfulness of sin as sin: 'we remember it', says a soul in Paradise, 'only for the sake of the eternal Worth' (*Par*. IX, 103–5). On the other side he is met by the four natural virtues—prudence, courage, justice, temperance—who say that they were ordained before the world began to be Beatrice's maidens (who has not often thought them so?), 'we will bring you to her eyes.' But they add that the other three—faith, hope, and charity—will quicken his own to see the joyous light which lies deep within those eyes. He is brought right up to where Beatrice and the Griffin face each other. 'Look,' they say; 'we have set you before the emeralds whence Love first shot his arrows at you.

    Posto t' avem dinanzi agli smeraldi
      ond' Amor già te trassi le sue armi' (XXXI, 116–17).

These then are the eyes of the Florentine girl; this is the origin of Amor. He looks; he sees her 'shining eyes' gazing into the eyes of the Griffin; he sees the double nature mirrored in hers.

      'Come in lo specchio il sol, non altrimenti
      la doppia fiera dentro vi raggiava,
      or con uni, or con altri reggimenti—

As the sun in a mirror, not otherwise shone the twofold beast within them, now with the one, now with the other nature. Think, reader, if I wondered in myself when I saw the thing motionless in itself and transmuting in its image—

      quando vedea la cosa in sè star queta,
      e nell' idolo suo si trasmutava.'

This is the imaged statement of the Image. It is this fact which, not then understood or expressed, underlay the whole *Vita*. It was not surprising that he had then quoted Homer: 'she seemed

The Re-assertion of Beatrice

the daughter of a God.' Love, that then 'unknown mode of being' had shown him in Beatrice a reflection of the exchanged Two Natures. They exist, said Saint Leo of Christ 'in reciprocity', and so they are mirrored in the beloved. They are, of course, a unity; and indeed in her the humanity is fallen. Also it is true of all, but seen in her. It is not, in those early days of the *Vita*, our business too assiduously to become portentous about it. Our bodies desire the good and ought innocently to have the good. The incarnate Beatrice is then our subject, and joy is to laugh for its own sake and not *because* of anything. It will—generally speaking—be an unfortunate day for Romantic Theology if it ever gets into the hands of official ministers of the Church. The 'stupor' will, with the best intentions, be hideously organized and encouraged. The covenanted mercies are their concern. This, uncovenanted, rides in our very nature—within and without the Church; say, rather, this is that ancient covenant which reveals what all the others support. 'My covenant shall be in your flesh.'[1]

Those three, who for want of better names, are called, abstractly, Faith and Hope and Love, entreat Beatrice in song. 'Turn, turn those holy eyes, to your faithful one' (and they call him that—*al tuo fedele*—for all the errors) 'who has taken so many steps to see you. By grace do us the grace to unveil your mouth to him, that he may see what second loveliness you are concealing.' She does. She gives her face to his eyes—'a disbramarsi la decenne sete—to satisfy their ten years' thirst' (XXXII, 2)—and he stands gazing. As—? certainly *as*—as any lover might, in Florence, in London, and the rest, now as well as then—*quod semper, quod ubique, quod . . .* it need not be claimed for all, only for many. He knows what is happening; it

---

[1] In the notes to his translation of the *Commedia* Mr. J. D. Sinclair has drawn attention to the Eucharistic relevance of the procession and appearance of Beatrice. This relevance would require another book than this to discuss, if it were possible to discuss it at all; one in which the Life of our Lord as enacted in the love-relationship could be touched on—which is the heart of Romantic Theology. It is sufficient here to render Patmore's maxim in *The Rod, the Root and the Flower*:

'. . the Holy Eucharist, in the beginning, is desired because it resembles the lower but still "great" sacrament of human affection; afterwards the lower sacrament is explained and glorified by its resemblance to the higher.'

The Re-assertion of Beatrice

was time, and now there is time for the others. The great doctrines are exposed. Dante says more, and yet no more, than those others have said: 'O splendour'—'isplendor' is, for Dante, always the reflection—'O splendour of the living and eternal light, who, that has grown pale under the shade of Parnassus or has drunk of its well, would not seem to have his mind hampered when he tried to render you such as you seemed when you appeared—there where the heaven harmoniously shadows you forth, when you loosed yourself into the open air?—

> O isplendor di viva luce eterna,
>   Chi pallido si fece sotto l' ombra
>   Sì di Parnaso, o bevve in sua cisterna,
> Che non paresse aver la mente ingombra,
>   Tentando a render te qual tu paresti
>   Là dove armonizzando il ciel t' adombra,
> Quando nell' aere aperto ti solvesti?'

XI

THE *PARADISO*

The validity of Beatrice has been re-established. Her second beauty glows. That is to say, not only is the original power and nature of the Image recognized, but its original power is recognized as now developed into a state of greater knowledge. It can be known with the whole court of intellect round it; and the kind of life which it involves is capable of infinite growth. In this sense it is at once exclusive or inclusive; it can be regarded in itself or in relation to everything else or in relation to God. Any of these studies is complex and holy, and any of the Images is capable of this centrality. Beatrice is not only a type of the love-relationship; she is a type of every relationship.

The *Paradiso* is concerned to exhibit beatitude; that is—proper relationship between men and men and men and God. So full of derivation and nourishment are these that they may well be named the in-othering of men and the in-Godding of men. It is not an exterior but an interior relationship which is in question. It is also, in a sense, the absolute relationship, or at least it is one than which nothing more can be imagined or expressed. This is, implicitly and all but explicitly, the poem's claim. Whether it succeeds is a matter upon which most of us are not very good judges. To begin with, both the subject and the method are of a kind with which we cannot easily make comparisons. The subject is beatitude; the method is a continual variation in light. These two are one. But the lack of comparison is, usually but unfortunately, a definite limitation to our judgement. Secondly, the great learned orations disturb us. We can believe that Dante, following Saint Thomas, put beatitude in an intellectual act. But when, quite apart from Saint Thomas, Dante exhibits a passion for learning (in both senses of the word), we do not easily feel this to be part of the total poetic effect. Nor, for all our appreciation of Christianity, whether from within or without the Church, do we easily think of a knowledge of the manner of the Incarnation as the climax of human existence; therefore the whole process

The Paradiso

of the 'in-Godding' a little misses for us its total consummation. Thirdly, we do not sufficiently realize, as was suggested in the last chapter, that the whole of the *Paradiso* was meant, verbally, to be very advanced poetry. The 'stupor' which Virgil feels in beholding the great preluding pageant was presented as a real 'stupor' before the poetry. The *Commedia* in its totality was meant to be an advance on the *Aeneid*. Possibly it is not. But we ought to feel that, philosophically and psychologically, the *Paradiso* was to be a poem which Virgil could not understand, and that it is at least doubtful whether our advantages in being able to look up Saint Thomas are entirely adequate to enlarge our poetic sense beyond that of Virgil. It is indeed arguable that Saint Thomas has been a little overdone as an exponent of Dante. It seems likely that Saint Thomas would have found some difficulty in apprehending Dante's whole Beatrician theme; and in any case, valuable as the explanatory expositions of Saint Thomas are for illumination of Dante, it is what is inside the poem and not what is outside which chiefly concerns us.

These are but stray comments on our difficulties. The fundamental fact is that the *Paradiso* is an account of the perfected universe. Dante is shown it by Beatrice, that is, by the means of his own particular Image, developing correspondently with the whole developing knowledge. But he hears the voices of many others, who have been led by and faithful to other Images, and of many who have been called to the other Way, the Way of Rejection. It is only courteous, in so great an Affirmation, to remember and honour so many holy rejections—here especially where the rejections and affirmations of human life are but memories; though indeed the intensity of them makes them something more than memories. The poetry itself has to overcome the element of time past and make it into time present. Rejections and affirmations are here, except for that re-discovery of the past, no longer separate; this is the unitive life of which we have heard. The figure of Beatrice herself is an example of this. The awareness of her in the *Paradiso* is of one who both was and was not and now is. She was affirmed, and then (by the holy consent to her holy withdrawal) delicately 'rejected'. She was Florentine, and then other than Florentine, and now both Florentine and other than Florentine. She is therefore in herself

The Paradiso

the *coincidentia oppositorum* of heaven. Her voice and her speech have a great range, but she herself is one. This makes her difficult to our imaginations; it is why the knowledge of the love for Dante which the second canto of the *Inferno* expressed is important. By that she becomes humanly credible.

There is, however, another side to the *Paradiso*. Besides being an image of the whole redeemed universe, it is also an image of the redeemed Way. It is, that is to say, an image of a redeemed love-affair—that is, of an ordinary love-affair, if things went as they ought to go. The poem can be enlarged or reduced as we choose. The important stages in the romantic consciousness are marked, and the classic conclusion. The *Paradiso*, like the *Purgatorio*, returns at its beginning to the first 'stupor'. The imaging of the Sacred Griffin in his two natures is the proof of this, for though the doctrinal consciousness is much more vivid than in the *Vita*, yet the thesis is that the vision is there at the beginning. But now there is no original or actual sin to prevent its actual development. It has its 'liberty and power' already within it, and the will being thus set, there remains but a knowledgeable enlargement of direction and arrival.

It is true that, after the first new cry: 'O isplendor di viva luce eterna', there is shown to Dante a vision of the evil that might have been; that indeed in some sense was, though only to the damage of the souls that will it, and not at all with any harm to the Divine City. He has been intensely gazing on Beatrice, and her 'holy smile—santo riso' has caught him again in its early net (XXXII, 5–6), where the attendant goddesses (Dee) murmur to him: 'Too fixedly!' He looks away, at the court of the Sacred Griffin—though what he says is more significant: 'As soon as my dazzled eyes could see again [after their ten years' thirst was satisfied] my sight re-formed on the lesser—I say the lesser, in respect of that more sensible, whence I perforce turned away.' Beatrice is the 'more sensible' object; the pageant of intellect the less. But they are one. Then the whole significant display—the keen vision-tranced face of Saint John its conclusion and seal—moves three arrow-flights through the empty forest: empty because of her fault who once believed the serpent, which perhaps (may one add?), since the mountain was then empty, was able to crawl upward to this forest itself, instead of being

The Paradiso

confined to the green vale below. They reach a great tree, robbed of all its foliage, and as they near it they murmur 'Adam!' for this is the tree of knowledge, and Adam and all his children have plucked flowers and fruit. It is natural growth in every sense—even including the Empire—natural order, natural right, the first thing given, the rooted image of all on this earth that is not we. The pageant surrounds it crying: 'Thou art blessed, Griffin, that thou didst not pluck with thy beak from this tree, sweet to taste, for the belly is twisted by the pain of it.' And, speaking this once only, the Sacred and twice-born (binato) Animal utters from its beak: 'So the seed of all justice is preserved.'

Against that cry—history and command at once—there follows a vision of all injustice. Dante sleeps again; when he wakes, the company of heaven has disappeared. The car is fastened to the tree; Beatrice is sitting on the ground; around her the seven lamped virtues wait. The car undergoes transmutations; an eagle plunges on it, and a fox; it is covered with plumage and then rent by a dragon; afterwards it puts forth heads and becomes a monster, upon which, like a fort on a mountain, a wanton woman sits; a giant stands by her and they kiss many times. Presently her wandering eyes alight on Dante, the only male thing about (except for the pure and spiritual form of Statius). The giant beats her savagely and finally drags the monster and the harlot on it far into the forest until they disappear from sight.

It is, no doubt, the Papacy and the French monarchy. It is also the Church and the World, the City and barbarism. It is an altered Beatrice and the ferocious Lion of the *Inferno*. It is luxury and malice under the tree of temptation, and disappearing into a forest then like the savage forest of the *Inferno*. It is, in fact, all the opposite of Dante now and all from which Dante has been barely saved—and this in its personal and in its general form. Beatrice, who at the sight has become so sorrowful that she is not unlike Mary at the Cross, explains something of it to Dante as they go on, and when he still does not understand, she tells him that this is 'because of the school he has followed'. He answers in surprise: 'I do not remember that I was ever estranged from you; my conscience does not prick me for it.' She answers smiling: 'If not, think how to-day you drank of Lethe;

The Paradiso

the mere forgetfulness shows how you sinned in a wandering will.'

They are at the edge of the forest; it is noon. Before them is the spring of two separating streams. 'O luce, o gloria della gente humana—O light, O glory of humanity'—the apostrophe is serious and yet at the same time half a jest, at least in the sense that each created thing is also so. He asks what these waters are. Beatrice answers: 'Ask Matilda'—as if the Active Life itself should have made clear to him the knowledge of Lethe which removes the memory of sin as sin, and Eunoe which recalls the knowledge of good as good. But Matilda protests—'come fa chi da colpa si dislega—as does he who frees himself from blame';—what is all this? She has already told him, and she is sure Lethe did not wash *that* away.

> 'Forse maggior cura
> che spesse volte la memoria priva
> fatta ha la mente sua negli occhi oscura',

Beatrice answers; 'perhaps some greater pre-occupation, such as often steals away our recollection, may have darkened his mind's eyes.' It is a perfectly grave answer, but (like the eyes and mouth of the lady herself) it coruscates with laughter. Since Matilda talked to him in the forest, Dante has been through the pageant of heaven, the loss of Virgil, her own return, the particular judgement, and the masque of the apostasy. 'Forse maggior cura—!' and she knows it as well as we do. In order to make Beatrice spiritual, there is no need to make her a complete fool. Both the ladies are gently laughing at him and each other. 'O marvellous smile of my mistress, which is only seen in her eyes!'

Matilda brings him to Eunoe; he drinks of it, and all the memory of all good done by him—it might be permissible to add, and to him—rushes back. He is freshened like trees 'with a new foliage'. Statius also drinks, but Statius and Matilda do not return, as Dante does. He is now, 'pure and prepared' to ascend among those imperial brightnesses the stars which have shone so often in the deep sky since they and the sky were first named in the *Convivio*, but now the heaven is deeper even than that of nobility, for the heaven and the stars are alike living. Across the green grass he walks back to Beatrice. She is to show him things which afterwards he is to write for the world; it is his function and hers to help him to it. It is the business of all lovers to love each other's function, and this is another reason why she will tell him all she can and show him all she can, including that great moment in the eighth or stellar heaven when she cries to him: 'Riguarda qual son io—look at what I am.' It is her business as it is his to write the poem. But at this last moment in the earthly paradise, she has turned a little to her left and is looking up straight at the noonday sun. His eyes follow hers, though he cannot bear it long; but in the brief time, as he stares dazzled, there seems to grow a second sun. Another day within the day is pouring round him— the day in which the Sacred Griffin and all its splendours live. This day striking on Dante's purified and invigorated flesh, 'transhumanizes' him. He is, it seems, as near as he can be before death, in the risen body; he is lifted by light—'che col tuo lume mi levasti.' A sea of the sun's flame shows in the heavens.

From now begins the movement through the nine heavens to the Empyrean, through the nine manifestations of glory to substantial glory. 'All things', the smile of Beatrice rather than her speech declares, 'move to different harbours through the great sea of being—lo gran mar dell' essere—not only creatures without intelligence, but those also who have intellect and love.' The two high creatures move in space and time still, but also through increasing knowledge of heaven. The stages of the Way are marked not only by a change in the apparent surroundings, but also by the ever-deepening beauty of Beatrice. The first of the eternal images shows lovelier and more significant at every term of their motion; the everlasting validity of the Florentine girl is strengthened by each new enlightenment. The first exposition is when Dante seems to himself to have entered a cloud—'lucida, spessa, solida, e polita—lucent, thick, firm, shining'—as if, living, he entered a still uncleft pearl. He in-pearls himself. How body enters body, dimension supports dimension (he says), we cannot tell; therefore we should more expressly long to understand the union of our nature with God's, that is, the Incarnation. This is at the root of that even physical co-inherence which is on this earth incapable of its full capacity. In this nearest heaven countenances appear, delicate, like pearls on white foreheads; they are those who were called to the con-

The Paradiso

ventual vows of the Rejection of Images, and have been compelled from their calling by violence, and have not (once free) returned. It is the heaven of the Moon, of the insufficient Rejection, but of a repented insufficiency.

In this heaven the condition of all the heavens is laid down. Piccarda, the sister of Forese Donati, is asked by Dante the question which so many in hell answered wrongly, and so many in purgatory delayed to answer. 'Do you', he says in effect, 'envy the happiness of others?'—or perhaps, since here in heaven such a question would be too crude, say, 'Do you desire, you who are here, to be higher, to see more, to be more loved?' 'Brother, the quality of love quietens our will; it makes us desire only what we have, and to thirst for nothing more. If we wished to be loftier, our desires would be in discord with his who sorts us. You will see that that cannot be in these circles, if love is indeed necessity, and if you recall the nature of love. It is the very form and being of the blessed to be held within the divine will, in which will all our wills are one. So that to be but what we are, from threshold to threshold in the kingdom, is to the whole kingdom a joy, as to the king who to his will in-willeth us (invoglia); and his will is our peace—it is that sea to which moves all that it creates and nature makes' (III, 70–87). Or indeed: 'Brother, we love; we love the divine will, we love as that chooses to love, we are in-willed to will, in-loved to love.'

This is the knot which unites the citizen with the City. It is the method of following whichever way of the Images, of serving Beatrice and the earthly City (in affirmation or rejection), and of knowing the great order of all. In the *Vita* love was communicated; here it is *necesse*. Love is fate; all luck is love. But as in heaven, so on earth. This is the first heaven of expansion beyond the young love of the exchanged images; were men unfallen, it is so that every romanticism would sweetly and gently enlarge; being fallen, we may still study it. Indeed, as Beatrice and all the blessed imply, Dante's question is great nonsense. For there is no other heaven—the hierarchy admitted, there is, it seems, no hierarchy at all; no higher or lower; all is here, in the first. 'Only,' and as if (lover-like) Beatrice exerted herself to explain to her lover, she seems to use an intense metaphor—'only—they have sweet life differently, by feeling more or less the eternal

The Paradiso

breath—per sentir più e men l' eterno spiro' (IV, 36). The swifter ardour of that sweet immingled life is all the difference any can know; passion is their law, not place. Anything else is democracy intoxicated with itself, the moon-lunacy of equality without degree, as without equality degree is only a sun-madness. Even in this world, even outside love, one does not *envy* Caesar or Shakespeare or the God-bearer; existence is equal, function hierarchical; at every moment the hierarchy alters, and the functions re-ladder themselves upward. To know both—to experience and to observe both—is perfect freedom.

This then is the air the Griffin breathes; without that there is simply no heaven at all. It is to be observed, however, that it is the *wills* of the blessed ones which also breathe it. This activity is not merely a resignation; it is a choice. They share that sweet life—vita—because they choose, by willing in God that others should know more. This is itself a joy, as the knowing (more or less) is itself a joy; they gain indirectly what they lose directly. This first heaven is the condition of all; its concern is the kind of affirmation made; its concern therefore is intention, especially (in the poem) intention as expressed in vows. We are in the purpose of establishing love—to Beatrice, to the City, to the First Mover. The vows here particularly spoken of are conventual, but a permitted vow is always a vow; and the vow of marriage need not be excluded, nor those of baptism and confirmation, nor those which a man should take, interiorly at least, to whatever for him is Florence or the City, nor any he finds he has taken. The secret order of the *Convivio* is now promulgated. Vows are the most extreme affirmation—excepting death for a thing—of devotion to a thing, therefore of its existence. The compact made thus with God—for that is what every vow is—is, it is declared, accepted in him, in that fate of love which is his will and our in-willed being; it is itself made fate. Accepted love is fate. If violence is laid upon such vows, the will of the troth-plight (in whatever kind) never consents to it; if ever, or as soon as, the violence is removed, it springs again to its own pledged and prolonged affirmation. The centre of Christian love, in this sense, is the affirmation of the existence of another soul and souls in the love-fate.

Beatrice defines and asserts this validity of affirmation: all this still in that first heaven. And then there occurs one of those

The Paradiso

sweet and tender passages which humanize (dared one say so) the *Paradiso* itself, intensely human as it is. She ceases. Dante begins to reply: 'O amanza del primo amanto, O diva'—'O loved of the First Lover, O goddess . . . my love is not so deep as to be able to change grace for grace, but let him who is able reply. . . . Lady, with reverence, one other question . . . I wish I knew if man can make reparation for broken vows with other good, so that he need not weigh too light on your scales.' Beatrice's eyes fill with such sparks of love that Dante, overcome, drops his own. Indeed the moment is too near that other moment of repentance and reconciliation for the reader not to feel the intense, the intimate, relevance. Whatever the grand metaphysics of heaven may formally assert, here the sin is half-recalled. 'O most loved, O divinity—can a man make *some* amends?' Her eyes sparkle with the passion of her answer: 'Oh if I flame on you now in a fire of love beyond all earth's, do not be astonished! . . . how the eternal light glows again in your mind—and only to see it, ever, ever wakens love—'she herself rushes on to a veiled allusion, excusing, explaining, all'—if anything else misleads love, it is only that light misunderstood. You want to know if—O!' She breaks into the great chant of exposition; she becomes again all-principled with love, but the detail has stood out; thus certainly, if lovers fall, should lovers forgive.

The compact must be kept, but the matter may, by high dispensation, be changed: this also is in the power of the interchanges of heaven—'converta'. But let it be done by authority, and let the second matter be offered in half as great proportion: vows are not rashly to be taken, nor, taken, easily loosed. God consented when you consented. This is the nearest man can come to heavenly justice; and it is here Beatrice speaks of the 'valour', the courage, of Dante's own eyes. It is the attributed courage of the early adoration—which requires courage—and the courage of inquiry. If his eyes have dropped it is not as they did by the rivers of purgatory, and he advances their courage again—to see about him the appearance of the second heaven. The spirits seem there to shoot towards him like fish in a pond: they exclaim: 'Lo, one who will increase our love—ecco chi crescerà li nostri amori' (V, 105). This is the carrying into consciousness of the Piccarda maxim: whoever the stranger is, they will gain increase of love

The Paradiso

by loving him. They invite him to ask what he will, and Beatrice encourages him:

'Di', di'
sicuramente, e credi come a Dii'.

—'speak, speak safely and believe these as gods'. The 'sicuramente' recalls the 'sicuri' of the entry into Dis, 'secure in the sacred words.' There is a safety in right speech, in the proper style; for speech also is an Image—to be used or not used as is convenient to heaven. Here all speech is what that angel's was —free and safe; inquiry is good, as when the Blessed Virgin herself inquired into mysteries: 'How shall these things be?'

The first heaven was a showing of Rejection, of spirits in the feminine, of final vows not quite fulfilled; the second is a showing of Affirmation, of spirits in the masculine, of final vocations not quite followed. It is distinguished by lawgivers and princes; and this character makes the entrance into it more lovely. As the lovers become aware of it, Beatrice grows so glad that 'the star itself was changed and laughed—la stella si cambiò e rise' (V, 97). Between Beatrice and the emperors is a largesse of smiles; this, in heaven, is the first image of the developed teaching of the *Convivio*; the girl and the City reflect each other. Hiding in his own emanation of light as if from excess of joy, an emperor speaks; it is Justinian—'Cesàre fui, e son Giustiniano—Caesar was I, and am Justinian' (VI, 10). In him and in the other lords of this light was also a certain lack; he defines it. They did good work; they laboured for the Republic; Justinian himself coded the imperial laws. But their desire swerved a little to themselves; it considered their own fame and honour; therefore they too in their affirmations were deflected from the eternal order. Milton also saw it exactly so: 'the last infirmity of noble mind.' The quality of love in them was therefore a little lessened. Yet that lessening of joy and brightness is itself brightness of joy, and they gain by what they lose, for the exact co-measure of deserving and obtaining is a delight. This is the only kind of irony that exists in heaven.

The speech of Justinian is a grand affirmation of the Empire. After an allusion to his own conversion to a belief in the Double Nature of Christ he recounts the high myth from the days of Aeneas to those of Charlemagne. It is to their proper work in this

The Paradiso

that all lovers are called. In the first heaven they were committed to a vow of real love (were they unfallen, indeed to real love; but being fallen, still to an effort towards it); in the second to a widening of it and to labour for it. The State (with a capital letter) is properly but a reflection of that voluntary state (without a capital); indeed it is that voluntary state universalized and public. The two here are one, in the knowledge of Beatrice and Dante. Justinian denounces both parties in Florence—both the Imperial and Papal; neither, in its party-spirit of greed, belongs to the public idea. He denounces them and ceases. This Affirmation has had its way; the showing of the second stage of romantic love is over.

As the great chorus breaks out, praising 'that clarity which makes super-illustrious those happy fires', Dante turns with a question, and immediately his heavenly progress is counter-pointed by a sudden revelation of his sensations on earth, now so far below. 'He does not seem unreal flesh', the spirits on the mountain-path had said of him, and here again he does not. 'The worship which in-dominates itself through all of me, though but by *Be* or *Ice*, bowed me—

>   quella riverenza che s' indonna
>   Di tutto me, pur per BE e per ICE,
>   Mi richinava' (VII, 13–15).

It is as commonly mortal as anything in the *Commedia*—the memory of the moment when, in the morning paper or in a book or in any overheard conversation, the name of the beloved (not then hers, but the one she bears) strikes the eye or the ear; or when someone not unlike her passes. Then for a split second the heart stands still; one is palsied and shakes, it is not she, and breath comes again. The worship has unexpectedly in-dominated us. She who had caused this in Dante—in what manuscripts of Boethius or Aristotle or Aquinas, or perhaps of Virgil himself—sees his movement and his check. She answers with one of those phrases upon our proper sensitiveness to which so much of the *Paradiso* depends. What she says is

>   'Secondo mio infallibile avviso,
>   come giusta vendetta giustamente
>   vengiatta fuisse, t' ha in pensier miso—

The Paradiso

According to my infallible advisement, how a just vendetta is justly avenged, hath sent thee into thought.' The first line is the test. Most of the English translations load Beatrice's voice with some such phrase as 'according to my unerring intelligence'. On the other hand, they make her say it (since Dante did) 'with such a smile as would make a man happy though in the fire'. It follows that, if she is to show such a rich and happy delight while she speaks, it must be vital in the words; she must be enjoying them and what they mean. So, of course, she is; she is enjoying—she is amused and delighted at—this astonishing fact of her infallible knowledge. This delight the reader in general misses, so that for him she is merely portentous. But she is not portentous, any more than the alliterations and verbal variations in the other lines are portentous. She and they are joyous. God has settled it like this; it is not her doing; ascribed to the only Omnipotence be all the glory. She is not 'putting it over' Dante, or only as much as any happy femininity would, in those celestial conditions, put it over a less quick masculinity. This union of laughter and knowledge, modesty and magnificence, humility and infallibility, may be difficult to imagine. The alternative is a cultured female psychiatrist, with an officially spiritual smile. It will not serve. Beatrice is saying—any lover to any lover—'I know what you are thinking', only (transhumanized) she is right. The phrase is imparadised by joy; we have to learn the joy by the phrase.

If, on the other side of Ariel's songs, Shakespeare had developed an intellectual heaven to which 'Where the bee sucks' was prelude, we might in English have had a comparison. But he did not; he stayed on the arch-natural verge. *The Tempest* may indeed be said to imagine an island of purgation, but we cannot press it. If there is a villain in a play, he must either become more villainous or less, and grow towards either damnation or purgation. That is merely the technique of narrative. In the later Shakespearian heroines there is indeed a touch of Beatrice, as in Imogen. 'My dear lord, Thou art one of the false ones', might have been said of Dante. It is as well as it is. Even Dante must, for the sake of his fame and our intelligence, have a 'compensation', and Shakespeare is that compensation.

The particular matter which, infallibly recognizing Dante's perplexity, Beatrice explains, has been discussed in Chapter VI.

The Paradiso

It is the nature of the Crucifixion in relation to the Roman Empire, and hence of the Manhood of Christ. She goes on to explain why God decreed this way of redemption rather than any other; this, she says, is hidden from those whose wit is not adult in the flame of love—'nella fiamma d' amor non è adulto' (VII, 60): say simply 'adult in love'. But to those who are—the full answer must be studied in the whole noble canto; briefly, it is that this is the most courteous way. Man might have made satisfaction for the sin? he could not; God might 'solo per sua cortesia—only by his courtesy' have forgiven? he would not; rather he would himself become Man that Man might make satisfaction. The greater became the less, that the less might be perfect with the Creator. 'Nor between the last night and the first day was, nor shall be, so high and magnificent a process ... for God was more large in giving himself that man might lift himself again than if of himself he had granted remission.' It is this, as one may say, handing over of the self to become another self which is the greater largesse of spirit, and this which is understood only by those adult in love. (It is, of course, often talked about by the adolescent.) The great oration ends with an allusion to the resurrection of the flesh. On the moment they are in the third heaven, that ascribed to Venus and to lovers. It is that of which Dante had spoken in the first canzone of the *Convivio*, which is here again recalled; it was the beginning of the philosophical analysis of love and wisdom, and it is recalled here in the heaven where the point of earth's coned shadow lies. The souls which rejoice in it are those who lacked something of a perfect love, in whom (as in those of the two lower heavens) there was some self-seeking. Dante speaks to three; each has a memorable point of exposition—coming exactly at that moment when the earth falls behind and the great doctors of the philosophy of love are about to be revealed in the fourth heaven.

The first of these points is exposed in the conversation with Carlo Martello, king of Hungary, prince of Provence, and once a friend of Dante. After he has spoken Dante says: 'Sire, since I believe the exalted joy with which your words in-pour me (m' infonde), there where all good has end and beginning, is seen by you as I see it, it pleases me the more; and still more

The Paradiso

because you see it by looking into God.' Dante is in-filled with joy—in God—by Carlo's speech; he rejoices again that Carlo knows this as he himself knows it; and he rejoices also that Carlo sees it in God. He has his own joy; he rejoices in Carlo's joy; and he rejoices in the eternal quality of that joy. That quality is further defined. Cunizza of Romano, admitting her weakness on earth ('I am refulgent in this place because the light of this star vanquished me') goes on:

> 'Ma lietamente a me medesma indulgo
> la cagion di mia sorte, e non mi noia,
> che parria forse forte al vostro vulgo—

but joyously I give indulgence to myself for the occasion of my fate, nor is it an annoyance to me, which would seem perhaps difficult to your vulgar.' She forgives herself (such virtue have Lethe and Eunoe) and her joy is undisturbed; and this—both the delight in her place and her self-pardon—would seem hard sayings to those not yet adult in love. 'Il ben dell' intelletto' is precisely for those who are so adult.

Another glory—'as a fine ruby in which the sun strikes—qual fin balascio in che lo sol percota'—shines by her; there, Dante says, brightness is acquired by joy, just as on earth joy breaks in a smile, but 'below' the spirits darken as their minds sadden. This new light is Folco of Marseilles, a troubadour, a Cistercian, a bishop, and a leader in the war against the Albigenses. (It is he to whom is sometimes attributed the cry: 'Kill all; let God find his own'; but this is more important.) He confirms Cunizza. 'Here we do not repent, but smile—non però qui si pente, ma si ride—non della colpa—not at the sinfulness, which does not return to mind, but at the Worth that ordained and fore-furnished us—

> ma del valore ch' ordinò e provide.'

This, now, is what seeing sin in God is. They remember the sin as occasion of love's potency; this too is possible, for a moment, to lovers on earth without any thought of the supernatural. The fault between them is a cause of joy; so only that the fault has been put by, it is possible even here to be gay in recollecting it. This natural delight is already a flash of our most courteous lord,

The Paradiso

and the souls in heaven supernaturally return his courtesy in accepting it.

But before Folco spoke, Dante had spoken. He asked Folco who he was, and he added:

> 'Già non attenderei io tua domanda,
> s' io m' intuassi, come tu t' immii—

I had not waited so long for thy request, if I me in-thee'd, as thou thee in-meest.' Or: 'If I in-thee'd myself as thou dost in-me thyself.' This is one of Dante's most concise and most intense sayings, and one of the most significant. He uses the prefix a number of times—by accident or design. The life of the Blessed Virgin 'in-heavens' her—'inciela' (III, 97). Each seraph 'in-Gods' himself—'india' (IV, 28); the ladies, often enough, have been 'innamorata'; Carlo Martello 'infonda'—inpoured—his joy. But this phrase is the most challenging, at the very point of the earth's coned shadow on 'the fair planet that hearteneth to love'. It is the very definition of all heaven, but especially of the heavens that are to follow; it is their mode of life. Something of this is known, on occasion, in the life of lovers; not, perhaps, in many; not, certainly, often. There is some kind of experience which can only be expressed by saying: 'Love you? I *am* you.' This is a natural thing; but then there is the moral duty. It is the moral duty of lovers, as they certainly at moments know, to plunge with love into each other's life—bringing power: power to resist temptation, to reject, to affirm, to purify, to pray. 'I will pray for you' is a good saying; a better—'I will pray in you.' This indeed is like the nature of the prayers for which the souls on the mountain terraces are asking. Those on earth fulfil the necessary task. And now it is more than ritual prayers; it is the life and inter-life of souls.

Just before Dante emerges from this heaven, he sees a light like the sun in water; it is Rahab. She is there because she saved the spies of Israel. It is, in a way, Dante's own position. He has lost much and been unfaithful in much; but he saved the spies of the heavenly kingdom—in the *Vita* and the *Convivio*. That's might have been the same—had she only meant something by her flattery; she did not, and is not. As Folco's voice compares the true harlot in heaven with the adulterous Pope on earth, the blazing

The Paradiso

hues disappear. Colour ceases. That fourth heaven into which, beyond the shadow of earth, they are come shows itself 'non per color, ma per lume—not by colour but by light'. It is the heaven of the sun.

>'Ringrazia,
>ringrazia il sol degli angeli, ch' a questo
>sensibil t' ha levato per sua grazia',

Beatrice says: 'give grace, give grace to the sun of the angels who to this sensible sun has raised you by his grace.' Dante obeys so immediately and so intently that a wonderful thing happens; for the first time, he altogether forgets Beatrice:

>che Beatrice eclissò nell' obblio (X, 60).

This—disturbs her? to laughter. It is one of the most concentrated moments. Dante forgets her; she laughs; and 'the splendour of her laughing eyes divided my united mind among many things'. She recalls him, but not to herself, to the intellectual splendours which are now about him. The Image quickens the soul to seek the Good, and as it is itself forgotten yet in that moment quickens the mind to ardours of intellect. The infidelity is heavenly, yet the laughter is not only that. 'The joyous laughter of the Florentine at finding herself at last forgotten is as simple and natural as the surroundings are complex and supernatural. It is precisely a girl laughing in her city whom we hear.' But it is a girl who has precisely excited her lover to his proper function; in this case, to know the doctrines it is his business to know.

It will be simpler now, with such unaccustomed verse, to observe the single general movement. All things now are known in God; the eyes of the Image continue to light the Way, which in its turn confirms and deepens the beauty of the eyes of the Image—that is, of the Image (conscious or unconscious in itself). The deepening beauty of Beatrice is a part of the poem; that is, it is (in the poem) known to us because Dante knew it. Her beauty is her own, but its publication is his; more—it is in his sight of it and worship of it that it grows deeper—so that all the infinite gratitude is not to be only on his side. In the exchange of their celestial love, she becomes more Beatrician by the measure of the Dantean knowledge.

The doctors are about them; the spirits are given a new name.

The Paradiso

It is the 'vita' which now speaks—'la gloriosa vita di Tommaso' (XIV, 6); 'Io son la vita di Bonaventura' (XII, 124). It is the summing up of the whole thing that had been Saint Thomas in what is now Saint Thomas, of all that Bonaventura had been in what is now Bonaventura. Dante has nine lines in which he describes (XIV, 1–9) the relation between the 'vita di Tommaso' and what we may call the 'vita di Beatrice'. The sound of the vibrations of their voices moves like the water in a round vessel, from centre to circumference and from circumference to centre, according as it is struck from without or within. The orations and philosophies, the praises of Francis and Dominic, are interchanged with the girl's voice; all testimony with a single experience. This consummation of union between vital image and intellectual image moves harmoniously through the sea of being. In this union the 'life' of Saint Thomas the Dominican begins to praise the life of Francis of Assisi, leaving it afterwards to Saint Bonaventura the Franciscan to praise the life of Dominic. Both these are great masters of the Rejecting Way, at least here, for Thomas does not bother to speak of the poem to the sun or the little brothers and sisters of whom we have heard so much or the birds, but rather dilates on the saint's union with Poverty—'la lor concordia e i lor lieti sembianti—their concord and joyous seeming'—on his thirst for martyrdom, and on 'l' ultimo sigillo —the last seal' of the Stigmata. So that, as is proper, honour and worship are paid on this affirming Way to the lords of Rejection, for this is confirmed by the speech that deals with Dominic. And many other names of both Ways are called—the 'vita' of Albert the Great, of Dionysius and Boethius, of Isidore and Bede, of Siger of Brabant and Joachim of Flora, of Hugh of Saint Victor and Solomon king of Israel. It is Solomon who utters in 'una voce modesta—a modest voice, such as perhaps the angel used to Mary'—why *that* comparison? because of what Solomon has to say, being urged to speak by Beatrice—it is he who foretells the resurrection of the Flesh. Beatrice has said that Dante needs (though the question has not yet reached even his mind, let alone his voice) to know whether the light with which the substance of the divine spirits 'in-flowers itself—

onde s' infiora
vostra sustanzia'—

The Paradiso

will be theirs eternally—and if so whether, on the resurrection of the body, the flesh will be an hindrance to the spiritual sight. Solomon answers that as long as Paradise lasts, the brightness will grow with ardour, and ardour with vision. 'Come la carne gloriosa e santa—when the glorious and holy flesh reclothes us, our persons shall be more pleasing by being more whole; and the free light which the Highest Good gives us shall grow greater, the light which conditions us to see him. It belongs to the vision to increase, and to the ardour kindled by it, and to the ray which goes out from it. But as coal gives forth flame, and by its own living brilliance of heat defeats it, maintaining its own appearance, so this glow which swathes us shall be overcome by the flesh which now the earth covers; nor shall so much light fleshlily weary us—so strong shall the organs of the body be to all that means delight (XIV, 37–60)—

> chè gli organi del corpo saran forti
> a tutto ciò che potrà dilettarne.'

This is the resurrection of the flesh. It is because of this prophecy that Solomon's voice is as quiet as the Angel of the Annunciation of the Divine Flesh; it is because of the hint of this that had been seen in the body of Beatrice that Beatrice puts the question in substitution for Dante. The hint had been real but remote. The brightness which her body shed directed attention to this future. The Resurrection—not only of the flesh but of all the past—was held in the word 'vita'; it is the whole life that here sings, of which in the past the flesh has been incident and means. As Solomon ceases, all the choir cry 'Amen!'—desiring their transcarnalized perfection.

As if the poem, whatever it defined, almost imagined that perfection to be already present, it draws the two Images of Dante and Beatrice into a deeper mystery, doubly related to the prophecy. The fifth heaven manifests a ruddy cross of souls, through which (but how Dante will not dare to say) Christ himself is lamped—'lampeggiava Cristo.' It is the first proposal of the union. The eyes of Beatrice had reflected the Twy-natured, but here the Twy-natured himself is conjoined to the moving lights. But the eyes are remembered. Nothing (Dante says) had been like this experience of inamourment ('io m' innamora'), and then half-checks himself as at a too-rash saying: what of his delight 'degli occhi belli'? No; not too rash (the accusation is only for the excuse), for those eyes themselves grew more effective here; he had never loved them till now—but he had not yet turned to them. This is the courtesy of the poem, but it is a courtesy of sheer fact. The cross glows. Its relevance to earth is twofold; first, it is composed of those whose special vocation and function was battle—the heaven of soldiers; and second, it is peculiarly the heaven of the families. It is here that Dante's own ancestor Cacciaguida appears, and Cacciaguida speaks of many great houses, chiefly of Florence and of the olden time. Launched into this awareness as Dante is, from the just-ceasing proclamation of the glorious and holy flesh, the evocation has a particular value; it is all of descent, tradition, and mortal blood in a pattern of sequent births. *Pietas* is here justified, but it is also actually here, as when Dante uses the ceremonial plural to address his ancestor. 'Voi siete il padre mio—You are my father . . .' (Since, in English, the Speech from the Throne was robbed of its plural, we have almost lost it altogether. It is a pity; it never excluded the singular, and it included a courtesy of recognition of greatness. It can certainly still be used in writing, though hardly in speech except in the first person. That even would not mean conceit— only function. The Majesty of England might be prayed to restore it in his ceremonial utterances.) It is true he is aware, as he does so, that a touch of pride moves not Cacciaguida but him. Beatrice smiles a little, and seems 'like that one who coughed at the first fault written of Guinevere'—just for a moment a hint of the false Francescan indulgence hangs in the divine sky, of the lingering at the foot of the mount. It passes; the chant sweeps on —to the famous prophecy of the exile (XVII, 55–60).

> 'Tu lascerai ogni cosa diletta
>   Più caramente, e questo è quello strale
>   Che l' arco dello esilio pria saetta.
> Tu proverai sì come sa di sale
>   Lo pane altrui, e com' è duro calle
>   Lo scendere e il salir per l' altrui scale.—

You shall abandon all those things most dearly loved—and this is that arrow which the bow of exile shall first shoot. You shall try how salt is the bread of others, and how hard it is to go up and

The Paradiso

down on others' stairs.' 'Others' in the *Paradiso* has so often meant joy, but here the word is sombre. Derivation shall be bitter; function hard. It is then that the virtue of that heaven comes home to Dante. It will (he foresees) need courage in that hour to continue his 'songs'. No-one was less an aesthete than Dante, nor more held poetry both at the least and at the greatest worth at once. But the writing of great poetry, it seems, especially of this intense, allusive, topical poetry, will need bravery. 'Alter your thought,' the voice of Beatrice murmurs, 'think that I am close to him who makes every injury light—colui ch' ogni torto disgrava.' He turns; he gazes. Her love and Love itself ray out on him—rather, Love rays on Beatrice and thence on him, with derived aspect; this is the 'isplendor'. He gazes; she smiles—

'Volgiti ed ascolta,
che non pur ne' miei occhi è Paradiso—

Turn and listen; not only in my eyes is Paradise.' The ruddy glow of courage, in death or in birth, pales; in the white glow of the sixth heaven the sacred spirits are moving like birds risen from a bank. They gather in one form, then in another; finally in the image of an eagle's head and neck and outspread wings. It begins to speak: 'Because I was just and righteous—giusta e pio—I am exalted in this glory . . .' The pronoun is an intense image of the way of life which this affirming justice involves. The eagle is composed of souls distinguished by and exalted for their just acts, their devotion to *pietas* and to greater things. Each of these souls in himself says 'I'. But the brain of the heaven of them all thinks 'We'. Yet the voice of this heaven says 'I' again. The ceremonial plural of Cacciaguida is made more real, and then carried into a closer unity. That plural involved, in some sense, all derivations which existed in Cacciaguida; he was himself, in that sense, not singular but plural; he was all his ancestors and all his past. So the Majesty of England or the Holiness of the Pope is inclusive of the English or of the Roman Church (I do not say it derives from them; it may indeed be that from which they derive). But since in all these instances, we contemplate a single being, the plural must to an extent remain ceremonial. Here however it is not so. The just all together are the eagle; their thoughts run together, and 'the feeling intellect',

The Paradiso

exalted to that degree, in each of them knows the thoughts of the others. Amongst themselves they are so, but to all else, to Dante, Beatrice, and the other blessed, their thought must speak more closely than that, and proclaim a greater identity. The only closer word is 'I', and therefore the eagle says 'I'.

The poem says all this, and more, in a line. It does not talk about this co-inherence, but only shows it. The souls who compose the eagle are called particularly 'burning lights of the Holy Spirit—lucenti incendi dello Spirito Santo' (XIX, 100–1), which might encourage those who would associate the whole idea of the co-inherence with the Third Person. Presently the single voice of the eagle changes into multitudinous songs, and they again to the single voice. The dispute here is on the relation of the heathen to the Church, and on the nature of predestination. The great maxim is (XX, 91–9): 'The kingdom of heaven suffers violence from warm love and living hope, which conquers the divine will—not in the manner in which man overcomes man, but conquers it because it wills to be conquered—ma vince lei, perchè vuole esser vinta—and, being conquered conquers by its own benignity—e vinta vince con sua beninanza.'

As if this maxim were seen in action, the eagle of co-inherent justice vanishes into the seventh splendour. The change is marked by the seriousness of Beatrice's countenance. 'E quella non ridea—she no longer smiled.' Dante could not (she tells him) endure her smile; her glance must be tempered to his need. At the same time 'la dolce sinfonia di paradiso—the sweet symphony of paradise' is silent—for the same reason. Quiet falls in heaven; both sight and hearing must be subdued—or rather the vision and the sound restrains itself through compassion for Dante's present capacity. What he becomes aware of is a new ascent, comparable to the movement from the third to the fourth heaven. There, as the shadow of earth was outpassed, the images began to be seen in God (VIII, 90); now God begins to be seen more clearly in the images. The change in vision is, like all changes in the *Paradiso*, a change in the stresses of light. The various phrases with which Dante, in canto after canto, describes Beatrice's increasing beauty, must have in them a poetic significance we have, in general, failed to grasp. The *Paradiso* has lain open to theologians, but hardly to critics.

The Paradiso

There is discerned before him a heavenly ladder, the entrance into the heights of contemplation. It is the contemplatives who possess it. A single light of those moving lights draws near; Dante inquires of him concerning this new silence.

> 'Tu hai l' udir mortal, sì come il viso',
> rispose a me; 'onde qui non si canta
> per quel che Beatrice non ha riso—

'You have', he said to me, 'mortal hearing and mortal sight; therefore there is no song for the same reason that Beatrice has no smile.' It is the spirit of the eleventh-century contemplative Peter Damian. Dante accepts the answer, but he desires an answer to another question—and it might be said that this other question also is related to the early experience in Florence. His curious and passionate intellect wants to know *why*. Almost the last poetry spoken by the sixth heaven in the eagle had adored the divine predestination—

> 'O predestinazion, quanto remota
> è la radice tua da quegli aspetti
> che la prima cagion non veggion *tota*!—

O predestination, how far is thy root removed from any sight which does not see the First Cause *whole*!' (XX, 130-2). Now in his second utterance in the seventh heaven, Dante renews the word: *why* was Peter Damian chosen for this interlocution—

> 'perchè predestinata fosti sola
> a questo offizio tra le tue consorte?' (XXI, 77-8),

He is not told; he cannot be. But if the poetry cannot do that, it can make the helpless answer an answer of such a kind that the helplessness opens into the depth of that Whole. The lines (82-102) do what so much theology does not do; they cause us almost to experience the reason that we cannot know. Why Peter? why Beatrice? why thus and thus? Peter, by communication of grace, can see much; he can behold 'la summa essenza—the supreme essence', but the depth of the Will in that—neither he nor the Seraph nearest to God can see. Why Beatrice?—

> 'So it was willed
> Where Will and Power are one; ask thou no more.'

The Paradiso

One moral indeed might be drawn: that it is not only Apologetics, but the *style* of Apologetics that matters. A thousand preachers have said all that Dante says and left their hearers discontented; why does Dante content? because an Image of profundity is there. Peter Damian goes on to say who he is and, like so many of these glories, denounces the sins of Christians on earth—especially, since he had been a bishop, of the bishops. Suddenly all the heaven breaks into a cry 'of such deep sound that there is no image of it, nor could I understand it, so overcome was I by the thunder'. He turns to Beatrice; she, swiftly and tenderly: 'Do you not know you are in heaven? that all heaven is holy? and all done there comes of a good zeal?' And she adds: 'If this cry shook you so much, think how the song and my smile would have transmuted you.' If you cannot bear the anger of heaven, how will you bear its joy? There had been a moment when Virgil on the mount had warned Dante of this, when he had spoken of those who feared the prosperity of others, and another moment on a lower terrace when Guido del Duca remembered that he had once become livid when he saw others merry; and on the steep side of the awful funnel was a marsh where those lay bubbling who hated the cheerful sun, and where one furious and envious spirit had clutched at the boat where two poets were. These and others are they who cannot bear the joy of heaven, nor even its hints and reflections; 'if a man cannot endure the joy he has seen, how shall he endure the joy he has not seen?' Dante had almost aimed the question at Piccarda: 'do you not desire a greater joy? do you not implicitly therefore envy and dislike those who have it?' 'Brother, we love.'

Another of the contemplatives, who still preserve Dante from their song as Beatrice still protects him from her smile, names himself; it is Benedict. He speaks of the last and absolute heaven, the presence of which begins to be felt now when all recognizable becoming is about to cease in being.—'There each desire exists, perfect, mature, integral; all parts are in it, there where they always were, for it is not in place nor does it in-pole itself, and our ladder goes there, where it is in-volved from sight—

> Ivi è perfetta, matura ed intera
> ciascuna disianza; in quella sola
> è ogni parte là dove sempr' era;
> perchè non è in loco, e non s' impola,

The Paradiso

e nostra scala infino ad essa varca,
onde così dal viso ti s' invola.'
(XXII, 64-9).

Man can bear anger—even heavenly anger—rather than heavenly joy (how did Dante know how the general preference for the *Inferno* was, in poetry at least, wholly to justify that passage?). But those who have, in their degree, known this ladder, who have in-loved themselves to love, can bear the joy. Benedict re-gathers himself to this college of joy, and the whole college gathers together, and like a whirlwind all sweep upward—quicker, and much quicker, than those souls which had skirred like doves at Cato's rebuke, there on the island at the foot of 'the cause and occasion of all joy—di tutta gioia'. Beatrice makes a gesture to Dante, and with the mere making, they are up the ladder—'si sua virtù la mia natura vinse—so did her virtue overcome my nature.' The phrase recalls the analysis of the *Convivio*—'her beauty has power to renovate nature in those who behold it.' One might perhaps—in a moment Beatrice is to show all earth spread out below—look back even further—to some gesture of the girl in Florence. Such gestures, a motion of the hand, a turn of the head, hint a profound significance; they are like the remote stars shining in an earthly sky, which are also virtues and heavens, and still stars. Beatrice was always Beatrice; she made 'un sol cenno—a single sign' and they have mounted contemplation. But the sign was likely to be one she would have made in her city, and like every lover Dante (to his degree) would have mounted contemplation there. The Image had been, and still remained, the ladder of his mind and soul. She had made herself that. 'Brother, we love.'

They rise; the planetary heavens are done. They are in the house of the Twins, in Gemini. It was Dante's own sign; astrologically, he ascribes to its influence 'tutto, qual che si sia, lo mio ingegno—all, whatever that may be, of my genius'. It is always easy to find relevancies, but perhaps Pleasantness may be allowed for a moment to think that sign peculiarly appropriate—to Church and Empire, to Beatrice and himself, to the woman and the city, to the two genders by which so much is known. It is pleasant to find a double-principled sign ruling over Dante's nativity, and his genius rained thence. 'Volgendom' io con gli eterni Gemelli—I rolled with the eternal Twins.' Beatrice, still

The Paradiso

gravely, speaks to him. She uses a word which is full of his past, and so at once unites it with his past and differentiates it. 'Tu sei si presso all' ultima salute'—'You are so near the ultimate Salvation'—perhaps the ultimate Salutation too. The earthly salutation had sprung from the girl's ineffable courtesy, and that itself from God 'solo per sua cortesia'; her largesse had been from his who is so 'largo' that he would himself be man to work redemption. 'Her aspect aids our faith'; her salutation also, and the ultimate Salutation is at hand. But so it had been, hidden in its image, in the street of Florence; so it had been, hidden in its image, in the council-chamber of the Priorate; so it had been, hidden in its image, in the manuscripts of Aristotle, Boethius, and Virgil.

Below him, as at his guide's will he looks down, are the seven heavens through which he has passed, the seven planets—also (in the quadruple meaning) the seven states of romantic, political, and spiritual being. Below them is an area of earth, with mountains, rivers, and seas. The great universe is 'beneath his feet'. It is real and intense, but he uses another word for what else in the space about him—still to call it space—is to be seen. He sees Beatrice herself gazing with suspense and yearning; he sees thousands of lights, and a sun above all, kindling all.

>'Per la viva luce trasparea
> la lucente sustanzia—

through the living light appeared the shining substance.' He had seen Christ flashing in the cross of courage; he now sees him as 'substance'. They have come to the heaven where that substance begins to appear in itself, and all the redeemed sustained and lit by it. It would be rash to say that we must not give to the words 'God' and 'Christ' in this poem any meaning which we do not find in the poem; it is not, I hope, rash to say that their primary meaning must be the meaning they take in the poem. It is 'Substance' as much as 'Christ' which Dante is seeing, and Substance dominating in everything. The word Substance is more useful. He cannot endure the vision; his mind loses hold; his eyes shut. It is then that the early salutation is confirmed. He hears the voice of Beatrice.

>'Apri gli occhi e riguarda qual son io;
> tu hai vedute cose, che possente
> sei fatto a sostener lo riso mio—

The Paradiso

Open your eyes; see what I am. You have seen things by which you are able to endure my smile' (XXIII, 46–8).

'Riguarda qual son io.' This is the great offer and the great demand. It has a double relevance. This is what Dante's poetry had all along been trying to do, from the very first moment. Beatrice and Love had then both been 'unknown modes of being'. He had imaged them in the *Vita*, then he had analysed them in the *Convivio*; he had both ways renewed them in the *Commedia*. Now? He sees again

> il santo riso,
> e quanto il santo aspetto facea mero—

'the sacred smile, and how deep and clear it made the sacred countenance.'

> If all the pens that ever poets held
> Had fed the feeling of their masters' thought,
> And every sweetness that inspired their hearts,
> Their minds and Muses on admired themes,
> If all the heavenly quintessence they still
> From their immortal flowers of poesy
> Wherein, as in a mirror, we perceive
> The highest reaches of a human wit—

Dante says: 'If all Polyhymnia's and her sisters' tongues should sound, they could not express a thousandth part of the truth.' Dante had not done it; much of the true glory of the human form remains to be patterned. But something he had done.

'Riguarda qual son io.' It was an offer 'degno di tanto grado—worthy of so much gratitude'. It is Beatrice becoming wholly Beatrician. She had hurled herself from heaven to save him; but now she has a second task, to show him what she is—that is, to show herself. It is a duty to contemplate; it is also a duty to be contemplated. She still fulfils it. The sacred countenance made clear by the sacred smile is there for his study. He sees? He sees at least all his and her past on earth and in heaven; he sees his passage with her through heaven, and therefore heaven in her. In the first heaven of recollection the soul, called to its vocation and in its vocation to its function, takes its vows of permanent love. It is open to distractions and subject to violence, but it is

The Paradiso

capable of fidelity through all. If it sustains this fidelity, it is still apt to be haunted by dreams of its own honour and glory; it desires sanctity rather on its own behalf than for the sake of sanctity. When this too is overcome, only the last preferences of earth remain to be discarded—not meaning by that any duty or delight derived from any of the Images, but all restless disturbance by mere inner or outer pressure. It is free then to understand (one way or another) the great doctrines; these were clouded at first, but are now clear. Its own rejections and its own affirmations image the equal-limbed cross; the cross of devotion is the unitive life, and all derivations are acknowledged and known. So therefore to the state of life that says 'I' and 'We' and again 'I'—in which it is a perfect voice. This is equality, and God is 'the Prime Equality—la prima equalità' (XV, 74). It is free then to mount swiftly through the contemplations till it can see at once all its own past and all the host of others. This is to be the course of any love-affair; this, till man refused it, was the development of all 'stupor'.

'Riguarda qual son io.' The poem cannot, for all it has said and will say, say more than that. The whole poem is, in effect, only the sigh which murmurs such a disclosure. It must get away now from Beatrice to the redeemed, and it is she who dispatches it. 'Perchè la faccia mia sì t' innamora—why does my face so inamour you . . .? there is the Rose in which the Divine Word made himself flesh.' The vision of the Substance withdraws. He sees indeed the image of Saint Mary the Bearer of Substance, as from this state of heaven where she for a moment shows herself she also recedes into the deepest heaven: 'chè si levò appresso sua semanza—she ascended after her seed' (or off-spring). Dante is left to the courts of the Church, the appointed Priors of that City. These understand what Substance is, and what is the multitude of the redeemed. Three chieftains descend to examine the new young soul upon it. Dante is a middle-aged man, a successful man, a great man, but here he is only a neophyte and a new student of the glory. So Saint Peter asks him concerning faith, and Saint James concerning hope, and Saint John concerning love. These three a little recall those other three of the opening of the *Commedia*, the three beasts. The Leopard then was almost as beautiful and gay and fierce as faith, and the Lion as strong and

The Paradiso

terrifying as hope, and the She-Wolf? Dante provided an Image for that comparison. The She-Wolf was full of all cravings: when the light which was Saint John descended it was so bright that it blinded Dante. He could not see anything, neither Beatrice nor the City. This is the heavenly 'strength of usurpation', as the She-Wolf is the hellish. Hell drives him altogether back to a place where 'the sun is silent'; heaven, like any 'stupor'—before the Image or before the more than all images—only blinds for a moment. Dante, in that blindness, answers concerning love, and how he came to know it. 'Doubly; by philosophic arguments and by authority.' By reason and revelation, that is, by the Church and Beatrice. And how does he love? 'All things proportionately to the good bestowed on each by the Eternal.' He loves, that is, in proportion as God would have him; he loves things because God loves them. So knowing faith, hope, and love, Dante sees, when his sight is restored, Adam; that is, he can in those three great capacities at last see Man. The centre and source of humanity (short of Christ), the first direct eternal Image of Christ, appears. But Adam has not said much concerning his sin and the Fall when suddenly the flame that is Peter begins to crimson, and the modesty of Beatrice to blush, 'as if at another's fault.' Peter begins to denounce the Paparchy. It will be remembered that the 'form' of the Church was the life of Christ—the life, that is, of the Second Manhood. In the presence of this great Father of the human race, the centre of the promulgation of the Second Manhood is denounced. Heaven crimsons, 'and such, I suppose, was the eclipse in heaven when the supreme Power suffered' (XXVII, 35-6). It is like a second and worse Fall; in the eyes of the Son of God the Papal Throne is empty—'vaca'. The Pope (so called) 'has made my (Peter's) burial-place a sewer for the blood and filth by which that perverse one (Satan) who fell from here is soothed below'. So denouncing and promising help, the three apostles and our common Father ascend once more.

There remain but two heavens—the *primum mobile* and the empyrean. Now, when Dante looks at Beatrice, he seems to see substance in her also—

'ridendo tanto lieta
che Dio parea nel suo volto gioire—

The Paradiso

laughing with such joy that God seemed to be rejoicing in her face' (XXVII, 104–5). And against that laughing Image, he sees the point 'from which heaven and all nature hangs—depende il cielo e tutta la natura'. Beatrice, impassioned with love, knowledge, and delight, launches herself on the final great expositions, which (being themselves Images) are not at all disproportionate to the mouth of the most glorious (but one) of all Dante's human images. These expositions are general but they are also particular. She is declaring the principles of creation and also of her created self; 'riguarda qual son io.'

> 'Concreato fu ordine e costrutto
> alle sustanzie—

'co-created was order and co-constructed with the substance' (XXIX, 31–2). This is as much true of her person as of the universe.

They are then in the heaven of those substances ('queste sustanzie') which are angels, the nine circles of whose lights surround the single point. But presently point and circles quench themselves. In the inter-pause there is nothing but Beatrice to see, as Dante (with a charming courtesy of candour) says:

> 'per che tornar con gli occhi a Beatrice
> nulla vedere ed amor mi costrinse—

there being nothing else to see, that and love compelled me to turn my eyes to Beatrice' (XXX, 14–15). But the courtesy was indeed greater than at first appears, for here, in the moment between the heaven of the angelic powers and the empyrean, she is given the whole poem absolutely to herself. Dante, in this single moment, will have nothing else distract his or our eyes. The perfect Image reaches its perfect height. She stands, alert and intelligential, beautiful and passionate, poised in the heaven from which her Maker has withdrawn for her sake his visibility; the Substance which is her spiritual off-spring has withdrawn; the divine God-bearer has withdrawn. This is Beatrice, said to have been called Portinari, a girl born in Florence, in 1266. Her lover begins his last praise of her—his last praise but for his last prayer. This beauty

> 'certo io credo
> che solo il suo fattor tutta la goda—

The Paradiso

—certainly I believe that only its Maker fully tastes it—

> Dal primo giorno ch' io vidi il suo viso
> In questa vita, infino a questa vista,
> Non m' è il seguire al mio cantar preciso;
> Ma or convien che mio seguir desista
> Più dietro a sua bellezza poetando,
> Come all' ultimo suo ciascuno artista.

From the first day when I saw her face in this life until the present sight, my song has not ceased to follow; but now the pursuit must cease from following her beauty further in verse, as at the last every artist does.'

She then, the measure and image of each state of being and of all, so poised, utters in that pause a sentence which, like any ritual formula or other word of power, seems to call up the effect it describes. 'Noi semo usciti fuore', she says, 'we have come out of the greatest body into the heaven which is pure light—

> al ciel, ch' è pura luce;
> luce intellettual piena d' amore,
> amor di vero ben pien di letizia,
> letizia che trascende ogni dolzore—

intellectual light full of love, love of the true good full of gladness, gladness surpassing every other sweet.' On the word 'a living light' wraps him, so swathing him with its glory that he cannot see beyond it. The voice continues:

> 'Sempre l' amore, che queta il cielo,
> accoglia in sè con sì fatta salute,

—always the love which stills heaven receives (all) into itself with such salutation.' Once the voice of Beatrice had been the salutation of love; now her voice is but the sign of the salutation of love. The whole of Dante's life and work had been to achieve that distinction and to understand it. It seems but a very slight distinction, but it is the whole purpose of the Way. He had set out on that Way in Florence at the age of nine, and again at the age of eighteen, and again from the savage wood at the age of thirty-five. Was so long, so beautiful, so horrible, so tedious, a Way necessary? It seems so, if indeed he was rightly to understand

The Paradiso

image and original. The salutation had at first been courtesy and largesse greeting him; now it laps him round; he and the august salutation are one. It is this lapping-round of which the early communication was a sign. As much as a man may be before death, he is again transhumanized into glory. As the voice strikes him, he receives power. The voice summons him into the energy of the light; he sees. His eyes now in the force of the light can measure themselves with any light. He sees a river of tawny light, between banks of glowing flowers, into which sparks from the river spring and drop and return. The voice beside him bids him drink—or be imaged as drinking; these appearances 'are the shadowy prefaces of their truth—son di lor vero ombriferi prefazii'. 'These things', it continues, 'are not in themselves *acerbe*—harsh or difficult—but the lack is on your side that you do not yet see them *superbe*—in their height of being.' He bends to the river—as he had been bidden to look so often ('riguarda qual son io')—and as he does so with this last temporal image of eternity, it changes. He passes into an awareness of the whole immense rose of all the blessed. 'Vedi nostra città quanto ella gira!—see our city in what gyres! see the thrones so full that few are still waited for—there where you are gazing his place expects the high soul—and on earth imperial—of that Henry who will come to direct Italy before she is prepared.' The Beatrician welcome to the near-coming Emperor—'before you are here, he will be'—is united with a final cry against the then Pope—'only for a little thereafter shall he be endured by God in the sacred office; he shall be thrust for his deserts where Simon Magus is, and shall force him of Anagna lower still.'

'I saw', said Bunyan, 'that there is a way to hell from the gates of the Celestial City', and so here. In the last single moment of them, all three images are caught up, and that not by type only but by persons—Beatrice, the Emperor Henry, the Popes Clement and Boniface. In that triplicity the shadow of the old Wolf lingers —the insatiable craving of 'him of Anagna'. It adds to the poetic value of the moment that it should be the Papal image which is to itself the means of damnation. 'Simon Magus is the operation and the worker of it'—to recall Francesca's line. The name of the false magical priest stands also for all that Dante might have been, for Geryon and the pollution. All that moment is especially

The Paradiso

pointed because it is the last utterance of Beatrice—'E farà quel d' Anagna entrar più giuso'. It is the fierceness of peace which speaks in her, and that is all the eternal peace can mean to 'him of Anagna'.

It is past. The white rose of humanity unfolds, and the golden-winged bees of the angelic orders—but all that is in Dante, and criticism need not be indecorous in mere repetition. Say, Dante contemplates the beatitude of mankind. He is again in 'stupor', but this time no longer at a small episode significant of the whole, but at the whole in which all episodes have their subdued place. There is no time nor distance; nor any kind of medium—'Dio senza mezzo governa—God rules without intermediary.' The stupor is not now of the mind. 'I turned with rekindled will to question—la mia donna.' He sees instead of her 'un sene'—a senior, a wise man; and he says suddenly—but only —'Where is she?' There is no cry as at the loss of Virgil. The wise figure—it is Saint Bernard—answers: 'Beatrice sent me; if you look—e se riguardi—you shall see her.' Unspeaking, he does, and he sees her also 'without medium'. Then he speaks.

'O lady, in whom my hope has strength, you who have borne to leave your footmarks in hell for my salvation—per la mia salute—I recognize the grace and virtue of all the things I have seen by your power and your goodness. You have brought me from servitude to liberty by all the ways and all the means possible to you. Guard your magnificence in me, that my soul, which you have made whole, may please you when it unknots itself from the body.'

> 'Così orai; ed ella si lontana,
> come parea, sorrise, e riguardommi;
> poi si tornò all' eterna fontana—

I prayed thus; and she, so far away as she seemed, smiled and gazed; then she turned herself to the eternal fountain' (XXXI, 79–93). The words 'sorrise' and 'riguardommi' have in them all the energy of their repetitions throughout the journey. It is so she is, in her passion, last seen. She turns, and though that turning is now her proper function, yet it has a minor function; it is to live again for him the vicarious life of heaven.

Bernard breaks in and bids him look 'till you see the queen of all this'. He speaks of the whole wonder, but two things only need be touched here. The first is 'the queen' herself. Bernard, saying what Virgil could not say, and invoking her, utters the great principle of this whole mode of being, the principle of exchanged derivation:

> 'Vergine madre, figlia del tuo figlio,
> umile ed alta più che creatura,
> termine fisso d' eterno consiglio,
> tu se' colui, che l' umana natura
> nobilitasti sì, che il suo Fattore
> non disdegnò di farsi sua fattura—

Virgin-mother, daughter of thy son, more extreme than any other creature in humility and greatness, fixed term of the eternal counsel, you'—this Image so characterized—'are she who has so ennobled human nature that its Worker did not disdain to become its work.' She is that point of substance in which Deity humanly subsists. She is the principle of motion in that substance. The 'off-springing' of the Empire and the Church is justice, opportunity, and vocation; the 'off-springing' of Beatrice is Love; the 'off-springing' of Mary is God. Before her the angel of the Annunciation gazes into her eyes—*guarda negli occhi . . . innamorata*—enamoured into flame. This is the topmost *salute*, salutation; the salutation of Salvation to his work and the salutation of angelhood and of manhood to the approaching Salvation. The eyes of Beatrice are seen no more; the eyes of Mary are seen instead. But, deeper and more piercing though these are, they are not alien. They are the eyes of the God-bearer, the last of the Images. But Beatrice, for Dante the first of the Images, had also been a God-bearer; only there the God had not, as here, fulfilled himself in the glorious and holy flesh. Therefore now Saint Bernard speaks of Beatrice to Mary on Dante's behalf—

> 'vedi Beatrice con quanti beati
> per li miei preghi ti chiudon le mani—

see Beatrice, with how many of the blessed, clasping hands for my prayers' (XXXIII, 38–9). It was to this that she had turned.

There is yet one more Derivation. All the principles of derivation lie in the Incarnacy, but the Incarnacy in its Person. Dante

The Paradiso

looks beyond Mary, down 'the ray of the high light which to itself is true'. Beyond the 'figlia del tuo figlio' he sees the figure of Man contained in and unseparated from God. He sees three circles 'di tre colori e d' una continenza—of three colours and one dimension': as Iris out of Iris, and breathed out of both a fire. At the depth of hell Satan chews men; but at the end of Paradise the great mathematical symbol shows Man distinct yet in-Godded. The pageant of the mountain had seemed to appear out of the air in the forest; a second sun had emerged from the first at the opening of the heavens; at their close, Iris out of Iris. How is the figure of our nature held in that second colour? 'I could not—but that my mind was struck by a flash, in which its will came to it —da un fulgore, in che sua voglia venne.'

Did it? He touched the whole vision with a phrase of that modesty to which a girl's greeting in a street had first converted him. 'Vidi . . . credo ch' io vidi,

> perchè più di largo,
> dicendo questo, mi senti ch' io godo.

I saw . . . I believe I saw, because, in saying this, it feels to me as if I had greater joy.'

XII

THE RECOLLECTION OF THE WAY

Of all this experience Dante says (*Par.* XXXIII, 58–63): 'I was like one who sees in a dream, and when the dream is gone the passion stamped (*impressa*) by it remains, and the other comes not again to mind; even so my vision has almost entirely disappeared, but the sweetness born of it distils still in my heart.' Wordsworth said something similar of the early Romantic sense (*Prelude*, II, 312–22):

> the soul
> Remembering how she felt, but what she felt
> Remembering not . . .

the vision or communication disappears, but the consciousness of the passion remains. It was then to Wordsworth a mood of 'shadowy exaltation', and perhaps, in many, some such recollection is all that remains of the 'stupor', especially during that period which has been called here 'the death of Beatrice'. We may complete the quotation from the English poet:

> The soul
> . . . retains an obscure sense
> Of possible sublimity, whereto
> With growing faculties she doth aspire,
> With faculties still growing, feeling still
> That whatsoever point they gain, they yet
> Have something to pursue.

This is applicable to the whole *Commedia*, until the last Canto. There, in the last four lines, there is a return, almost in so many words, to the simile used in that famous dream of the *Vita*. The dream occurred after Beatrice had refused him her salutation; Love said: 'I am as the centre of a circle to which all parts of the circumference are equal, but with you it is not so.' In the

The Recollection of the Way

Paradiso she had again turned from him, and after that he had seen all, and he wrote:

> 'All' alta fantasia qui mancò possa;
> Ma già volgeva il mio disiro e il *velle*,
> Sì come rota ch' egualmente è mossa,
> L' amor che move il sole e l' altre stelle—

Power failed the high imagination; but the Love which moves the sun and the other stars rolled my desire and my will, as if they were a wheel which is moved equally.' The final line is known everywhere. But the final line has a subordinate verb, and not the chief verb of the sentence. The important thing to Dante was not so much that Love moved the sun and the other stars, as that Love rolled his own desire and will. It is clearly more convenient for us to recollect the sun and the rest rather than our desire and will; that is why the last line is so popular. But it is the desire and will which, in the poem, are fully in the Empyrean; the sun and the other stars are (literally) below that heaven, and (allegorically) they are lesser states of that heaven.

It is the simile of the equally-rolling wheel which recalls the earlier circle simile. For now, to Dante as well as to Love, 'all parts of the circumference are equal'; with him 'it is so'. This distinction between the two states, as was said of the Salutation, has been the whole purpose of the journey. The wheel which is he rolls in the Empyrean; that is, in the world of substance. His motion is a motion in true substance; indeed, his desire and will are the motion; that is, he is himself the motion. This is now his function, for which he was created—to be exactly that perfect motion in substance, and this is the chief statement in the last four lines. Nevertheless, the sun and stars have their poetic place; they ease the imagination from the single flash—'fulgor' —in which it perceived *how* the Image of Man 'came together with the circle—

> come si convenne
> l' imago al cerchio, e come vi s' indova—

and how it in-dwelled there'. They allow the mind to relax (if such a word may be used of such a state) towards the creation. The eyes of Beatrice are permitted to turn again towards the gyres of the eternal and roseal City.

The Recollection of the Way

The operative word of the last line is 'move—moves'. The sun and stars are in movement, engaged on their similar functions. They too are movements in substance. As was explained to Dante, all the heavens are, in fact, one heaven. He has to know them separately, but they are all one, only known in distinction by their 'feeling, more or less, the eternal breath'. All then are seen in that simultaneously understood City, with all their times and places; all the small roses and all the mighty are in this Rose. If Dante—say rather, if Beatrice—had been able to look back—or rather, considering the last line of the poem, if they were able to follow that returning Way—But, of course, they were; it was precisely this which the freedom of the City granted them; the wheeling desire and will looked out on the sun and the other stars. The second Iris derived from the First; our Image was fixed in it; the eyes which see that Image deepest are the eyes—'da Dio diletti e venerati—loved and venerated by God'—of Mary, of her from whom the Image in the Iris is derived, as she herself is imaged by every soul in heaven. It is therefore that the other images can now be seen, beginning with Eve, herself the mother of all lives, between whom and Mary is a great interchange—for 'the wound which Mary closed and anointed she who is so beautiful at her feet opened and thrust' (*Par.* XXXII, 4–6), in which exchange both have a complete joy; so that the shapes of all who wound and all who heal here courteously rejoice together. Between all the human images the golden bees of the angelic creation fly, and the introduction of that other creation adds a strangeness and a touch of 'stupor', and consequently an added exaltation to the whole; for even here the human perfection is in relation to some quite different perfection; humanity itself is not self-enclosed. In that state it becomes again possible to talk 'of every *when* and every *where*—ogni *ubi* ed ogni *quando*' (*Par.* XXIX, 12), for here was the state in which Dante first saw, reflected in the eyes of Beatrice, the point from which 'depende il cielo e tutta la natura—from which heaven and all nature hangs'. He saw it reflected in her eyes before he turned to see it in itself, and this therefore is the moment of the opening downwards of that reflection which is the principle and cause of all the images, which indeed is what makes things images, and that not only of things towards God

The Recollection of the Way

but of things towards each other. The full working out of this possibility has to be seen (in God) below this. Beatrice—that is, not only Beatrice but every relationship according to proper vocation—'imparadisa—in-paradises' the mind (*Par.* XXVIII, 3), which has already been 'innamorata—in-amoured' (*Par.* XXVII, 88). This is possible to each of that great crowd who have been seen 'triumphing' in Christ; but not before they are seen as a whole. It will be remembered that Dante could not bear the full heavenly smile of Beatrice until after he had seen Christ glorious in his saints—a figure of profound significance, for it was the earlier subdued smile of Beatrice which had brought him to Christ and his saints; and here again is a continual exchange of power between one image and all the other images. This certainly is the principle—discovered or undiscovered—of every love-affair, by which (now) is meant every affair of love.

That celestial power, in such continual exchange, moves always towards earth as always up from earth. The ladder of the great contemplatives is just below that Saint John whose glory blinds Dante, though in the Earthly Paradise it was Saint John who had seemed to Dante to be in trance, with closed eyes. I suppose a small additional image might be borrowed there from poetry—say, from the *Commedia* itself; for a line which seems to us great but of which we do not understand the full significance will lie vibrating but quiescent, whereas when we do understand something of the significance it seems to have relevancies of all kinds, and we are defeated by it in quite another way. Such pause and progress in exploration is the paradisal counterpart of the sleeping and waking in the *Purgatorio*. In hell there is no progress, only insignificant monotony. The descent from and in that blinding power leads contemplation to the great eagle of earthly justice, and so to the cross of the courageous and of the families. This is the heavenly knowledge (in the eagle) of all commonalty, of all proper balance—the 'I' for the 'We' and the 'We' for the 'I'—and (in the cross) of time and transition, and of exile. So that, this way, the idea of exile has a double meaning, for the temporal exile of Dante is the result of the act of the self-exiled from heaven. It is the topmost note—and the first in this descent—of immediate personal suffering from sin; those above know—like Adam our lord and father—that they were sinners, and denounce

The Recollection of the Way

sin on earth, but this is the prophecy of sin on earth shooting direct arrows, and the salt bread and hard stairs express it. As for the families and the history of Florence, there is the tale of physical derivation in time. Birth, in itself, had been known above; giving birth was the function of the God-bearer, but that was single, and it was 'the cause and occasion' of all the rest. This is the spectacle of the rest. The eagle of justice and the cross of courage are, respectively, humanity seen simultaneously and humanity seen sequentially; they are complementary.

Below these are the wheels of pure light which are the heaven of the sun, and of the philosophical intellects of the City. There are two great stages of ascent in heaven, as there are two great pits of descent in hell. The wise and accurate doctors of this stage correspond to the false pollution of Geryon, as the ladder of the contemplatives above corresponds to the abyss of the giants below —the giants are even less intelligent than Geryon, just as the contemplatives are wiser even than the doctors. But though we can say 'below' in one case, we cannot rightly say 'above' in the other. Hell is a funnel; heaven is a rose. The narrowing inorganic rock of the one is the chosen antitype of the intensifying organic heart of the other. The wheels of the doctors mark a sudden change in Paradise, more intense than that only from one heaven to another. Descending knowledge, issuing downwards from those wheels, finds itself in a heaven already touched with the shadow of earth. The three heavens of this lowest order need to be touched by it with a particular tenderness, for they have in them a marked insufficiency of their own. This must, theologically, be true of all the heavens; only, in the poem, it is made spectacular here. Below the heaven of the doctors Dante has not once worthily forgotten Beatrice; in so far as he ever did forget, it was of the nature of sin. But sin here, as the heaven of Venus sings, is known only as an occasion of glory; 'sin shall have worship in heaven', as the Lady Julian said. Lovers, citizens, nuns, are the symbols of the three grades. And then, still sinking, and issuing from the lowest, the sweetest and most childlike of the heavens, the descending knowledge—memory—is aware of two suns, but that one in which all paradise dances is lost behind the other, the lower, sun; and suddenly there is landscape—a great forest, trees, earth, streams, men and women walking.

The Recollection of the Way

One might certainly imagine that here too, as in another wood of which somewhere we heard (in a nightmare—forgotten all but the soul's 'how she felt') were three creatures—something like a leopard, gay and dangerous (the first three heavens and their 'spotted vanity'), and something like a lion strong and noble (the second three heavens and their universal intellect and proportion), and a third not at all like a wolf, but a twy-natured existence, whose craving for souls is greater than that of any wolf's for food. The Sacred Griffin moves in its own forest, the paradise of earthly function; a pageant plays itself which can be seen when it breaks out of the air to welcome or threaten a mounting soul, but for the rest is known only to the air and the recesses of that primal wood.

All this while the human memory, as it sinks, has been aware of the eternal Images—of the God-bearer, of Beatrice, of Adam, of the three apostolic lords, of the City above and the City below, of teachers and poets and friends, of lovers and nuns; rather, has been accompanied by them. But now, it recalls how, in a whirl of accusation, the most constant of the Images had appeared. She was one whose eyes once reflected the point beyond all points, and also the two Natures of the Griffin. But the human memory recollects that once it did not understand that. It is blessed enough now to be able, with the *Convivio*, 'to bless the times past, and well may it bless them.' It says: ' "Had I not passed by such a way, I should not have had this treasure; I should not have had means of joy in the City to which I approach," and therefore blesses the way it has gone.' Especially it blesses the great master who before Beatrice came and when Beatrice disappeared was all that was not Beatrice, all that was not the direct point of experience, all the offices of others that served its own *vita*, and its *vita nuova*. It sees all the degrees of that new life on earth and after, how arch-natural, and how natural. If it recollects its sins, it recollects, with them, its purifications; if it recollects its own lack of love and courtesy, it recollects, with that, the love and courtesy of others; it is fulfilled by others, as (it may dare to hope) in some way, known or unknown—what does that matter?—it is a fulfilment of others. At least, before the purifications, it can still for ever acknowledge its debt—'tu duca, tu signore, et tu maestro', 'la gloriosa donna della mia mente.' Dante himself called both

The Recollection of the Way

Virgil and Beatrice light—'O degli altri poeti onore e lume—O honour and light of other poets'; 'O luce, O gloria della gente humana—O light, O glory of the human race.'

But in that light it sees also something else—the whole opposite of itself which it might have become. It sees the little vile side-paths through the wood, opening before those who walk in a coma of themselves, and oblivious of those shining natural 'membra—members' which were more beautiful than anything else in all Nature and all art. It sees the valley where 'la gloriosa donna' does not come, and Virgil hardly except as a faint ghost, though certainly there it did turn to that ghost of poetry and found recollection and 'salute'. It sees the great sad gate, which can only properly be understood by those who know Paradise, for it is the light of Paradise which has engraved itself over the gate. Within, are those who know the worst—'the expense of spirit in a waste of shame.' Shakespeare, in his darkest play, wrote that

> the worst is not
> So long as we can say, This is the worst.

It is perhaps a note of Dante's different greatness that the souls here can both feel the worst and say that it is the worst; their extreme consciousness, without intellect, is itself the pain. But into this 'low hell' there is no need to go again. It is, all of it, without intellect, however enormous it may seem to those in it, and yet also very narrow for most—and very small to the redeemed, no more than a little snake slipping for a moment out of a rocky cleft into a grassy valley. The soul looks back rather to its real beginnings, its birth and its re-birth—its re-birth as particular to each soul as its birth, but for Dante, as for many, the experience of the natural eyes of a laughing girl in a city street.

Those eyes are named all through the *Commedia*. In the *Convivio* (IV, ii) it was said that Philosophy contemplated herself 'when the beauty of her own eyes is revealed to her. And what else does this say but that the soul in philosophy not only contemplates truth, but also contemplates its own contemplation and the beauty of it . . .?' In the *Commedia* this act of knowing is the subject throughout; so it had been, in a lesser way, in the *Vita*. In the *Commedia* Beatrice is a poetic image; being in a poem, she cannot well be anything else, though of course her relevance, like

The Recollection of the Way

that of any other poetic image, may extend outside poetry. The most extreme supporters of the femininity both of Beatrice and of the Lady of the Window never supposed that in the poem Beatrice could be anything else, however great and wide a relevance they may suppose her to have outside. The allegory of her is (Dante said) at least fourfold, perhaps multifold. She is, in the whole *Paradiso*, his way of knowing, and the maxim is always 'look; look well'. Attention is demanded of him and her expositions are the result of his attention. She is, in a sense, his very act of knowing. It is in this sense that the *Paradiso* is an image of the whole act of knowing which is the great Romantic way, the Way of the Affirmation of Images, ending in the balanced whole. Indeed the entire work of Dante, so inter-relevant as it is, is a description of the great act of knowledge, in which Dante himself is the Knower, and God is the Known, and Beatrice is the Knowing. To say so is not to lessen Beatrice in herself to a mere quality of Dante, or only in the sense that, had we her *Commedia*, Dante would have been a quality of hers. All images are to excite qualities in us; so, in fact, Virgil taught in his great rationalization of love during the night in Purgatory—Virgil, himself a lesser master of knowing. We have only hints and fragments of her story; it is perhaps preserved for us after we have 'condescended' to understand Dante's. Her eyes are his knowing; the beauty and wonder of his knowing deepens with the heavens; they are not in the hells because there is no true knowing in hell; they are not in the purgatories because he is only learning again what he forgot. But they are on earth and they are in heaven. Unsatisfied desire sees itself, in her, satisfied; satisfied desire sees itself, in him, unsatisfied. His actual knowing, even so, is a reflection; the Twy-Natured is reflected in it, and the final Point Itself. Those eyes yield, in the end, to the eyes of the God-bearer. Then the Knower begins to know after a quite other manner, about which nothing can be said. It is, in a way, astonishing (but blessed) that this great poet should have said so little in the ordinary speech of Christians; he omits so much that any small Christian versifier would have put in. The God-bearer appears intensely, but how little! how little, in so long a poem, our most courteous Lord himself! But then she is the primal motion in substance, the motion being an exchange in unity—

The Recollection of the Way

'figlia del tuo figlio.' After that, in the poem, the Knower knows altogether, or remembers how once he did know altogether, 'because I feel my joy increase.' He hears still the running of the wheels of desire and will, the ever-humming speed of 'il ben dell' intelletto'.

Beatrice is his Knowing. To say so is not to reduce her actuality nor her femininity. The reason for the insistence on her femininity is simple—it is that this is what Dante insisted on, and that we ought perhaps to take Dante's poetry as relevant to our own affairs. Perhaps also we ought not. But if we ought, then the whole of his work is the image of a Way not confined to poets. That Way is not only what the poem is 'about'; it is (according to it) what Love is 'about'. It is what Love is 'up to', and the only question is whether lovers are 'up to' Love. Were they, the *Vita* and the *Paradiso* would be the only way. The complex art of this knowledge is certainly not confined to romantic love of the male-female kind. Wherever the 'stupor' is, there is the beginning of the art. Wherever any love is—and some kind of love in every man and woman there must be—there is either affirmation or rejection of the image, in one or other form. If there is rejection—of that Way there are many records. Of the affirmation, for all its greater commonness, there are fewer records. 'Riguarda qual son io'—we have hardly yet begun to be looked at or to look.

INDEX

Adam, 193, 217
Adam of Brescia, 140
Adrian V, 167
Aeneid, see Virgil
Affirmation, Way of, 9, 48, 51, 63, 83, 157, 172, 191
   secret order, 97, 100
   danger of, 105, 110
Apostacy, 90, 97, 124, 132, 144, 193
Aquinas, St. Thomas, 37, 55, 60, 72, 84, 97, 175, 190, 200
   appearance of, 206
Aristotle, 43, 75, 76, 80, 81, 175, 200, 214
Athanasius, St., 9
Augustine, St., 50
Authority, 74, 90

Beatrice, first appearances of, 7, 18, 79, 123
   salutation of, 22, 214, 219, 222, 224
   death of, 16, 31, 34, 47, 52
   identity and character, 17, 66, 101, 105, 218, 232
   and the Lady of the Window, 41, 47, 55, 58
   duty to Dante, 71, 124, 181, 215, 222
   and Virgil, 112, 153, 161, 165
   and laughter, 65, 153, 194, 201, 205, 210
   and St. Mary, 34, 112, 177, 193, 222
   return of, 71, 179
   as compensation, 100
   and apostacy, 124, 132, 135, 144, 193
   and the mountain, 145
   and Purgatory, 146
   and the double nature, 187
   'riguarda', 195, 214, 218, 232
   consummation, 218, 221

Benedict, St., 212
Bernard, St., 112, 221
Boethius, 52, 200, 214
Bonaventura, St., 24, 206
Boniagiunta, 170
Boniface VIII, 131, 134–6, 139, 167, 217, 220
Browne, Sir Thomas, 100
Browning, 39
Brunetto Latini, 130, 136, 169
Bunyan, 220

Can Grande della Scala, 56, 113, 182
Carlo Martello, 202
Cacciaguida, 208
Casella, 150
Cato, 148, 213
Cimabue, 158
City, image of the, 11, 14, 76, 127, 130, 135, 138, 141, 155, 164
   divine, 25, 33, 70, 84, 180, 196, 220, 226
   of Dis, 125
Clement V, 86
Co-inherence, 92, 172, 195, 204, 210
Coleridge, 7, 17, 18, 26
Cunizza, 203

Dante Alighieri
   experience of Beatrice, 7, 18, 27, 37, 179
   death of Beatrice, 31, 34, 47
   life of, 39–41, 98, 104
   marriages, 41, 46
   exile, 41, 97, 159, 208, 227
   and the Lady of the Window, 41
   the four meanings of his writings, 56, 66, 68, 70, 76, 97, 117
   and apostacy, 124, 144

Index

Works:
  Commedia, 15, 16, 40, 43, 44, 47, 49, 96, 100, 145, 215, 227
    writing of, 100, 230
  Convivio, 7, 42, 45, 48, 69, 119, 170, 197, 199, 202, 213, 229, 230
    examination of, 44
  De Monarchia, 40, 73, 167, 175
    examination of, 90
  'Donne, ch' avete', 19, 26, 102, 171
  Inferno, 73, 97, 103, 134, 140, 163, 167, 213
    discussion of, 113
  Paradiso, 23, 79, 101, 103, 134, 135, 140, 231
    discussion of, 190
  Purgatorio, 81, 96, 102, 103, 115, 135, 167
    discussion of, 145
  Vita Nuova, 13, 45, 52, 69, 104, 123, 133, 134, 171, 196, 215, 224, 230
    discussion of, 17
    revision, 21-2, 32
Dionysius, 8, 206
Dis, City of, 125, 142
Dominic, St., 206

Eagle, 155, 178, 209, 227
Emperor, image of the, 72, 93, 97, 143-4, 199, 220
Eucharist, the, 188
Eunoe, 115, 194
Eve, 226

Farinata, 126, 130
Flattery, 133
Florence, 11, 14, 82, 86, 88, 98, 120, 124, 138
  image of the City of, 39
Folco of Marseilles, 203
Forese Donati, 170, 196

Fortune, 121
Fox, George, 154
Francesca, 117, 127, 130, 142, 150, 182, 208
Francis, St., 206

Galahad, 101
Ganymede, 155
Gemma Donati, 41, 46
Geri dell Bello, 137
Geryon, 97, 132, 182
Giotto, 158
Griffin, 178, 183, 187, 193, 197, 229
Guido dell Duca, 160
Guido of Montefeltro, 83, 97, 139
Guido Guinicelli, 172

Henry VII, 89, 98, 220
Heresy, 125, 142
Hippocrates, 178
Homer, 20

Image, 7
Incarnation, 77, 97
'Intelletto, il ben dell' ', 21, 170

James, St., 216
Joan (Primavera), 28, 32, 175
John, St., 178, 216, 217, 227
John the Precursor, 29, 111
Julian of Norwich, 91, 152, 228
Justinian, 95, 199

Keats, 69
Kierkegaard, 46

Lady of the Window, 41, 45, 105, 123, 186, 231
  discussion of, 52
Lancelot, 83, 97, 101, 118, 139
Leo, St., 188
Leopard, 109, 123, 131-2, 155, 216

Index

Lethe, 145, 187
Lion, 109, 127, 178, 216
Loyola, 100
Luck, 121
Luke, St., 178
Lucy, St., 156, 166
Lully, Raymond, 100
Lussuria, 118-19, 121, 127

Malory, 83
Marlowe, 151, 215
Marriage, 15, 38, 49, 51, 83, 119
Mary, St., 30, 61, 76, 156, 161, 199, 206, 216, 218, 226
   and Beatrice, 34, 112, 177, 193, 222
   'figlia del tuo figlio', 158, 222
Matilda, 175, 187, 194
Medusa, 125
Milton, 13, 40, 102, 108, 110, 144
Montanists, 51
Myrrha, 140

Nobility, 72, 77, 79
   fruits of, 75

Paolo, 117, 127
Patmore, 13, 49, 69, 90, 188
Peter, St., 216
Peter Damian, St., 211
Piccarda, 196, 212
Plato, 79
Pope, image of the, 87, 93, 95, 134, 217
Pre-destination, 211

Rahab, 204
Rejection, Way of, 8, 13, 51, 157, 172, 191
Romanticism, 14, 33, 35, 36, 49, 63, 81, 101, 116, 117, 122, 132
Romantic Love, 14, 16, 29, 38, 47, 49, 135, 153, 188

Rome, 86

Satan, 143
Scartazzini, 18
Shakespeare, 13, 40, 47, 69, 144
   Antony, 94
   Imogen, 71, 201
   Julius Caesar, 93, 94
   King Lear, 17, 132, 230
   'Let me not', 24
   Midsummer Night's Dream, 11
   Othello, 71, 131
   Tempest, 201
   Troilus, 88
Shaw, Bernard, 182
Simon Magus, 220
Sinclair, J. D., 161, 168, 188
Sinon, 140
Siren, 165
Sollazia, 76, 119, 170
Solomon, 206
Stars, 77, 170, 194
Statius, 168
Styx, 122
Stupor, 7, 80, 110, 176, 188, 191, 221
Substance, 214, 216, 218, 222
Substitution, 158

Thaïs, 133, 135, 136, 154, 160
Tyndale, 59

Ugolino, 129, 142, 154
Ulysses, 129, 137

Virgil, 11, 12, 45, 76, 110, 136, 214
   and the *Aeneid*, 15, 94, 112, 191
   as the City, 70
   and Paradise, 70, 111, 169, 174
   his expositions, 121, 160, 162, 212
   and Statius, 168

Index

and the return of Beatrice, 176
disappearance of, 179, 221

Wolf, 109, 123, 127, 217
Wordsworth, 16, 69, 70, 83, 88, 102, 148, 153

and Dante, 11–13, 31, 35
Prelude, 12, 19, 20, 52, 64, 80, 89, 224

Yeats, 33

www.ingramcontent.com/pod-product-compliance
Lightning Source LLC
Chambersburg PA
CBHW022148180426
43200CB00028BA/318